The Blue Ridge Parkway

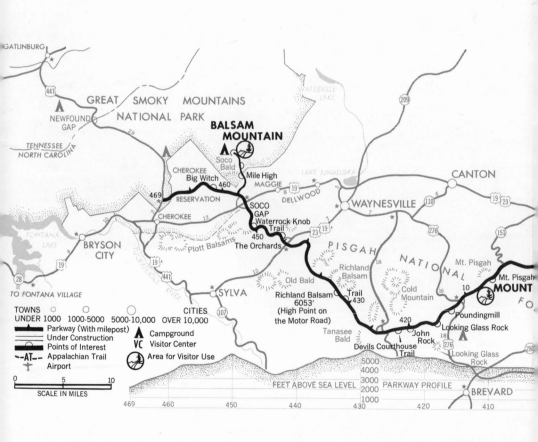

GATLINBURG

GREAT SMOKY MOUNTAINS
NATIONAL PARK

441

NEWFOUND
GAP

TENNESSEE
NORTH CAROLINA

WATERVILLE
LAKE

209

**BALSAM
MOUNTAIN**

Soco
Bald

CHEROKEE
Big Witch

460

Mile High

CANTON

469

RESERVATION

MAGGIE

DELLWOOD

8 19

LAKE JUNALUSKA

110

6

19 23

CHEROKEE

12

SOCO
GAP
Waterrock Knob
Trail

WAYNESVILLE

7

450

23 19

450

The Orchards

BRYSON
CITY

Plott Balsams

PISGAH NATIONAL

276

151

Mt. Pisgah

FONTANA
LAKE

19

441

SYLVA

12

Old Bald

Richland
Balsam

18

Cold
Mountain

16

10

Mt. Pisgah
MOUNT

28

TO FONTANA VILLAGE

107

Richland Balsam
6053'
(High Point on
the Motor Road)

Trail
430

FO

420

Poundingmill

Looking Glass Rock

TOWNS
UNDER 1000   1000-5000   5000-10,000

CITIES
OVER 10,000

Tanasee
Bald

John
Rock

18

276

280

Parkway (With milepost)
Under Construction
Points of Interest
--AT-- Appalachian Trail
Airport

▲ Campground
VC Visitor Center
🌲 Area for Visitor Use

Devils Courthouse
Trail

Looking Glass
Rock

0   5   10
SCALE IN MILES

5000
4000
3000
2000
1000

FEET ABOVE SEA LEVEL

PARKWAY PROFILE

BREVARD

469   460   450   440   430   420   410

THE
BLUE RIDGE
PARKWAY

HARLEY E. JOLLEY

KNOXVILLE ⊍ THE UNIVERSITY OF TENNESSEE PRESS

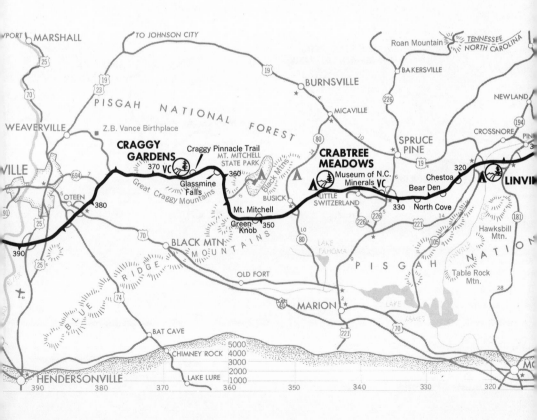

Library of Congress Catalog Card Number: 68-9777

Clothbound editions of University of Tennessee Press books are printed on paper designed for an effective life of at least 300 years, and binding materials are chosen for strength and durability.

The map on pages ii-viii, showing the Parkway as it appeared in 1968, is used through the courtesy of the National Park Service. The author of course assumes the responsibility for any errors.

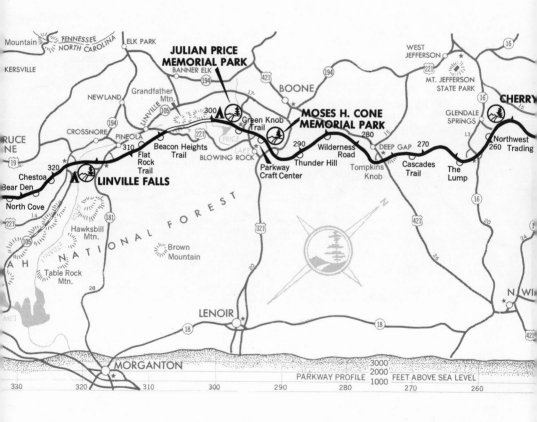

Preface

THE BLUE RIDGE PARKWAY, part of the National Park system, is a unique approach to national recreation. Built along the crest of the Blue Ridge Mountains, the 469-mile highway is designed to provide a ride-a-while, stop-a-while motor vacation, with facilities for camping, hiking, picnicking, lodging, and eating. The scenery and driving thrills are now so popular that more than eleven million visitors travel the Parkway each year. Yet few of these millions have any inkling of the dreams, labors, controversies, lobbying, and politicking that were brought into play to make the magic of the mountain scenery available to them.

Conceived as a make-work project in 1933, the Blue Ridge Parkway has been under construction since 1935 and is operated under the jurisdiction of the Department of the Interior. Originally, the Parkway was expected to be a scenic highway linking the Shenandoah and Great Smoky Mountains National Parks, with the states of Virginia,

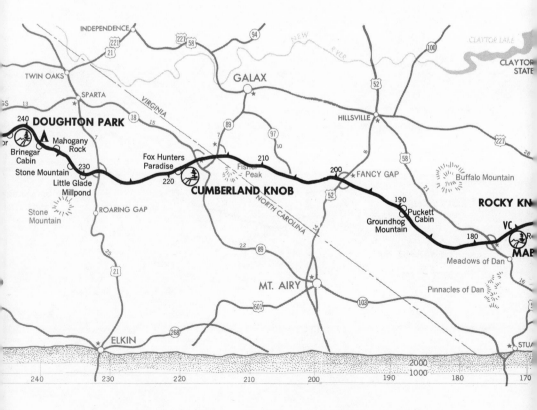

North Carolina, and Tennessee sharing the route. When the time came for determining the location, however, a major controversy developed between Tennessee and North Carolina. In the end North Carolina, by applying a host of arguments and pleading directly through Ambassador Josephus Daniels and others to Secretary of the Interior Harold L. Ickes and President Franklin D. Roosevelt, obtained more than half of the mileage; Tennessee got none.

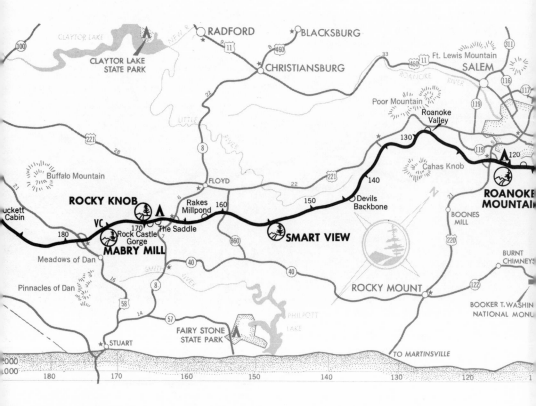

Acknowledgments

To PRESENT PARKWAY OFFICIALS, and to former superintendent Sam P. Weems, ex-chief naturalist Donald H. Robinson, and former supervisory architect Edward H. Abbuehl, I am indebted beyond payment for the untiring cooperation which aided the research on this project. To Dr. Herbert Kahler, ex-chief historian, National Park Service, and his colleagues of the Eastern National Parks and Monument Association, I express appreciation for their encouragement and aid in the form of two summer grants. The Piedmont University Center also provided financial aid for the research, and this assistance is hereby gratefully acknowledged. The late Senator Harry F. Byrd, Theodore E. Straus, Earl W. Batten, Jarrett Blythe, and William Mathis, as well as many others, were most helpful in sharing the wealth of their personal knowledge and in providing historical leads. To each of them I express my special thanks.

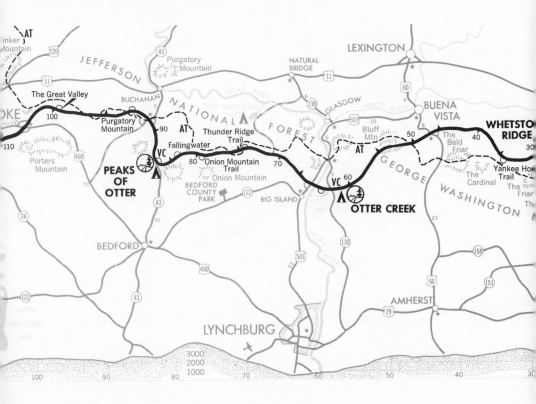

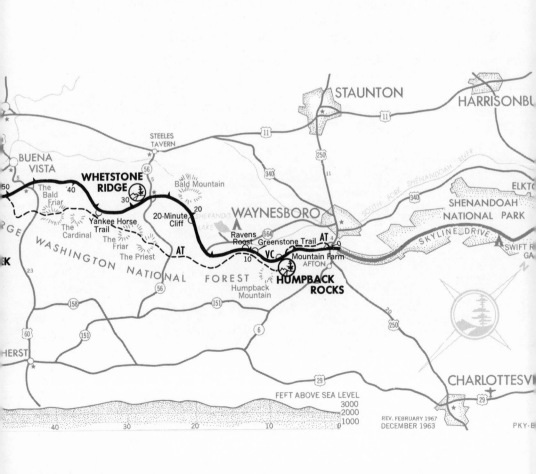

STAUNTON

HARRISONBU

11

250

BUENA
VISTA

STEELES
TAVERN

11

340

11

WHETSTONE
RIDGE

56

ELKTO

Bald Mountain

340

WAYNESBORO

SHENANDOAH
NATIONAL PARK

The
Bald
Friar

40

30

SKYLINE DRIVE

20-Minute
Cliff

20

SHERANDO
LAKE

SWIFT R
GA

Yankee Horse
Trail

Ravens
Roost   Greenstone Trail

AT
0

The
Cardinal

The
Friar

AT

VC

The Priest

10

VC

Mountain Farm

WASHINGTON   NATIONAL

FOREST

AFTON

HUMPBACK
ROCKS

23

56

Humpback
Mountain

20

158

151

250

RGE

EK

60

151

6

HERST

60

29

CHARLOTTESV

29

FEET ABOVE SEA LEVEL
3000
2000
1000

40   30   20   10

REV. FEBRUARY 1967
DECEMBER 1963

PKY-B

Contents

Preface   page v
Acknowledgments   vii
Maps and Illustrations   **xi**
1   *A Road of Peace*   3
2   *Visions of a Mountaintop Road*   9
3   *"I Did It"*   21
4   *"I Ask Your Cooperation"*   33
5   *"Run It This Way!"*   45
6   *A Godsend for the Needy*   50
7   *Slicing the Pie*   57
8   *One Little Indian*   93
9   *"It's Good fur a Road"*   102
10   *"The Most Visionary Thing"*   122
11   *Fulfilling the Promise*   130
    Things to see and do along the Blue Ridge Parkway   137
    Blue Ridge Parkway Log   143
    Bibliography   158
    Index   165

Maps and Illustrations

1. Route of the Blue Ridge Parkway *page* ii
2. Proposed Crest of the Blue Ridge Highway 14
3. Proposed Eastern National Park-To-Park Highway 16, 17
4. Proposed Shenandoah-Great Smoky Mountains National Parkway 60
5. The Maloney Route 62, 63

ILLUSTRATIONS

Following page 12

The Blue Ridge Parkway, showing the first milepost at Rockfish Gap, Virginia, and the last milepost at the Oconaluftee River, North Carolina
A low-altitude Parkway scene
The mountains of the Blue Ridge area
Fog amid the mountain peaks
Mabry Mill
Camping along the Parkway
Bush Creek Gap and mountain laurel

Following page 28

A typical road in the Blue Ridge Mountains
Billboards characteristic of most public highways
Bridge made from stone of the area
A rail fence along the Parkway
Oxen used in farm work
A dogtrot cabin
A valley as seen from the Parkway

Following page 76

Blue Ridge patriarch
People of the mountains
A Blue Ridge couple
Evidences of hardship and lack of medical attention
A bark-sided cabin

Poverty evident in houses of mountain people
Blue Ridge families
Differing mountain fence styles

Following page 92

Placing dynamite in preparation for blasting
Clearing away stone to avoid clutter
Breaking up rubble after dynamiting
Laborers employed in building the Parkway
Rock crushers
"Jumbo" method of tunnel-building
Tunnel construction in the 1960's
Continuing construction on the Parkway

Following page 108

Rocks and faults exposed during blasting for the Parkway
Visitor centers at Peaks of Otter and Humpback Rocks
Examples of building tools used in the Blue Ridge Mountains
Waterrock Knob and rhododendron
Museum of North Carolina Minerals and Doughton Park coffee
    shop
Flame azalea and lady's slipper
Bridge at Buck Creek Gap

Following page 124

Weaving and blacksmithing exhibits
Gristmilling at Mabry Mill
Puckett Cabin
Asheville North Fork Reservoir
National Park Service rangers with visitors
Picnicking at Craggy Gardens
Molasses mill

The Blue Ridge Parkway

AUTHOR'S NOTE: The attractions which appear in *Italics* in the Blue Ridge Parkway Log (at the back of the book) have also been described in the text, especially Chapter 11, and in the section, "Things to see and do along the Blue Ridge Parkway."

A Road of Peace

EARLY IN JUNE, 1959, a full-blooded Cherokee Indian, as part of a colorful ritual celebrating a recent development in the now famed Blue Ridge Parkway, lifted his arms heavenward and in his rhythmical native tongue uttered these words (translated): "Where once there was only a buffalo trail, where Indian campfires once blazed . . . where once the red man and the white man fought . . . there is a road of peace and we are thankful." [1]

The Indian speaker could have added just as easily that the road of peace is a road of history and conflict, a road that slices through an area filled with legends and memories of the historical great, the near-great, and the never-great-but-nonetheless-important figures who followed the call of the "Horn in the West." A ride along the highway opens windows on a cultural history more than two centuries old. Where the hard-surfaced thoroughfare now runs, Indians held tribal powwows, and the earliest settlers made their overnight campfires as they headed west for greener pastures. Thomas Jefferson and George Washington speculated in land that now lies near the road. Young Andrew Jackson crossed from the eastern to the western side of the Ridge to make his political fortune. Across the same mountain, but in the opposite direction, trudged the Moravians as they sought a new home in the American wilderness. Daniel Boone and David Crockett hunted the land as if it were their own private game preserve. Indian hunting and raiding parties coursed up and down the length of the Blue Ridge. Armies— pioneer militia, Revolutionary, and Civil War—left their punitive mark on the land. The remains of turnpikes, canals, and narrow-gauge railroads reflect the romantic "boom and bust" era of transportation. And the mud-chinked log cabin, the split rail fence, the loom and spinning wheel, the long rifle, the old grist mill, the ancient broad-axe, all of which did so much to tame this frontier land, still linger for public view and wonderment.

Exciting as it was, however, the conquering of the wilderness did not mark the end of the region's drama. Beneath the calm and peaceful quiet which now typify the great road, there lies a background of

[1] John Parris, "Ceremony Joins a Storied Road with Smoky Park," Asheville *Citizen*, June 6, 1959, p. 1.

twentieth-century discord. Had the highway been named "Controversy Parkway," there would have been ample justification because
from the very beginning disputes have been associated with it—even
about such matters as its origins and "father." Moreover, several of
these issues were not minor altercations such as commonly arise when
a new highway is built. They were major controversies, fought for the
most part over the question of the proposed route of the parkway, and
of such magnitude as to arouse the concern of the President of the
United States, the Secretary of the Interior, an American ambassador,
numerous United States senators and representatives, at least three
state governors, an Indian tribe, many chambers of commerce, and a
host of other persons. But that was in the 1930's; and in the years since,
the conflict has been almost forgotten in the myriad details inherent in
the construction of the Blue Ridge Parkway. What remains are old letters, the memories of old-timers, and a magnificent highway on top of
a range of mountains that effortlessly wipes out the turmoil of the past.

He who travels the Parkway today quickly discovers that it is a road
of unlimited horizons. One of the great attractions of the route is that
it follows the very crest of the ridges that form the backbone of the
Southern Appalachians. In its role of opening this vast mountain region to the motoring public, the Parkway provides a grand balcony
from which to view the diverse natural wonders of the area. Thus a
trip along the scenic route is well calculated to produce a marvelous
sense of being on top of the world, with only one's imagination to
bound the horizons.

But within the confines of these horizons, one finds an abundance
of additional nature-given bounties. Not the least of these is the color
of the mountains and of the vegetation. Color, in fact, has long been
associated with the region. There is an omnipresent blue haze which
hangs heavily over the upper reaches of the mountains and is believed
to have inspired the name of the Ridge. The Virginian William Byrd,
writing in 1728, was one of the earliest commentators to note this phe-
nomenon. While surveying the boundary between Virginia and North
Carolina, he recorded the discovery of a range of mountains to his
northwest that seemed to lie off at a vast distance and "lookt like
Ranges of Blue clouds rising one above another." [2] And so they look

[2] William K. Boyd (ed.), *William Byrd's Histories of the Dividing Line
Betwixt Virginia and North Carolina* (Raleigh, N. C.: The North Carolina Historical Commission, 1929), 124.

today. Blue, however, is only one of the hues that create the splendor
of the Parkway. There is the pristine white of the flowering dogwood,
which displays its blossoms in the early spring, and the more creamy
white of the early blooming Fraser magnolias. And rivaling them for
dominance, as spring begins to unfold, are the white to pale pink petals
of the shadbush ("service berry") and the rich pinks of the redbud.
Then, in late April or early May, glistening as though it had been
sprayed with a florescent paint, the flame azalea presents an ostenta-
tious show of oranges, yellows, and golds of almost unbelievable bril-
liance. By mid-May the delicate pinks of the mountain laurel have
begun to appear, and in late May and early June the catawba rhodo-
dendrons fill such areas as Craggy Gardens and the Bluffs with purple
so rich that it seems to be double-dyed.

Indeed, throughout the spring and summer there is a steady procession of color, with a seemingly endless variety of wildflowers, flowering shrubs, and trees providing their unique loveliness. Then, as if to
say, "Huh, you ain't seen nothing yet!" the autumn colors begin
emerging and appear to saturate the whole world. The sumacs, the
dogwoods, the gums, and the sourwoods begin the process with varying tints of copper and red, usually by mid-September or earlier; and
with each day, a new patch of color is added to the landscape. Yellows
and golds are provided by the birch, buckeye, tulip poplar, beech, and
hickory trees. The sassafras tree displays mitten-like leaves of vivid
orange. The mountain ash colors whole mountainsides with its deep-
hued red berries, and the maples top off the show with brilliant shades
of scarlet. Then, as a last gesture, when others are fading, the oaks give
forth the final tones of red. As color fades from the leaves, the Parkway environs take on the subdued hues of winter; but when the chill
winds come, the higher regions assume an entirely new color—the
jewel-like sheen of rime ice that festoons the trees and shrubs and
sparkles as richly as diamonds.

Closely allied to the resplendent plant life is the unique climate of
the Blue Ridge. Even as early as the 1850's the Swiss-American geol-
ogist Arnold Guyot was writing: "The climate of this elevated region
is truly delightful. . . . The nights are generally cool, and the mildness
of that healthy and bracing air is both invigorating and exceedingly
pleasant." [3] The tourist industry of North Carolina and Virginia has

[3] Myron H. Avery and Kenneth S. Boardman (eds.), "Arnold Guyot's Notes
on the Geography of the Mountain Districts of Western North Carolina,"
North Carolina Historical Review, XV (July, 1938), 288.

long capitalized on the invigorating climate; rainfall is abundant (in the United States only the Pacific Northwest has more) and contributes richly to the lushness and variety of vegetation; temperatures run fifteen or more degrees below those of nearby lower elevations. As a result, the Parkway country, in the very middle of the Blue Ridge Mountains, has become a great vacation land with regular colonies of summer residents.

Summer residents and Parkway visitors alike have come to expect generally sunny skies but soon learn that periodic showers and even fog may quickly change their horizons. Characteristically, rain may fall on one side of the mountain and not on the other. A superintendent of construction for the Parkway recalled, "We had a hard time getting the boys on the east side of the mountain to come to work when it was raining on their side. We kept telling them to come to the job regardless of the weather because oftentimes the rain didn't reach all of the project." [4] The fog, like the rainfall with which it is usually associated, may occur at any season of the year. Sometimes thin, it will float in billowing wisps over the roadway. Again, it may be as heavy as a leaden mantle and completely enshroud the tops of the ridges. It is sometimes deceptive; a visitor might leave Waynesboro, or Roanoke, or Asheville in brilliant sunshine and within a few miles encounter fog on the Parkway so thick that further travel becomes hazardous. On the other hand, the fog is capable of presenting some wonderful, eye-catching scenes: masses of fog occasionally settle on and completely obliterate the lower mountainsides, causing the higher peaks and ridges to appear as islands and the shoreline of a vast ocean.

The result of this abundant rainfall and the mild climate, coupled with the varying elevations of the Blue Ridge, is a veritable botanist's paradise. A two-hour trip from the foothills of the Blue Ridge to its higher elevations discloses as many plant-life zones as would be encountered in driving a thousand miles north from central Georgia to central Quebec. A wider variety of wildflowers grows here than is found in all of Europe, to say nothing of the many species of trees and flowering shrubs that are present.

With such a climate, it is natural that the Parkway should also be a road of varied animal life. Wild animals do abound, and they add to

[4] Interview with William Mathis, onetime Parkway construction superintendent, September 3, 1963.

the excitement of traveling. One of the most frequently seen animals, and one of the most commonly mis-identified, is the ground hog or "whistle pig." Feeding along the roadside, he seems to halt his activities and pose for the visitor—as long as the automobile keeps moving. But the moment a car slows down or stops, he scurries into his hole, and the traveler goes home telling about the big "beaver" he saw up on the Parkway. There are, indeed, beavers in the area, mostly in the vicinity of such places as Otter Creek (Milepost 84), where they have actually constructed lodges adjacent to the roadway. Bear and elk inhabit the forests along the way, but they are seen infrequently. Deer are far commoner, and a few albinos have been reported. Foxes, opossums, squirrels, skunks, chipmunks, and many other smaller species inhabit the region and are often seen. Partly because it lies astride a major bird migration flyway, the Parkway offers unusual opportunities to the bird watcher, especially in the early spring when more than one hundred species may be identified. And, yes, there are some snakes, including the timber rattler and the copperhead, but it is the rare visitor who encounters one.

Nature has provided still another attraction in the form of geologic formations. The mountains through which the Parkway runs are considered to be among the oldest in the world. One authority has said that compared to the Blue Ridge, the Himalayas are in their swaddling clothes, the Andes are in precocious days, the Rockies have reached middle age, and the Alleghenies have barely turned their faces toward the sunset of life.[5] Thus, the rock along the way contributes fascinating pages to nature's geology textbook. The cuts made during the process of construction have exposed the rocks common to the province—granites, gneisses, schists, diorites, and slates. And, with an eye to both frugality and aesthetics, the Parkway builders added a man-made contribution by using many of these stones to fashion attractive bridges, tunnel facings, and retaining walls. Moreover, at the time the engineers were locating the roadbed, they consciously provided for excellent views of such geological wonders as the granite Looking Glass Rock (3,969 feet), the quartzite Grandfather Mountain (5,938 feet, highest point of the Blue Ridge), and the greenstone Humpback Rocks (3,210 feet). Also, the state of North Carolina and the National

[5] William J. Showalter, 1933 chief of Research Division, National Geographic Society, as reported in the Richmond *Times Dispatch*, December 14, 1933, p. 4.

Park Service joined to create a museum of North Carolina minerals (Milepost 331.0), featuring such minerals as mica, feldspar, kaolin, and tungsten.

Millions of visitors have already enjoyed these natural wonders, and predictions call for even more. Located within easy driving distance of more than half of the national population, the Parkway attracted more than eleven million to its facilities in 1967; at least fifteen million visitors are expected in 1975. Many of them find pleasure in simply traveling to the mountains and driving for a day or an afternoon, at a leisurely pace along the scenic route, free from the pressures of their urban boulevards. Others pack their travel trailers, campers, or automobiles and head for one of the Parkway's high elevation campgrounds, frequently staying for weeks at a time. Those who prefer hiking and climbing are excited by the opportunities offered by the many trails and peaks along the way. Wayside museums, campfire programs, and nature walks provide relaxation and a change of pace for persons of all ages. Families and young couples have discovered that picnicking along the Parkway is delightful, and in season the picnic areas are usually crowded. All in all, visitors from every state in the Union and from many foreign countries have enjoyed and marveled at the great highway.

Thus, the Blue Ridge Parkway of today might rightly be called nature's department store, offering exciting variety to a broad spectrum of persons. Campers, bird watchers, rock hounds, botanists, picnickers, or those who simply wish to escape the polluted air of cities for a refreshing drive in the mountains—all may find much of what they seek on the pleasant miles of the Parkway. Most of all, however, the Parkway is American history, past, present, and future waiting to be enjoyed. The tranquillity that now permeates the region is qualified by this past history and especially by the events of the last thirty years. The following chapters tell of the controversies that raged at the inception of the Blue Ridge Parkway—and even during its construction—in an effort to explain how the "Road of Peace" came into existence.

Visions of a Mountaintop Road  2

2

FROM THE FOUNDING of Jamestown onward, easily accessible water transportation combined with the plantation system to retard road-building in the South. In the North the Boston Post Road connected New England with New York as early as 1673. By 1795 the pressure of westward migration had brought about the first organized road improvement, the Lancaster Turnpike, a private road running 62¼ miles westward from Philadelphia.[1] In contrast, for years no roads of importance linked Virginia with North Carolina. Edward Moseley's map of 1733, said to be the oldest North Carolina general road map, shows only an Indian trading path connecting the mountain districts of the two colonies. Some forty years later John Collet's "Compleat Map of North Carolina" indicated that two roads ran across the mountains between Virginia and North Carolina.[2] When the first contingent of Moravians trekked to North Carolina from Pennsylvania in 1753, they came down the Great Road from Pennsylvania through the Shenandoah Valley. As they passed Augusta Court House (Staunton, Virginia) they declared, ". . . and there the bad road began." Their diary says that thereafter the farther they went the more difficult travel became. Frequently the travelers were forced to cut down trees and use grubbing hoes to clear a passage for their wagons. Occasionally block and tackle were required to keep the wagons from slipping over the mountain's edge. Thus, it is not surprising that the journey from Augusta Court House to Bethabara (Staunton, Va., to Winston-Salem, N. C.) required three weeks.[3]

By 1780 one of the best known roads across the Blue Ridge was the Yellow Mountain Road. It was part of a North Carolina intra-state highway system running via Wilmington, Fayetteville, Salem, Wilkesboro, Morganton, and McKinney Gap, across the Blue Ridge, over the Unakas, and into Sycamore Shoals, a frontier outpost on the Watauga

[1] Albert C. Rose, "Historic American Highways," *Annual Report of the Board of Regents, Smithsonian Institution, for the Year 1939* (Washington, D. C.: Government Printing Office, 1940), 500.

[2] Based upon maps reproduced in Capus Waynick, *North Carolina Roads and Their Builders* (Raleigh, N. C.: Superior Stone Co., 1952), 74, 246.

[3] Adelaide L. Fries (ed.), *Records of the Moravians in North Carolina* (Raleigh, N. C.: Edwards & Broughton Printing Co., 1922), I, 77–78.

River. It is believed that this trace was originally blazed by the fron-
tiersman James Robertson, using information provided by Daniel
Boone. Even prior to this time Boone, in traveling from his home on
the Yadkin River to the western waters, had laid the now famous
Boone Wilderness Trail.[4]

Both Virginia and North Carolina passed many road laws in the following years, but most roads remained scarcely worthy of the name.
The average one was little more than a path meandering haphazardly
across fields and through forests.[5] Increased demands for better roads
brought the development of such privately sponsored building efforts
as the Howardsville Turnpike, long a main artery for transporting
goods from the Kanawha Canal at the James River to Howardsville
and other points along the Blue Ridge. Private turnpikes were never
adequate to meet public needs, but throughout two hundred years
neither North Carolina nor Virginia took effective action to improve
their highways. In fact, until the twentieth century their roads were
built and maintained by the counties rather than by the states.[6] Some
counties levied special road taxes, employed convict labor, and used
improved methods of road-building; but the more isolated and rural
areas received little attention.[7]

An authoritative 1911 report described transportation conditions in
the Southern Appalachian regions as dismal.[8] Railway facilities were
rated poor, and most of the settlements were twenty to thirty-five
miles from the nearest railroad. Few of the mountain roads were
graded or otherwise improved. Inhabitants therefore found transportation generally slow, difficult, and expensive. Some, but relatively
little, road improvement had been made throughout the Blue Ridge
area by the 1930's. The ten poorest mountain counties in Virginia and
North Carolina had 310 and 500 miles, respectively, of improved highway in 1928.[9] The Federal Land Planning Committee in 1935 revealed

[4] John Preston Arthur, *Western North Carolina: A History from 1730 to
1913* (Raleigh, N. C.: Edwards & Broughton Printing Co., 1914), 232.

[5] Hugh Talmage Lefler and Albert Ray Newsome, *North Carolina: The History of a Southern State* (Chapel Hill: University of North Carolina Press, 1934),
300.

[6] *Ibid.*, 585.

[7] Blackwell P. Robinson (ed.), *The North Carolina Guide* (Chapel Hill: University of North Carolina Press, 1955), 94.

[8] Leonidas Chalmer Glenn, *Denudation and Erosion in the Southern Appalachian Region*, U. S. Geological Survey Professional Paper No. 72 (Washington,
D. C.: Government Printing Office, 1911), 10.

[9] Rupert B. Vance, *Human Geography of the South: A Study in Regional*

that many of these counties were acquiring their first gravel roads, and numerous localities were said to be accessible only by horseback or "jolt wagon." [10] The best that some counties could boast was that they had a paved road, often the only one in the county, leading from the county seat to the state capital. Others, like Floyd County, Virginia, did not have a single paved road at the time construction began on the Parkway.[11] Thus, the mountain communities eagerly welcomed any prospect of a new highway. To them the possibility of a paved road through the mountains, as began to be rumored in late 1933, stimulated hopes of ending their isolation and improving their economy.

CREST OF THE BLUE RIDGE HIGHWAY

Man's dreams and visions are frequently years in advance of his accomplishments. Even in the building of the Parkway this was true. In September, 1935, the first shovelful of dirt was turned to begin the highway, but years before, a dreamer had been hard at work in laying out a similar route. The coming of the automobile had created a renewed interest in highway-building. Good roads associations sprang up with the express purpose of promoting construction of roads that would, in turn, stimulate development of agriculture, commerce, and natural resources. Commercial utility became the measure of a road's success. It is therefore somewhat amazing to learn that as early as 1909 a visionary project had been planned and the actual survey work begun for a pleasure road along the summit of the Blue Ridge. This road had been looked upon as a means of providing a scenic drive that would make available to the public the spectacular natural beauty of the mountains. Recreation rather than commerce was its reason for being. Even the name implied its purpose: "The Crest of the Blue Ridge Highway." [12]

Resources and Human Adequacy (Chapel Hill: University of North Carolina Press, 1932), 255.

10 U. S. Federal Land Planning Committee, "Maladjustments in Land Use in the United States," *Supplementary Report of the Land Planning Committee to the National Resources Board* (Washington, D. C.: Government Printing Office, 1935), Pt. VI, 21.

11 Interview with Edward H. Abbuehl, Parkway supervisory landscape architect, July 16, 1962, Roanoke, Va.

12 Joseph Hyde Pratt, *Highway Work in North Carolina: Containing a Statistical Report of the Road Work during 1911*, North Carolina Geological and Economic Survey Economic Paper No. 27 (Raleigh, N. C.: E. M. Uzzell and Co., 1912), 27–33.

The father of the Crest of the Blue Ridge Highway was Colonel Joseph Hyde Pratt, head of the North Carolina Geological and Economic Survey. This man readily understood the impact that the new-fangled automobile would have on travel. If properly catered to, the new machine could do much to promote tourism and the economic growth of North Carolina. With this in mind he drew up plans for and began promoting construction of a scenic highway along the summit of the Ridge. He described his road as probably the most ambitious undertaking ever made in highway construction in North Carolina. With pride he asserted that it was destined to be one of the greatest scenic roads in America, surpassing anything in the East and rivaling those in Yosemite Valley and the Yellowstone National Park.[13] A report by Pratt included one sentence which expressed why he thought his brainchild was worthwhile: "The grandeur of the scenery along this highway, comprising, as it will, extensive vistas into the Piedmont region, nearer views of valleys, and mountain tops, and ridges, with here and there a most attractive waterfall; and the highway crossing and passing streams of clear crystal water and penetrating the dense evergreen forests of balsam and spruce, whose deep shade always casts a feeling of awe over the traveler as he passes through them, will make the ride over this highway one never to be forgotten." [14]

The scheme called for a highway and a chain of hotels extending from Marion, Virginia, to Tallulah Falls, Georgia. The northern end was to connect with the Bristol-Washington road and the southern, with a good highway leading into Atlanta, Georgia. From Marion the route was to pass close to White Top Mountain, a resort center in southwest Virginia, and enter North Carolina via Ashe County. Then passing through Boone, Blowing Rock, Linville, Altapass, Little Switzerland, Asheville, Hendersonville, Brevard, Toxaway, and Highlands, the road would enter Georgia near Rabun Gap. The estimated length was 350 miles, most of it lying in North Carolina, and the estimated cost was $5,000 per mile.[15] Highest roadway elevation was to be at Steppe's Gap, only eight hundred feet short of the top of Mount Mitchell. None of the route was to have a grade of more than 4½ per cent.

[13] *Ibid.*, 27.
[14] *Ibid.*
[15] Thomas F. Hickerson, "The Crest of the Blue Ridge Highway," *Journal of the Elisha Mitchell Scientific Society*, XXVIII (December, 1911), 160.

From Rockfish Gap, Virginia, to the Oconaluftee River in North Carolina, the Blue Ridge Parkway winds 469 scenic miles, connecting the Shenandoah and Great Smoky Mountains National Parks. *Courtesy (top left) Stella Anderson, Skyland (N.C.) Post; and Blue Ridge Parkway*

Streamside scenes such as this helped bring more than 11,000,000 visitors to the Parkway in 1969. *Courtesy Blue Ridge Parkway*

One great attraction of the Parkway is its location, hugging the back-bone of the Southern Appalachians. *Courtesy Blue Ridge Parkway*

Masses of clouds and fog occasionally cause the higher peaks and ridges to appear as islands in a vast ocean. *Courtesy Blue Ridge Parkway*

Mabry Mill (Mile 176.2) features an old-time mountain industry the year long. *Courtesy Blue Ridge Parkway*

The National Park Service has repeatedly enlarged its camping facilities. *Courtesy N. C. Dept. of Conservation and Development*

The native stone bridge at Buck Creek Gap (Mile 344.1), skillfully integrated with the terrain, illustrates both the art and frugality of the Parkway designers. Mountain laurel (left) grows prolifically along the Parkway and thrives at elevations up to 5,000 feet. It blooms mainly in May and has a light pink flower. *Bridge picture courtesy N. C. Dept. of Conservation and Development; flower courtesy Blue Ridge Parkway*

The road was to be twenty-four feet wide from ditch to ditch, and nine feet of that would have a sand-clay or gravel surface.[16]

At a meeting of the North Carolina Good Roads Association on August 1, 1912, Pratt reported that for the past three years he and his men had been surveying the route. He stated that because of the scanty population and the nature of the country through which the route passed, the highway would require private subscription. Thus it would be a toll road rather than a public one. Construction had already begun in July, 1912, with a crew of one hundred men building from Altapass toward Linville. The Appalachian Highway Company had been chartered to lay the road, and it hoped to have a fifty-mile stretch open for automobile travel by the following summer. Pratt indicated that all the people along the way were interested in the project and were giving the right-of-way as well as buying stock. He closed his address to the association by saying that the enterprise was one of the largest ever attempted in the South, or even in the United States. "But," said he, "the plan is feasible. It is started; it is going to be completed; and we are going to be proud of the Crest of the Blue Ridge Highway!" [17]

The portion of the highway between Altapass and Pineola, North Carolina, was actually completed; but the project, unfortunately, was abandoned when the pressure of World War I made it necessary to divert manpower, material, and funds into other channels. Although the dream of Pratt and his colleagues fell by the wayside, the vision of a scenic mountaintop highway remained. Almost three decades later it was revived and so vigorously supported by a new group of boosters that it became a reality. Their arguments in support of the road as well as much of the proposed route corresponded closely to those advanced by Pratt. Today, as one travels the Parkway between Mile 317.6 and Mile 318.7, he drives along the approximate roadbed of this pioneer effort at a Crest of the Blue Ridge Parkway.[18] A large part of the remainder of the Parkway follows relatively closely that charted for its

16 Joseph Hyde Pratt, *Proceedings of the Annual Convention of the North Carolina Good Roads Association*, North Carolina Geological and Economic Survey Economic Paper No. 30 (Raleigh, N. C.: Edwards & Broughton Printing Co., 1912), 95.

17 *Ibid.*, 96.

18 Edward H. Abbuehl, "History of the Blue Ridge Parkway," paper read before Blue Ridge Parkway Rangers' Conference, Roanoke, Va., February 8, 1948, p. 1, in the files of the Superintendent, Blue Ridge Parkway, Roanoke, Va.; hereinafter referred to as Abbuehl, "History."

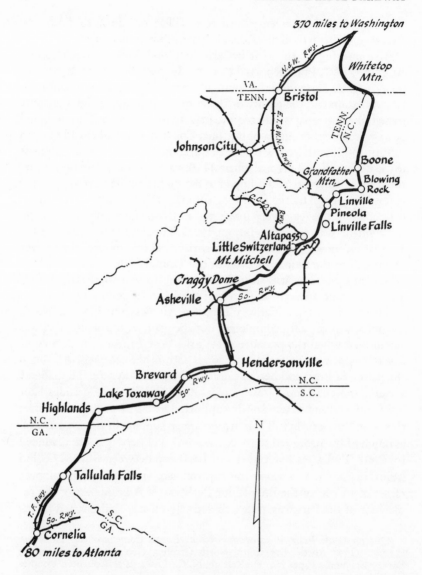

Proposed Route of the Crest of the Blue Ridge Highway. *Based on the original map, courtesy of North Carolina Geological and Economic Survey.*

predecessor. Thus to Joseph Hyde Pratt should go first honors for conceiving what eventually became the Blue Ridge Parkway.

FEDERAL PARK-TO-PARK HIGHWAY

Following the First World War, little was heard of a Blue Ridge highway for several years; but by 1930 federal park-to-park highways had become topics of conversation and, naturally, of political maneuvering. The most prominent booster of such highways was Congressman Maurice H. Thatcher of Kentucky. He proposed a system of highways that would link several of the federal parks. His idea was to build a road beginning in Washington, D. C., which would come down through the Shenandoah National Park in Virginia, take in the Natural Bridge, and move by way of Roanoke and Wytheville into North Carolina. There the cities of Boone, Blowing Rock, Pineola, Asheville, and Waynesville would be touched upon, and the route would continue to the Great Smoky Mountains National Park. That park would be linked with the Mammoth Cave National Park project, Abraham Lincoln's Birthplace, the Kentucky Blue Grass region, Jamestown, George Washington's Birthplace, Mount Vernon, and Washington, D. C.[19]

In the summer of 1930 Thatcher, in the course of a tour along the proposed route, stopped in Knoxville and unwittingly aggravated an eastern Tennessee-western North Carolina feud. The cities of Knoxville and Asheville had long been rivals for the Great Smoky Mountains tourist trade. One irate North Carolinian said that Colonel David C. Chapman and other Tennessee boosters had told Thatcher that it was not only unnecessary but also a waste of time to ask tourists to spend a vacation in North Carolina. This advice was based on the opinion that visitors could see all of the worthwhile portions of the Smokies by remaining within Tennessee.

When this report reached the ears of interested North Carolinians, they immediately began counteraction. While the Tennesseans were lobbying so that the highway would favor them and bypass the Carolina towns,[20] western North Carolina civic leaders, seeking to insure for their region a fair share of any federal park-to-park highway that

[19] Letter with map, Arno B. Cammerer to Governor John G. Pollard, May 8, 1931, in John G. Pollard Papers, Box 6, Virginia State Library, Richmond.
[20] Fred L. Weede to Verne Rhoades, September 6, 1930, in North Carolina Park Commission files, Waynesville.

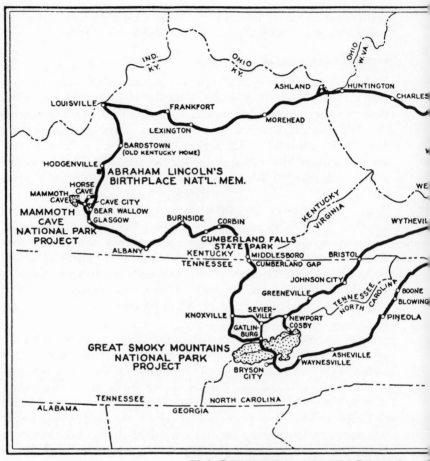

EASTERN NATIONAL P

Agreed on in Conference at Washington D.C., April 4,193

Map prepared in cooperation with East

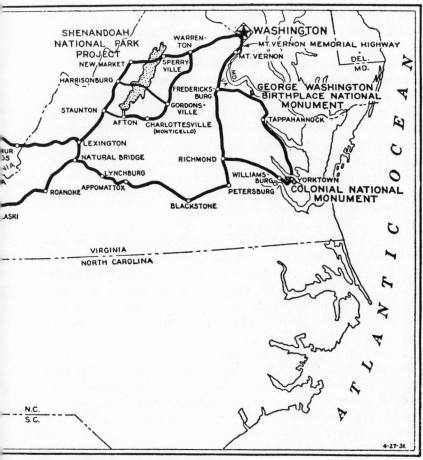

K- TO- PARK HIGHWAY

tatives of interested State authorities participating.

onal Park to Park Highway Association

might result from Congressman Thatcher's activities, appealed to the North Carolina Park Commission for support. The commission adopted a resolution declaring that the proposed road should be routed via Asheville, Linville, Blowing Rock, Boone, Jefferson, Sparta, and thence to Wytheville. In addition, the North Carolina State Highway Commission was requested to make effective representation of their desires at a park-to-park conference scheduled in Louisville, Kentucky, September 20, 1930. The resolution also authorized enlisting Congressman Robert L. Doughton's support.[21] The Carolinians were fearful that the Tennesseans would lobby them out of the picture unless they threw all their effort into the fight. This friction between the two states foreshadowed a major struggle which reached a climax when a park-to-park highway was finally authorized.

Tar Heel interests actually were in jeopardy, according to a delegate sent to Washington to protect them. When he and a fellow delegate arrived at a conference called by Congressman Thatcher, they found a large map with a routing of the park-to-park highway on the table; the road followed the Lee Highway straight from Virginia into Tennessee and by-passed North Carolina. The Carolina men immediately protested. They drew another route which veered off the Lee Highway at Wytheville, Virginia, ran into North Carolina via Jefferson, Boone, Blowing Rock, Linville, Marion, and Asheville, and then connected with the Great Smoky Mountains National Park. The next day their work was championed by Congressman Doughton, Senator Josiah W. Bailey, and others. "And," reported the delegate, "we succeeded in getting it adopted. Otherwise North Carolina would have been left out." [22]

Thatcher had in the meantime become president of the Eastern National Park-to-Park Association, which had been formed to agitate for the promotion of such a highway system. For various reasons, he failed to obtain the support necessary to make it a reality. Thus, it was not until 1933, from an entirely different source, that there emerged the basic idea, planning, groundwork, and authorization for what is now the Blue Ridge Parkway. Even so, Thatcher's project, despite the fact that it was intended to utilize existing highways rather than con-

---

[21] Minutes, North Carolina Park Commission, September 13, 1930, in Commission files.

[22] Letter, Finley H. Coffey to Governor J. C. B. Ehringhaus, October 14, 1933, in J. C. B. Ehringhaus Papers, Box 152, State Archives, Raleigh, N. C.

struct new ones, did advance the idea of a park-to-park highway. It also aroused state and civic groups to the possibility of a scenic highway and stimulated an interest that culminated in the establishment of the Parkway. Today, the North Carolina portion of the road follows closely the Thatcher routing.

PARKWAY PRECEDENTS

The term *parkway* has become almost as significant in the twentieth century as *turnpike* was in the nineteenth. Yet parkway legislation and construction are of remarkably recent birth. The modern parkway idea, as it is understood in the United States today, had its origins in county and municipal undertakings such as the Westchester County Parkway in New York.[23] Parkways, like highways, may serve either a commercial or a recreational function. For both, the recreational role is amazingly large. According to a report made by the Natural Resources Board to President Franklin D. Roosevelt, more than half of the traffic over the 1933 highway system of the United States was recreational traffic.[24] The same authority estimated that 60 per cent of the total use of the American automobile was for recreational purposes. The increasing population and its need for outdoor travel made construction of scenic highways highly desirable.

The first legislative reference to a federal parkway or its equivalent is found in an Act of Congress of May 23, 1928, which provided for the establishment of the Mount Vernon Memorial Highway and specifically called for the "planting of shade trees and shrubbery and for other landscape treatment, parking, and ornamental structures," as well as right-of-way provisions to protect adequately the beauty of the highway.[25] On May 29, 1930, came the second federal parkway legislation, making provision for the acquisition, establishment, and development of the George Washington Memorial Parkway. Legislation authorizing what is now the Colonial National Parkway was enacted by Congress on July 30, 1930. Under its provisions a highway

23 U. S. Federal Land Committee, "Public Works and Rural Land Use," *Report of the Land Committee to the National Resources Planning Board* (Washington, D. C.: Government Printing Office, 1942), 146.

24 U. S. National Resources Board, *Report on National Planning and Public Works in Relation to Natural Resources Including Land Use and Water Resources with Findings and Recommendations* (Washington, D. C.: Government Printing Office, 1934), 220.

25 *Congressional Record*, 70th Cong., 1st Sess., LXIX, Pt. 9, 9382–83.

with a right-of-way not exceeding five hundred feet was authorized to connect Jamestown, Williamsburg, and Yorktown.[26] The next important parkway development was an anti-Depression measure. The National Industrial Recovery Act of June 18, 1933, authorized the Publics Works Administrator to prepare a comprehensive program of works which would include construction, repair, and improvement of public highways and parkways.[27] The Blue Ridge Parkway was a product of that program.

The basic principle underlying all these acts was to provide for the construction of parkways in a manner that would protect yet make available for public enjoyment the outstanding points of scenic beauty along the route. A particular aim was to prevent the erection of billboards, signs, or other objects that might mar or detract from the natural beauty. With this concept and these precedents in mind, it is somewhat easier to understand why a *parkway* rather than an ordinary state or federal highway was chosen when the time came to build a road linking the Shenandoah and Great Smoky Mountains National Parks.

[26] A. E. Demaray, "Federal Parkways," paper read before Council Meeting of the American Planning and Civic Association, January 24, 1936, in National Archives, National Park Service, Record Group 79, Washington, D. C.
[27] U. S. *Statutes at Large*, XLVIII, Pt. I, 204.

"I Did It"

3

TODAY, MILLIONS OF VACATIONERS are driving, camping, picnicking, and visiting museums along the crest of the Blue Ridge Mountains on a magnificently engineered parkway that is one of the most scenic and heavily traveled thoroughfares in America.[1] As late as a generation ago, few visionary and even fewer "sane" men would have believed that completion of such a project was possible. For centuries this land, the most inaccessible of the mountain reaches, had provided passage for only the hardiest of humans and the most sure-footed of animals. Yet man's vision, combined with his engineering skill, brought forth on the mountaintop a strip of asphalt running 469 miles from ridge to ridge and gap to gap in such a gentle fashion that it was the driving equivalent of a city boulevard. Those miles connect two national parks and include some of the most spectacular scenery in the eastern United States.

The list of those who played prominent roles in the origin and development of the Parkway includes a President of the United States, a United States ambassador, numerous cabinet members, the heads of federal agencies such as the Bureau of Public Roads and the National Park Service, United States senators and congressmen, governors, lawyers, engineers, architects, and even Indian chiefs. Like the Tennessee Valley Authority and Social Security, the Blue Ridge Parkway was a Depression-born project that gained enough momentum in the depressed years to prove its merit and earn permanent status.

To identify the particular persons charged with planning and implementing the construction of the Parkway is relatively easy, but to name the man who actually thought of the idea first is a difficult and perhaps impossible task. In July, 1953, Hugh Alexander, member of the House of Representatives from North Carolina, wrote to the National Park Service in Washington, D. C., asking the identity of the originator. From Acting Director Hillory A. Tolson came this reply: "Careful examination of the records of this Service fail to reveal conclusively what individual or individuals organized the idea for the

[1] Speech, Secretary of the Interior Stewart Udall, as reported in the Asheville *Citizen*, August 19, 1961, p. 3.

building of the Blue Ridge Parkway." [2] Tolson further noted that the question of whether any one individual is solely responsible for advancing the original idea for the beginning of any particular project is always subject to controversy. He informed the congressman that this was especially true in the case of the proposal to build the Blue Ridge Parkway.[3]

A combination of many factors made the idea of a parkway linking the Shenandoah and Great Smoky National Parks possible, and not the least of these was that the time was singularly propitious. Both parks were newly established, and their scenic importance was well known. Moreover, the Skyline Drive had recently been built through the Shenandoah National Park for the purpose of making its beauty accessible. The first Civilian Conservation Corps camp in the United States had been established in Shenandoah County, Virginia, to relieve unemployment and preserve the natural resources. Its members had helped build the road in the park, and this use of surplus manpower was fresh in mind.[4] Too, there were the precedents of the Crest of the Blue Ridge Highway and the more recently suggested Eastern National Park-to-Park Highway. Finally, the Virginia Highway Department and the Department of Conservation had themselves seriously considered extending the Skyline Drive[5] southward. As early as July, 1933, the Virginia Highway Commissioner had received communications relative to obtaining the right-of-way for extending the Drive into the Natural Bridge Forest.[6]

In normal times, such a large construction project as building a parkway might have been considered impractical, but the alarming number of unemployed persons in 1933 made the proposal most attractive to government planners. President Franklin D. Roosevelt was

[2] Tolson to Alexander, September 22, 1943, in National Archives, National Park Service, Record Group 79.

[3] Ibid.

[4] Theodore C. Fearnow and I. T. Quinn, "Action on the Blue Ridge," Trees, 1949 Yearbook of Agriculture (Washington, D.C.: Government Printing Office, 1949), 587.

[5] From the very beginning there has existed considerable confusion in many minds about the distinction between the Skyline Drive and the Blue Ridge Parkway. The former is the proper name for the drive through the Shenandoah National Park; the latter is the official and correct title for the scenic route linking the Shenandoah and Great Smoky Mountains National Parks.

[6] Virginia Department of Highways, "Right of Way, Extension Skyline Drive," July 2, 1934, in files of Virginia Highway Department, Richmond.

willing to experiment, and Harold L. Ickes, Roosevelt's Secretary of the Interior and director of the Public Works Administration as well, was willing to offer him support. Still, the question remains, who suggested to them the actual idea for the parkway?

The number of claimants to that honor is remarkably small. The chief contenders for the title are the following:

Harry Flood Byrd, United States senator from Virginia;
Thomas H. MacDonald, chief, Bureau of Public Roads;
John G. Pollard, governor of Virginia;
George L. Radcliffe, United States senator from Maryland and regional advisor of Public Works Administration, District No. 10 (including North Carolina, Tennessee, and Virginia); and
Theodore E. Straus, one of Senator Radcliffe's advisors and also a member of the Public Works Administration, District No. 10.

The question of who actually thought of the Parkway idea was of little concern to these men in the 1930's. The chief objective was building the road itself, and each person had his own job to do. However, as the problems were overcome, as the Parkway grew longer, and as the years passed, people wondered more frequently who had really suggested the original plan. Byrd has claimed it was he, and Straus has made the same claim for himself. MacDonald, Pollard, and Radcliffe have seemed uninterested in the matter.

In a 1962 interview[7] Senator Byrd declared:

At the dedication of the Shenandoah National Park, President Roosevelt, Harold L. Ickes, and I were riding together from Panorama to Big Meadows. I suggested to Mr. Roosevelt that it would be a fine idea to connect the two parks, the Shenandoah National Park and the Great Smoky Mountains National Park, by extending the Skyline Drive. He quickly agreed that it was an excellent idea but stated that we must begin up in New England. The President then said to me, "You and Ickes get together for the right-of-way." The New England governors were contacted but were not interested. In the meanwhile I was made chairman of the right-of-way commission. And that is how it got started.

A 1959 feature article by Ozzie Osborne in the Roanoke *World News* related an almost identical quotation. In it the senator added that he and Ickes were told to make the necessary arrangements and that the

[7] June 3, 1962.

President would make an initial allotment for the parkway from public funds.[8]

That the Shenandoah National Park was not dedicated until July 3, 1936, does not necessarily discredit the senator's statement. President Roosevelt, Secretary Ickes, and Senator Byrd were together in the Shenandoah National Park at an earlier date, on August 11–12, 1933, for the inspection of a Civilian Conservation Corps camp. The Skyline Drive had been under construction since 1931, and they most certainly could have driven over part of it. Except for being mistaken about the occasion, Senator Byrd's memory was probably quite correct about the conversation relative to the parkway linking the two national parks.[9]

At the dedication of the James River Bridge, Blue Ridge Parkway, on June 11, 1960, Conrad L. Wirth, director of the National Park Service, told his audience that not only was Senator Byrd the first to suggest the Parkway to Roosevelt, but also it was largely because of his efforts that the states of Virginia and North Carolina donated the right-of-way for the road.[10] In a letter to the editor of the Roanoke *Times*, September 11, 1951, one person claimed that Byrd, who "was at that time on more friendly terms with the President than he was in later years," suggested the Parkway idea when Roosevelt made his first visit to the Shenandoah National Park, which was August 11, 1933. The writer of the letter was Hunter Miller, a Virginia state senator who had been active in promoting the Parkway through the Peaks of Otter section of his constituency. He also had been involved in many of the political manipulations of that period and was well posted on Byrd's activities.

The man most likely to know the truth was Ickes. In a magazine article, December, 1933, he related how, "the other day," he had listened to Senator Byrd sketch his vision of a road a hundred feet wide from the Shenandoah to the Great Smokies National Park. Moreover, he said that the President had amplified the picture by declaring that he would like to see the road begin at the Canadian border and sweep

[8] Roanoke *World News*, April 10, 1959, p. 1.

[9] Letters, Sam P. Weems to Hunter Miller, December 17, 1953; Herbert E. Kahler to regional director, Region One, National Park Service, March 10, 1954; Guy B. Edwards to Weems, December 14, 1953, all in files of the Superintendent, Blue Ridge Parkway.

[10] Department of the Interior, Information Service release, June 11, 1960, in National Archives, Department of the Interior, Record Group 48.

down through the Green Mountains and the Berkshires to the Blue Ridge, there joining the senator's road. Ickes' approval of the project was well expressed in his article: "This will be a great thing, a, great thing for the interior life of our people." [11]

At first glance this evidence would seem to prove Byrd's "first," but a time element enters the picture. The exact date to which Secretary Ickes refers in his "the other day" is not known. One of Byrd's strongest supporters believes that it was "the time you [Byrd] went to him for an allocation to build the Blue Ridge Parkway, just after we had had the meeting in Washington, at which time it was agreed that it should be built as a free road and not as a toll road." [12] If this opinion is correct, Ickes would have heard Senator Byrd outline his vision of a road sometime on or after October 17, 1933, the date of the meeting in Washington. In all probability the date Ickes referred to was either August 11–12, 1933, the time of the ride through Shenandoah Park, as claimed by Byrd, or possibly October 9, 1933. On the latter date Byrd sent the governor of Virginia a telegram saying that he was "delighted to advise had a most satisfactory conference with Secretary Ickes in regard to proposed Skyline Road. He has requested that we present to him promptly definite request for this project." [13]

If either of the October dates is the one referred to by Ickes, then Senator Byrd was not acting as an originator of the Parkway idea but as spokesman for a group seeking federal funds for the construction of a scenic highway, previously conceived. The Richmond *Times Dispatch*, September 23, 1933, carried front page sub-headlines reading, POLLARD WINS SENATOR'S SUPPORT FOR HIGHWAY LINKING SHENANDOAH TO SMOKY MOUNTAINS. The article claimed that Byrd had accepted, in Richmond the previous day, the chairmanship of a Virginia committee seeking federal funds to construct a scenic highway from the Shenandoah to the Great Smoky Mountains National Park. Byrd's successful labors as chairman are highlighted in a letter he received on October 10, 1933: "You have interested the President, Secretary Ickes, and the higher officials of the states concerned and doubtless these gentlemen will be guided by you to the desired goal." [14] When offi-

11 "The National Domain and the New Deal," *Saturday Evening Post*, CCVI (December 23, 1933), 10–11.
12 Letter, Miller to Byrd, October 10, 1933, copy in files of the Superintendent, Blue Ridge Parkway.
13 Telegram in *ibid.*
14 James A. Anderson to Byrd, October 10, 1933, in files of Virginia Highway Department.

cial authorization for construction of the Parkway materialized, the
governor of Virginia eulogized, "I want to congratulate you on having initiated this worthy project, and having obtained the President's
approval thereof. . . . You will thus add another item to the long list
of obligations which the State owes you." [15] One of Byrd's most ar-
dent champions declared that Theodore E. Straus or some representative of the National Park Service might have conceived the idea, but,
so far as the public was concerned, Senator Byrd was the first to suggest extending the Skyline southward. He was the one responsible for
procuring the first sixteen million dollars allocated for construction.[16]

Thomas H. MacDonald, chief of the Bureau of Public Roads, was
at one time credited by Senator Byrd with having been the originator
of the Parkway. At a meeting held in Byrd's office in Washington,
D. C., October 17, 1933, to discuss the proposed parkway, the senator,
as chairman, opened the discussion with the comment that the basic
idea was to extend the Skyline Drive some five hundred miles, following the crest of the mountains and connecting the two parks. He
quickly added, "The idea, I might say, originated with Mr. MacDonald of the Bureau of Public Roads, and we are here today to devise
ways and means to consummate this great project, which I believe
when completed will be the greatest scenic road in the world." [17]

MacDonald, however, gracefully declined the honor. He insisted
that Byrd was overmodest in giving him credit for the idea: "It is one
of the outgrowths of a conversation that has taken place with Senator
Byrd and others of Virginia and of those States that are interested, and
Mr. Radcliffe and Mr. Straus of the Public Works Administration,
and numerous other individuals have already taken part in bringing
into a rather definite concept this whole idea. I should be the last to
claim any personal credit for the idea. . . ." [18] Despite MacDonald's
disclaimer, and bearing in mind that Byrd may have been demonstra-
ting his well-known political astuteness in paying the chief of the
Bureau of Public Roads such a high compliment, there is further indi-
cation that MacDonald may have been the man who suggested the
idea. The editor of the Asheville *Citizen* wrote a letter to Straus in-

[15] Letter, Pollard to Byrd, November 27, 1933, in files of Superintendent, Blue
Ridge Parkway.
[16] Letter, Miller to Weems, December 10, 1953, *ibid*.
[17] Minutes, October 17, 1933, in files of Virginia Highway Department.
[18] *Ibid*.

quiring, "Isn't it true that you were the first to suggest the plan for the parkway?" To this Straus replied, "It is true that I created the initiative in connection with this Parkway which eventually became a reality. But the thought was suggested in a private interview to Mr. Radcliffe and myself by Mr. MacDonald of the Bureau of Public Roads as a possible Regional matter, after he had discussed how the Boulevard from Washington to Mt. Vernon was made a reality by getting persons from the outside interested." [19]

A comparison of the 1933–34 testimony of Byrd and Straus regarding MacDonald's suggesting the idea and their testimony on the same subject in the 1950's and 1960's would seem to indicate that time had mellowed both of their memories somewhat in their own favor and at MacDonald's expense. At any rate, no further source material has been found that can substantiate or eliminate MacDonald as a claimant for the original suggestion honor.

John G. Pollard, in his capacity as chief executive of Virginia, had much opportunity and reason to concern himself with a possible federal project as immense and important as a park-to-park highway routed through Virginia. Numerous advantages would accrue to the state—jobs, tourist money, and a recreational asset, to say nothing of the political potential. Thus, it is not surprising to find that he, too, was credited with conceiving the Parkway. A news article in the Richmond *Times Dispatch*, September 23, 1933, stated, "The plan is so new that the cost has not been calculated. Neither Governor Pollard, whose idea it is, nor Henry G. Shirley, chairman of the State Highway Commission, would venture a guess." No supporting evidence has been found to indicate that it was Governor Pollard's idea. It is doubtful, therefore, that he was responsible for anything more than serving as a willing audience and encourager of those dreaming of such a project. At most, he implemented the dream by appointing the necessary men, such as Byrd, to do the important leg- and brainwork required to promote such an undertaking.

The origination claims of Radcliffe and Straus are so closely allied that they should be considered together. Senator Radcliffe, in his position as regional advisor, District No. 10, Public Works Administration, would logically have been and was interested in work projects

---

[19] Letters, Robert McKee to Straus, February 24, 1934; Straus to McKee, March 12, 1934; both in Straus's private files, Baltimore, Md.

that had the potential of employing numerous people and producing a worthwhile product. Radcliffe and "one of his advisers, Theodore E. Straus, contacted Mr. MacDonald, Head of the Public Roads Administration, and, in the discussion of several projects, Mr. Radcliffe mentioned that if something could be done connecting the Shenandoah National Park with the Great Smokies National Park it would work in with his administrative function" as Public Works Administration advisor.[20] The exact date of this contact is not known, but it probably preceded the Richmond meeting of September 22, 1933, which brought formulation of plans that resulted in authorization of the Parkway.[21]

Straus, a close associate of and advisor to Radcliffe, has over the years insisted that to the two of them should go the major credit for presenting the idea and initiative that created the scenic road. He has also been careful to stress his own contribution: "Being a member of Senator Radcliffe's Advisory Board . . . the question of highways came solely under my jurisdiction, but naturally the results of my effort should go to his credit." [22]

Both Straus and Radcliffe were guests of honor at a luncheon given by Virginia's Governor Pollard, September 22, 1933. They had come to Richmond to participate in a meeting of the representatives of municipalities of Virginia who had gathered to have the aims and purposes of the Public Works Administration program explained to them. At the luncheon Radcliffe, Straus, Byrd, and others engaged in conversation with Pollard concerning the possibility of extending the Skyline Drive to the Great Smokies. One of those present later recalled the meeting and wrote Straus that "I am sure you and Sen. Radcliffe had a most important part in the inception and culmination of this great parkway." [23]

Of all the claimants Straus has been the most insistent that it was he who first envisioned the Parkway. Once, after having read a pioneering history of the Parkway[24] Straus wrote a letter to the associate director of the Service complaining that "somehow or other you hesi-

[20] Abbuehl, "History," 1.
[21] Ibid.
[22] Letter, Straus to A. E. Demaray, March 30, 1940, in National Archives, National Park Service, Record Group 79.
[23] James A. Anderson to Straus, April 8, 1940, in Straus's private files.
[24] Abbuehl's "History."

Although this photograph was taken at the turn of the twentieth century, it illustrates well the condition of roads and travel in the Blue Ridge Mountains in the 1930's. Many residents of the area had solid doubts about whether a road such as the Parkway could be built. One mountain lady jeered, "One of them hard surface roads like they have below the mountains? Why, Lord have mercy, nobody a-livin' could put one of them through here." The people were skeptical, but they were hopeful, too. Such a road offered a mud-free highway, rising property values, construction work, new business, a steady stream of tourist money, and an end to years of isolation. *Courtesy U.S. Government Printing Office*

A particular aim of the Public Works Administration in building the Parkway was to provide relief from the billboard jungles of public highways. *Courtesy Blue Ridge Parkway*

Owners of land adjacent to the Parkway were urged to fence their property and make it more appealing to the eye. *Courtesy Blue Ridge Parkway*

Oxen were still being used in the Blue Ridge region when work on the Parkway began. These giant animals stand 6 feet high at the shoulder and weigh more than 1½ tons. *Courtesy Blue Ridge Parkway*

By the 1930's the dogtrot cabin had largely been replaced by the frame house. The design is simple—two rooms or portions of a house, separated by an open breezeway (dogtrot), but connected by a single roof. Because the basic design is so simple, it has often been adapted for use in more sophisticated structures. *Courtesy Shenandoah National Park*

The Parkway provides a balcony overlooking the valleys below.
Courtesy Blue Ridge Parkway

tate to give me the real credit for my endeavors, avoiding the fact that it was entirely through my efforts this project is now a reality." He argued that for a period of nearly a year he had directed every move that was made relative to the road, and, hence, the results came from his work. Therefore, he requested that "the fact prevail that it was through my suggestion to Gov. Pollard that the creation of the Parkway Project came into existence." [25] In reply Straus was sent a revised version of the Parkway history with the assurance that there had been no intention at any time of slighting the efforts of anyone who had been connected with the project. The revised version contained, too, a statement that must have highly pleased Straus. It told of the September 22, 1933, meeting in Richmond and then said, "After the meeting, at a luncheon in the Executive Mansion . . . the possibility of such a parkway was proposed by Mr. Straus and received the approval of Gov. Pollard, who immediately appointed a Virginia Committee, requesting Senator Byrd to act as its Chairman." [26]

Fred L. Weede, manager of the Asheville Chamber of Commerce during the 1933–34 period, has always been convinced that Straus was the father of the Parkway. Weede was one of the handful of persons who successfully masterminded North Carolina's efforts to secure routing of the road through the Asheville area. In a letter of encomium he wrote Straus, "You were the originator of the idea and were the one who first set the wheels in motion." [27] He assured Straus that the Asheville Chamber of Commerce and the communities of western North Carolina had not forgotten that he had been particularly active in the project from the beginning; "we cherish the hope that some of these days we shall have an achievement to celebrate. We are hoping that in the van of a most notable procession riding over the most scenic parkway in the world will be Mr. Theodore Straus and that when the caravan reaches Asheville, and glasses clink, we can tell you more completely just how highly we regard you and what you have done." [28] Years later Weede again wrote Straus and assured him, "I always recognized you as the father of the idea." [29]

[25] Straus to Demaray, March 25, 1940, in National Archives, National Park Service, Record Group 79.
[26] Demaray to Straus, April 2, 1940, in *ibid.*
[27] Weede to Straus, July 13, 1935, in Straus's private files.
[28] *Ibid.*
[29] Weede to Straus, January 27, 1954, in *ibid.*

The associate director of the National Park Service in November, 1933, wrote a letter introducing Straus to the superintendent of the Great Smoky Mountains National Park with these words: "This note will present to you Honorable Theodore E. Straus, Member of the Regional P.W.A. Board, District No. 10, Baltimore, Maryland. Mr. Straus is the man who was largely responsible for the advancement of the Parkway which is to connect the Shenandoah and Great Smoky Mountains National Parks." [30]

North Carolina's Senator Robert R. Reynolds must have been convinced of Straus's origination claim because in 1940 he brought to the attention of the Senate, and entered into the *Congressional Record*, an article from a Baltimore newspaper entitled "A Baltimorean's Part in a Great Project." The theme of the article, written by Louis Azrael, was that Straus "not only made the suggestion which started the Blue Ridge Parkway movement, he also participated in and is still participating in carrying the project to fulfillment." [31]

In Straus's personal papers there is a diary-type memorandum pad; on September 22, 1933, Straus noted therein that he and others had met in "conference in the governor's office till 11:25 A. M.," following which Straus was at the "Meeting Hall of Delegates State House till 1:30 P. M., then to Executive Mansion for Luncheon." Straus's entry also included a seating chart, indicating that Senator Radcliffe sat beside Governor Pollard and Straus sat adjacent to Radcliffe. On the same page, in a different ink, different pen, and probably entered at a later date, there was an entry reading, "Suggested the Blue Ridge Parkway," presumably meaning that it was he who did it.

Throughout the years Straus has maintained an alert guard over his origination stake. In June, 1950, he informed the assistant director of the Park Service that newspaper accounts indicated the President would soon dedicate the Parkway and that he wanted to know whether "as originator of this project, will I have the opportunity to be present at its dedication?" He was tactfully referred to the superintendent of the Blue Ridge Parkway, who cautiously told him that "as Mr. Demaray wrote you, I am only an advisor to the Program Committee for the Parkway dedication; however, I will be glad to submit

[30] Demaray to J. Ross Eakin, November 20, 1933, in Straus's private files.
[31] *Congressional Record*, 76th Cong., 3rd Sess., LXXXVI, Pt. 15, p. 3180.

your name to the Invitation Committee and tell them of your interest in the Blue Ridge Parkway." [32] Straus was not to be diverted this easily. He sent the Parkway superintendent another letter explaining that his interest stemmed from the fact that he was the originator of the parkway; hence, "I am surprised that with the dedication on hand, some one in charge has not already communicated with me." [33]

As it happened, the emergency created by the Korean War caused an indefinite postponement of the dedication ceremonies, and this somewhat thorny matter of protocol and invitation was left hanging in the air. But so far as Straus was concerned, the issue was not dead. On May 21, 1962, in response to an inquiry as to whether he was the true originator of the Parkway, Straus replied:

> You are correct. I am the originator of the mountain road connecting the Skyline Drive and the Smoky Mountains in North Carolina, 467 miles long, now the Blue Ridge Parkway. I was connected with the Works Progress Administration for District No. 10 and in September, 1933, we had some business with the Gov. of Virginia in Richmond. ... I had charge of the Roads in connection with the W. P. A. and suggested the now Blue Ridge Parkway.[34]

Later, in a private interview, he repeated basically the same information.[35]

In sum, the currently available material indicates that the idea of a park-to-park highway was in existence as early as 1930, that many men in influential places had considered the prospect of a scenic highway connecting the Shenandoah and Great Smoky Mountains National Parks, and that the existing depression coupled with the reception accorded the Skyline Drive made the extension of that road a very logical project for serious consideration.

To identify the single individual who first conceived the idea would require the talents of a Sherlock Holmes and is most likely not possible of accomplishment. However, Byrd and Straus and their many associates must be given credit for providing the vision, the political

[32] Straus to Demaray, June 22, 1950, in Straus's private files; Weems to Straus, July 7, 1950, in files of Superintendent, Blue Ridge Parkway.
[33] Straus to Weems, July 10, 1950, in files of Superintendent, Blue Ridge Parkway.
[34] Letter, Straus to the author, May 21, 1962.
[35] Interview with Straus, July 30, 1962, Baltimore, Md.

know-how, and the dedication to public service that culminated in the authorization and construction of the Parkway. Great credit is due, too, to Congressman Doughton from North Carolina and others who quickly gave the project their support and with dedicated labor carried it to completion. The result of their effort has been aptly described as "the most important public improvement in Virginia and North Carolina since railroad days." [36]

[36] National Park Service, "Development Outline," January 20, 1938, in National Archives, National Park Service, Record Group 79.

"I Ask Your Cooperation"  4

LUNCHEON MEETINGS occasionally shape the course of history, and the one held in the governor's mansion in Richmond, Virginia, in association with a meeting of the League of Virginia Municipalities did so, too. It was here, on September 22, 1933, that plans were laid which launched the Blue Ridge Parkway project. One of those present recalled, in 1940, the "very delightful luncheon which we had with Governor Pollard at the Mansion in Richmond . . . at which time the Parkway . . . was suggested." [1] Another participant later remembered "that the possibility of the Parkway was discussed at the luncheon and Senator Radcliffe took considerable interest in it. I also believe that Willis Robertson and Senator Byrd probably approached the matter with the President when they had him at a CCC camp in the Shenandoah National Park." [2]

The Richmond *Times Dispatch* for September 23, 1933, carried a front page streamer announcing, $7,500,000 PLAN FOR SCENIC ROAD HEADED BY BYRD. A later article indicated that Governor Pollard had appointed the senator as chairman of a Virginia committee charged with the responsibility of seeking federal aid for the construction of a scenic highway linking the Shenandoah and Great Smoky Mountains National Parks.[3] The scheme was expected to require an expenditure of about $7,500,000 and to provide jobs for approximately 10,000 persons. Construction costs were estimated at $20,000 to $25,000 per mile. The proposed highway, as a toll road, was to be self-liquidating.[4]

Governor Pollard followed Byrd's appointment by wiring the governors of North Carolina and Tennessee that:

SENATOR BYRD HAS AGREED TO ACCEPT THE CHAIRMANSHIP OF A COMMIT-
TEE TO SECURE A SCENIC HIGHWAY CONNECTING SHENANDOAH NATIONAL
PARK WITH THE GREAT SMOKIES. FUNDS TO BE FURNISHED BY NRA AND PROJ-
ECT LIQUIDATED BY TOLLS. UNDERSTAND THE PRESIDENT GREATLY INTER-

[1] Letter, B. F. Moomaw to Straus, April 9, 1940, in Straus's private files.
[2] Letter, Anderson to Moomaw, April 27, 1951, copy in files of Superintendent, Blue Ridge Parkway.
[3] Richmond *Times Dispatch*, October 10, 1933, p. 5. Later, other members included Hunter Miller, Bedford; C. J. Harrader, Bristol; W. B. Smith and Junius P. Fishburn, Roanoke; and J. A. Johns, Charlottesville.
[4] Richmond *Times Dispatch*, September 23, 1933, p. 1.

ESTED. WILL YOU APPOINT A COMMITTEE TO COOPERATE WITH VIRGINIA
COMMITTEE.[5]

On September 24, 1933, came the report that Senator Byrd had
"moved quickly in an effort to close the deal as a Public Works project
providing employment for hundreds of idle men." [6] The senator was
quoted as saying that the project would not incur any state indebted-
ness to Virginia or other states because it was to be financed with federal funds through a nonprofit corporation. President Roosevelt was
credited with suggesting the highway be made a toll road as a means
of self-liquidation.[7]

In Washington, D. C., September 26, 1933, a Virginia delegation led
by Byrd presented its proposals to MacDonald, at the Bureau of Public
Roads. In the course of the meeting, suggestions were made that the
road be extended to the Mammoth Cave in Kentucky and that a nonprofit organization be chartered to do the work. It was also recommended that tolls be charged to liquidate the Public Works loans.[8]
Because the proposed parkway later became the responsibility of the
National Park Service, the reaction of its associate director as indicated
in a letter to the director is noteworthy: "I have seen something in the
newspapers about this project but in view of the fact that it is purely a
state project I have not been particularly excited about it. . . . Despite
the apparent interest in this project I am rather doubtful that it will be
approved because of the enormous expense involved." [9]

Seeking to enlist the support of the governors of Tennessee and
North Carolina, Senator Byrd sent them a telegram that is highly significant in Parkway history because it not only invited support for the
project but indicated the tentative mileage that each of the three states
might expect to obtain. It also set forth the possibility that the scenic
highway would be established as a toll road. The telegram read:

I JUST HAD A TALK WITH THE PRESIDENT WITH RESPECT TO THE CONSTRUC-
TION OUT OF FEDERAL FUNDS OF A SCENIC HIGHWAY CONNECTING THE SHEN-
ANDOAH AND GREAT SMOKY PARKS STOP PLAN ᛁ TO FINANCE FROM FEDERAL
WORKS PROGRAM WITHOUT OBLIGATION ON THE PART OF THE STATES EXCEPT

[5] Pollard to Hill McAlister of Tennessee and Ehringhaus of North Carolina,
October 5, 1933, in Ehringhaus Papers.
[6] Richmond *Times Dispatch*, September 24, 1933, p. 8.
[7] *Ibid.*
[8] *Ibid.*, September 27, 1933, p. 12.
[9] Office memorandum, Demaray to Cammerer, September 26, 1933, in National Archives, National Park Service, Record Group 79.

1220S

WESTERN UNION

CLASS OF SERVICE
This is a full-rate Telegram or Cablegram unless its deferred character is indicated by a suitable sign above or preceding the address.

SIGNS
DL = Day Letter
NM = Night Message
NL = Night Letter
LCO = Deferred Cable
NLT = Cable Night Letter
WLT = Week-End Letter

The filing time as shown in the date line on full-rate telegrams and day letters, and the time of receipt at destination as shown on all messages, is STANDARD TIME.

Received at

CFB391 166 GOVT   SN WASHINGTON DC 7 149P   1933 OCT 7 PM 2 39

MINUTES IN TRANSIT	
FULL-RATE	DAY LETTER

HON J C B EHRINGHAUS=
GOVERNOR OF NORTHCAROLINA RALEIGH NCAR=

I JUST HAD A TALK WITH THE PRESIDENT WITH RESPECT TO THE
CONSTRUCTION OUT OF FEDERAL FUNDS OF A SCENIC HIGHWAY
CONNECTING THE SHENANDOAH AND GREAT SMOKY MOUNTAIN PARKS
STOP PLAN IS TO FINANCE FROM FEDERAL WORKS PROGRAM WITHOUT
OBLIGATION ON THE PART OF THE STATES EXCEPT AS TO
MAINTENANCE OF ROAD STOP THIS MAINTENANCE CAN BE READILY
GIVEN BY THE STATES BY REASON OF THE LARGE AMOUNT OF
INCREASED GASOLINE TAX DERIVED FROM THE TOURISTS ATTRACTED
TO THIS ROAD STOP THE PRESIDENT SUGGESTA A SMALL TOLL SO AS
TO MAKE THIS A SELF LIQUIDATING ENTERPRISE STOP TENTATIVE
SURVEY INDICATES A DISTANCE OF FOUR HUNDRED MILES TOTAL COST
SIXTEEN MILLION DOLLARS STOP HUNDRED SEVENTY FIVE MILES IN
VIRGINIA HUNDRED FORTY MILES IN NORTHCAROLINA AND NINETY
FIVE MILES IN TENNESSEE STOP THIS ROAD WILL BE THE GREATEST
SCENIC ROAD IN THE WORLD AND WILL ATTRACT MILLIONS OF
TOURISTS STOP I ASK YOUR COOPERATION IN THE PROJECT AND IF
YOU APPROVE WOULD APPRECIATE A TELEGRAM TO SECRETARY ICKES=
HARRY F BYRD.

Senator Byrd's telegram to the governors of North Carolina, Virginia, and Tennessee proposing construction of a Blue Ridge parkway.

AS TO MAINTENANCE OF ROAD STOP THIS MAINTENANCE CAN BE READILY
GIVEN BY THE STATES BY REASON OF THE LARGE AMOUNT OF INCREASED GAS-
OLINE TAX DERIVED FROM THE TOURISTS ATTRACTED TO THIS ROAD STOP THE
PRESIDENT SUGGESTS A SMALL TOLL SO AS TO MAKE THIS A SELF LIQUIDATING
ENTERPRISE STOP TENTATIVE SURVEY INDICATES A DISTANCE OF FOUR HUN-
DRED MILES TOTAL COST SIXTEEN MILLION DOLLARS STOP HUNDRED SEVENTY
FIVE MILES IN VIRGINIA HUNDRED FORTY MILES IN NORTH CAROLINA AND
NINETY FIVE MILES IN TENNESSEE STOP THIS ROAD WILL BE THE GREATEST
SCENIC ROAD IN THE WORLD AND WILL ATTRACT MILLIONS OF TOURISTS STOP
I ASK YOUR COOPERATION IN THIS PROJECT AND IF YOU APPROVE WOULD AP-
PRECIATE A TELEGRAM TO SECRETARY ICKES.[10]

Meanwhile, Byrd and Colonel J. A. Anderson, a Virginia Public
Works engineer, had been in conference with Ickes regarding the possibility of making the Parkway a Public Works project. They were
given encouragement and were told to submit an official application to
Ickes, as administrator.[11] Byrd, pleased, telegraphed the news to Governor Pollard and assured him that the matter was being expedited in
every possible way, including a Washington meeting of all interested
parties called for October 17, 1933.[12]

In the interval Byrd had received telegrams from Governor Mc-
Alister of Tennessee and Senator Bailey of North Carolina expressing
the keen interest of their states and pledging support.[13] Governor Ehringhaus of North Carolina delayed his answer because of the possibility that a toll would be levied on the proposed highway. As a
political candidate and governor, he had labored to remove all tolls
from the North Carolina highway system. It therefore might be politically embarrassing if he gave official sanction to a toll road in North
Carolina even if that highway were federal. This stand by the governor foreshadowed an official North Carolina refusal to support the
proposed parkway if its construction hinged upon the levying of a
toll.[14] However, Ehringhaus wrote Byrd informing him that the following persons had been appointed as "members of the Park-to-Park
Scenic Highway Committee to represent this State": Senator Josiah
W. Bailey, Raleigh; Senator Robert R. Reynolds, Asheville; Congressman Robert L. Doughton, Laurel Springs; J. Q. Gilkey, Marion; R. L.

10 Byrd to Ehringhaus, October 7, 1933, in Ehringhaus Papers.
11 Richmond *Times Dispatch*, October 10, 1933, p. 5.
12 Byrd to Pollard, October 9, 1933, copy in Office of Superintendent, Blue
Ridge Parkway.
13 Richmond *Times Dispatch*, October 10, 1933, p. 5.
14 Numerous letters, *passim*, in Ehringhaus Papers.

Gwyn, Lenoir; John P. Randolph, Bryson City; Reuben B. Robertson, Sr., Canton; Francis O. Clarkson, Charlotte; Charles Hutchins, Burnsville; and Haywood Parker, Asheville.[15]

Although the governor of North Carolina was taking a cautious stand because of the toll issue, officials from Virginia and Tennessee were eagerly indicating their willingness to support and promote the proposed highway. Straus, in the Public Works Administration, received from Virginia a telegram stating:

> GOVERNOR POLLARD GOVERNOR ELECT PERRY AND STATE HIGHWAY COMMISSIONER SHIRLEY PLEDGE THEIR EFFORTS TO SECURE WITHOUT COST TO THE UNITED STATES GOVERNMENT NECESSARY RIGHTS OF WAY OVER PRIVATELY OWNED LAND FOR THE SKYLINE DRIVE IN VIRGINIA. THE STATE HIGHWAY COMMISSIONER IS READY TO PROCEED WITH THE SURVEYS IMMEDIATELY.[16]

And from Tennessee came a similar pledge:

> REFERENCE SHENANDOAH SMOKY MOUNTAIN PARK TO PARK HIGHWAY TENNESSEE HIGHWAY DEPARTMENT WILL GUARANTEE FREE RIGHTS OF WAY OVER PRIVATELY OWNED LAND STOP HIGHWAY DEPARTMENT WILL FURNISH SURVEY PARTIES TO WORK UNDER THE DIRECTION OF MR. MACDONALD.[17]

On behalf of Virginia, Colonel Anderson began considering ways of expediting the project and bringing it to fruition. He finally told Senator Byrd that there were three possible means of consummating the plan: formation of a private nonprofit corporation, which could build a toll road and turn it over to the states for operation and maintenance; creation of a public body (similar to the Triborough Bridge Authority), which would be eligible for federal aid and could liquidate construction costs by charging tolls; and adoption of the project by the federal government.[18] Two days later Colonel Anderson expressed the opinion that "the proposed scenic highway ... can be made a national parkway under the Federal Emergency Public Works Act and thus be a free rather than a toll road, as first suggested." [19]

With the political efficiency that had characterized his career as

15 Letter, October 14, 1933, in *ibid.*

16 Anderson to Straus, November 13, 1933, in National Archives, National Park Service, Record Group 79.

17 O. F. Goetz to Straus, November 10, 1933, in National Archives, National Park Service, Record Group 48.

18 Letter, Anderson to Byrd, October 10, 1933, in files of Virginia Highway Department.

19 Richmond *Times Dispatch,* October 12, 1933, p. 1.

governor of Virginia, Byrd had in the meantime summoned representatives of the interested federal agencies and states to his office in
Washington, D. C. There, on October 17, 1933, the concerned parties
gathered to lay plans for making the proposed parkway a reality.
Those present, according to the minutes of the meeting, included Senator Byrd (chairman), Senator Reynolds of North Carolina, the director and assistant director of the National Park Service, the chief of
the Bureau of Public Roads, representatives of the Public Works Administration, plus state delegations from North Carolina, Virginia, and
Tennessee, and others.[20]

When Senator Byrd called the meeting to order, he explained that
the purpose of the conference was to devise a plan whereby a scenic
highway could be constructed through Virginia, North Carolina, and
Tennessee to link two great national parks. As discussion progressed,
MacDonald expressed enthusiasm for a scenic highway that would
lead people into a higher altitude and give them "the right kind of sur-
roundings to offset the enervating influences of the lower altitudes." [21]
Yet, he was not enthusiastic about the proposal to build the project as
a toll road. He argued that enough returns could be obtained from
concessions or other activities related to the operation of the road to
permit long-term liquidation of costs.[22]

The toll issue brought immediate response from E. B. Jeffress, chairman of the North Carolina State Highway and Public Works Commission. He informed the conferees that as a representative of the state
of North Carolina he could not accept a toll proposition under any
circumstances. He explained that the North Carolina Highway Commission in 1921 had adopted a policy of buying out all toll roads, toll
bridges, and toll ferries in the state. Governor Ehringhaus, whom he
was representing, supported this policy and advocated the abolition of
all tolls on the highway system. Therefore, Jeffress felt compelled to
make plain North Carolina's position.[23] This inspired Colonel Anderson to tell the group that he had been working on the project and had
prepared three plans, "two of which we do not think anything of because they put tolls on the road." The chairman directed him to explain the one he approved and to disregard the others, whereupon

[20] Minutes, October 17, 1933, in files of Virginia Highway Department.
[21] Ibid.   [22] Ibid.
[23] Undated statement by E. B. Jeffress, in files of North Carolina State Highway and Public Works Commission, Raleigh.

Colonel Anderson stated, "It is to consider this as a Federal project—
a Parkway connecting two great National Parks in the East, and let it
be financed entirely as a Federal Project, with the assistance of the
Highway Departments of the several states." [24] To Senator Byrd's
question about the amount involved, Radcliffe replied, "The amount
requested is $16,000,000 based on 414 estimated miles at $40,000 a
mile." [25] He added that the undertaking would furnish four thousand
men employment for two years, constructing a twenty-foot roadway
with six-foot shoulders.

The proposal to finance the entire parkway as a 100 per cent federal
venture eliminated further objections on this score. Other aspects
were then considered. Senator Reynolds, ever mindful of the fact that
his Tar Heel constituents derived a considerable portion of their income from the tourist industry, indicated why he considered the
Parkway desirable. "If I am not mistaken in 1929, followed by 1930,
the American tourists spent at home and abroad something like five
billion dollars. In 1929 and 1930 the statistics will show more money
was expended in travel to the automobile man, the gasoline man, and
various sundry others interested in tourist travel than in anything in
the United States of America. We want to get these tourists in Virginia, Tennessee, and North Carolina." [26] Jeffress, also concerned for
Tar Heel interests, suggested that the "highway run directly south
from Roanoke to the North Carolina Line, and follow the crest of the
Blue Ridge to the point where the Blue Ridge turns east, and from
there around by Mount Mitchell into Asheville, and by Waynesville
into the Great Smoky Mountains National Park." [27] Many months
later, and after much vigorous debate between Tennessee and North
Carolina interests, this was the route finally chosen.

While routing was being discussed, the director of the National
Park Service, Arno B. Cammerer, introduced the idea of a "loop road"
in the vicinity of the Great Smoky Mountains National Park, suggesting that the road fork at the northern tip of the park, with a terminus
at Cherokee, North Carolina, to match a similar one at Gatlinburg,
Tennessee. He further intimated that he would like to see the parkway continued northward from the Shenandoah Park to the nation's
capital.[28] Neither of his suggestions materialized.

[24] Minutes, October 17, 1933, in files of Virginia Highway Department.
[25] *Ibid.*   [27] *Ibid.*
[26] *Ibid.*   [28] *Ibid.*

To enhance the possibility of success, Straus recommended that a steering committee be appointed with a regional advisor at its head. Radcliffe was named chairman, with MacDonald, Cammerer, and the chairmen of the state highway commissions of the three states serving with him. The prestige, personality, and political ability of the committee members greatly increased the likelihood of success for the proposal. As the conference was about to close, Radcliffe asked, "As a matter of procedure, how would it be for several of us to see Secretary Ickes today and present to him very briefly what the idea is?" [29] This suggestion was quickly approved, and a statement was drawn up setting forth the basic features agreed upon. The first draft of the recommendations asked $16,000,000 for construction of a parkway from the southern tip of the Shenandoah National Park in Virginia to the Great Smokies. At Cammerer's suggestion the amount of funds requested was boosted to $20,000,000 to make possible the addition of a sixty-five-mile link between Washington, D. C., and the Shenandoah National Park. Senators Byrd and Reynolds personally took the request to Ickes' office.[30]

The reason that the recommendation was sent to Secretary Ickes is made plain in a statement by a member of the Virginia committee: "I remember very distinctly asking Senator Byrd if he thought he could get Congress to appropriate money for the project. . . . He said it would not be necessary to ask Congress to make any appropriations, that the President had turned over to Secretary Ickes many millions of dollars to be used in putting unemployed back to work . . . ." [31]

At this point, Congressman Thatcher, leading spokesman for the Eastern National Park-to-Park Highway, again set forth his idea. He was trying to convince Ickes that it would be better to use such funds as were available to develop his park-to-park highway system rather than finance an entirely new project. Secretary Ickes told the congressman that when the proposed parkway was first brought to his attention, he understood that part of the expense would be borne by the states involved, with the Public Works Administration lending its aid; the final proposal, however, called for a purely federal project. Thatcher must have been highly pleased when he read the next remark by Ickes: "I do not believe that the Federal Government would be justi-

[29] *Ibid.*
[30] Richmond *Times Dispatch*, October 18, 1933, p. 1.
[31] Miller, letter to the editor, Roanoke *Times*, September 11, 1951.

fied in entering into such a project at this time. . . . If the states involved would be interested in the improvement of the Eastern Park-to-Park Highway along lines of the regular policies adopted by the Public Works Administration, we would be glad to consider the project." [32]

In a letter to Senator Radcliffe, Secretary Ickes reiterated his conviction that the parkway should not be financed solely by federal funds. He declared that when Senator Byrd first suggested the matter it was on the basis of at least a substantial contribution toward the cost by the three states it would cross. Moreover, he said he could not recommend it as a wholly federal enterprise because its main service would be to the states and not to the parks. He pointed out that it "would seem just as logical to insist that a main highway connecting Washington and New York should be at the joint expense of those two cities because it connects them." [33]

It is evident from the foregoing that the Secretary had not been convinced that the highway should be underwritten entirely by the federal government, as had been hoped by the project's backers. The press was informed of his attitude, and the public was told he felt that Virginia, North Carolina, and Tennessee should make contributions on the grounds that "It is so important to these three states." [34] William E. Carson, chairman of the Virginia State Conservation and Development Commission, immediately rebutted with a statement declaring that Ickes' position was not well taken because "Virginia is presenting to the National Government the Shenandoah National Park at a cost of about $2,000,000 and this might well be considered her contribution to the . . . drive just as North Carolina and Tennessee are presenting their park which will cost in the neighborhood of $10,-000,000." [35] How effective this argument was is not known; but a short time later Virginia's Highway Commissioner Shirley received information asserting, "If the State of Virginia could guarantee Mr. Ickes that rights-of-way could be secured for the Skyline Drive [extension] without cost to the United States, the money would be available for the building of the drive in Virginia." The informant was

[32] Ickes to Thatcher, October 30, 1933, in National Archives, Department of the Interior, Record Group 48.

[33] Ickes to Radcliffe, October 19, 1933, in National Archives, Department of the Interior, Record Group 79.

[34] Waynesboro *News-Virginian*, October 31, 1933, p. 1.

[35] *Ibid.*

relaying a telephone message from Straus. Shirley was also told, "It is
my understanding that with these assurances the Drive would be built
as a Federal project, no toll allowed." [36] While Virginia authorities
worked on this angle, Secretary Ickes assured Byrd that the matter
would be taken up personally with President Roosevelt within a few
days.[37]

In the interim it was announced that Ickes had decided to eliminate
that portion of the project which would have linked Washington,
D. C., with the Shenandoah Park. He had also decreed that the "boulevard between the two parks would be considered a parkway and
would be administered as a regular national park." [38] This development was of the utmost importance because the *parkway* designation
and assignment to the National Park Service meant that every aspect
of the routing and construction of the road would conform to the
high standards and aesthetic desires of the Service.

Two days later Governor Pollard released the news that Ickes had
assured him of approval for the project if the property owners would
donate a 200-foot strip right-of-way. Virginians were told that their
share of the federal funds would be $12,000,000 if the landowners
would cooperate. The governor urged his fellow citizens to donate
the necessary land if for no other reason than to increase the value of
their own property.[39] Senator Byrd supported him by saying that
Secretary Ickes had consulted the President and was prepared to discuss practical details of construction provided assurance of free right-
of-way could be given. To comfort the economy-minded among his
constituents, Byrd said, "This road project will be financed exclusive-
ly by Federal funds. No obligation whatever will rest upon the States
of Virginia, North Carolina, and Tennessee, except to furnish the
right-of-way of 200 feet." [40]

On November 16, 1933, almost exactly one month from the initial
planning meeting held in Byrd's office, Secretary Ickes conferred with
a large delegation of senators, congressmen, governors, and others
from Virginia, Tennessee, and North Carolina. To their great joy, he

[36] Letter, Anderson to Henry G. Shirley, November 8, 1933, in files of Virginia
Highway Department.
[37] Waynesboro *News-Virginian*, November 10, 1933, p. 1.
[38] *Ibid.*
[39] Richmond *Times Dispatch*, November 12, 1933, III, 1.
[40] *Ibid.*

assured them that President Roosevelt had approved their plans for a scenic parkway and that "whatever it takes" would be provided from Public Works Administration funds. He must have smiled with pleasure that night when he made his diary entry: "Everyone in the delegation was delighted and said many complimentary things." [41]

Governor Pollard quickly made the news known and told reporters that the landowners were "crazy about the idea" because mountain land that previously had been worth less than six dollars an acre would have its value considerably increased by parkway construction. Pollard was of the opinion that "the landowners will probably be falling over each other in their effort to present the right-of-way through their property." [42] In the enthusiasm of the moment it seemed that he was quite correct in his assumption that landowners would eagerly offer free right-of-way, yet in many instances this did not prove true. In counties where the landholders were anti-Administration, procuring rights-of-way occasionally became burdensome. [43]

With construction tentatively approved, the question arose as to who should be held responsible for supervision, construction, and maintenance of the parkway. The chief of the Bureau of Public Roads stated that "if this parkway is to be built as a Federal project it will have to be under the jurisdiction of a Federal agency and the proper agency for this purpose, in my judgment, is the National Park Service." [44] Secretary Ickes thoroughly agreed. He therefore assigned the parkway to the National Park Service and told its director to cooperate with the Bureau of Public Roads in initiating the work, with this to be done at the earliest possible date. At the same time, Radcliffe was appointed by Ickes to serve as chairman of an advisory committee to coordinate federal and state interests. [45]

The many hours of correspondence, telephoning, telegraphing, pleading, and planning for the desired parkway were climaxed by an authorization of funds. At a meeting of a Special Board for Public

[41] *The Secret Diary of Harold L. Ickes* (New York: Simon & Schuster, 1954), I, 123.

[42] Richmond *Times Dispatch*, November 17, 1933, p. 2.

[43] Abbuehl, "History," 2.

[44] Letter, MacDonald to Straus, November 10, 1933, in National Archives, National Park Service, Record Group 79.

[45] Memorandum, Ickes to Cammerer, November 18, 1933, in National Archives, Department of the Interior, Record Group 48.

Works, December 5, 1933, Colonel Henry M. Waite, deputy administrator of the Public Works Administration, submitted the following resolution:

> Resolved that the Administration and this Board include in the comprehensive program a certain project of the Office of National Parks, Buildings and Reservations, Department of the Interior, for the construction of a scenic highway connecting the Shenandoah and Smoky Mountains National Parks, and that the sum of $4,000,000 be allotted and transferred to the Office of National Parks, Buildings and Reservations, Department of the Interior to finance the same.[46]

The resolution was adopted; and on December 19, 1933, E. K. Burlew, administrative assistant and budget officer, notified the director of the National Park Service that, in accordance with the provisions of the National Recovery Act of 1933, an allotment of $4,000,000 had been consigned to the Service for the construction of a parkway to connect the Shenandoah and Great Smoky Mountains National Parks.[47] Thus, the Parkway received official approval and entered the federal budget and payroll as a "Depression baby" and a "make-work project."

[46] Minute Book, Special Board for Public Works, December 5, 1933, p. 12, in National Archives, National Park Service, Record Group 79.
[47] Demaray, "Federal Parkways."

To THE PRESENT GENERATION, bred on turnpikes, expressways, and interstate highways, and daily accustomed to gigantic earth-moving equipment, the construction of a road through almost any terrain presents no major problem. But in 1933, when the Blue Ridge Parkway was being projected, the building of a hard-surfaced highway along the crest of the Blue Ridge Mountains posed construction problems of such magnitude that many people doubted whether they could be overcome. One mountain lady was quoted as deriding the rumor of parkway construction by slapping her knee and laughing: "One of them hard surface roads like they have below the mountains? Why, Lord have mercy, nobody a-livin' could put one of them through here." [1]

Although many residents of the area through which the contemplated parkway would run had solid doubts about its becoming a reality, they were elated at the prospect. Such a road not only offered what was for them a rarity, a mud-free highway, but also promised to enhance the value of their property, provide construction jobs, bring in new business, and end long years of isolation, as well as guarantee a steady stream of tourist money. They were well acquainted with the practice of donating right-of-way clearances in return for access to a road and were keenly aware of the benefits to be derived from a good, all-weather highway. Many persons were eager to contribute a portion of their land in order to facilitate road-building. To the various responsible governmental authorities came letters volunteering land donations, local help for obtaining the right-of-way, and civic support for the project, in additon to approval for the undertaking. [2]

Each community lying between the Shenandoah and Great Smoky Mountains National Parks was determined to secure a portion of the road. Officials were besieged with routing pleas. For example, the Board of Supervisors, Carroll County, Virginia, urged consideration of a route leading "through the Pinnacles of Dan following the crest

[1] William G. Lord, *The Blue Ridge Parkway Guide* (Asheville, N. C.: The Stephens Press, Inc., 1962), 3-C.
[2] The files of the Virginia Highway Department are especially rich in this material.

of the Blue Ridge Mountains through Carroll County along the route known as the Appalachian Trail." [3] This group assured the authorities that "the Government could not find a more suitable route for a Sky Line Drive in the State of Virginia, for relief purposes as well as a geographical survey, this route being a natural scenic beauty and will open up a territory much needed for the use of the general public and a much needed link in the Highway System." They also displayed an awareness of the political efficacy of a properly turned compliment, closing the resolution with this shrewd sentence: "If selected everyone from Maine to Florida will enjoy the beauty and enhance the wisdom of those responsible for the selection of said route." [4] From Hillsville, Virginia, came information that an enthusiastic meeting of citizens had appointed a committee to show a preliminary survey party "all the courtesies possible" and to attend to "the comfort of your party as far as possible while you are in our midst." [5]

An attorney from Floyd, Virginia, told Virginia officials that the counties along the Blue Ridge, both in Virginia and in North Carolina, were very anxious to have the scenic highway located along the crest of the mountains. They knew, he said, that in order for this to be accomplished they would have to provide free right-of-way and were seeking right-of-way relinquishment forms. His letter reported an organizational meeting held at Hillsville, December 8, 1933, in which representatives from Floyd, Patrick, Carroll, and Grayson counties in Virginia plus several counties and cities in North Carolina had enthusiastically made plans to encourage the construction of the parkway and insure its coming their way. [6]

Very quickly, interested groups, such as chambers of commerce, took an active part in stimulating public support for the project and in expediting an early start of construction. The Mount Airy, North Carolina, Kiwanis Club held a booster banquet to which representatives from the various counties along the prospective parkway route were invited. A report of the banquet said that there were approximately "100 present and the tables held miniature replicas of mountain ranges with highway signs denoting the various gaps and points of

[3] Resolution, Board of Supervisors, Carroll County, Virginia, November 6, 1933, in files of Virginia Highway Department.

[4] *Ibid.*

[5] Letter, J. F. Caldwell to Shirley, December 23, 1933, in files of Virginia Highway Department.

[6] Kyle M. Weeks to Joseph F. Hall, December 9, 1933, in *ibid.*

interest along the scenic route." [7] An invitation had been sent to the Virginia Highway Commissioner with this comment: "The people of this mountain section are highly enthusiastic over the route of the Scenic Highway through here and . . . we want to cooperate in every way we can to further its construction." [8]

As might have been expected, job seekers applied for all sorts of positions. From a man in Ripplemead, Virginia, came a letter saying, "I notice in the papers that the Federal Government is going to build 350 miles of Skyline Roads in Va. If the State Highway Department is going to have charge of this work I want to have your consideration of my application for a position as foreman." [9] Also, indicating the progress of aviation, the Charlottesville Flying Service filed a request seeking a contract for an early aerial survey of the various routes proposed for the parkway.[10] From a Bedford, Virginia, politician came another plea for jobs: "I assume that you will have a lot of extra surveying to be done in this section in connection with the locating of the Skyline Drive, and if so I wish you would please give me the privilege of recommending two or three young men here in Bedford who are anxious to get some work of this kind." [11]

Several of the residents of the mountain counties along the crest of the Blue Ridge wrote their political representatives advocating support of the scenic highway. Typical in content, if not in phraseology, was the following letter received by Congressman Doughton of North Carolina:

> Dear Mr. Doughton,
>   I am writing you in Regard to Scenic Highway as us people that lives along the crest of the Blue Ridge Has been cut off from the outside world & We would be glad to give the Right a way to get the Road. Hoping you will do all you can to get the Road built along the crest of the Blue Ridge.
>
>   With Regards, . . .[12]

Asheville, North Carolina, as the leading western North Carolina

---

[7] Roanoke *World News*, August 11, 1934, p. 1.
[8] *Ibid.*
[9] R. Lacy Johnston to Shirley, November 20, 1933, in files of Virginia Highway Department.
[10] Letter, Charlottesville Flying Service to Shirley, December 8, 1933, in *ibid.*
[11] Letter, Miller to Shirley, November 17, 1933, in *ibid.*
[12] Daniel Wagoner to Robert L. Doughton, November 27, 1933, in Robert L. Doughton Papers, File Book 2. University of North Carolina, Chapel Hill.

tourist city, was acutely interested in the proposed road because of its potential for funneling a great number of visitors into the town and its nearby area. The local chamber of commerce had several dynamic leaders, such as Manager Weede, and they quickly turned their talents to promoting the establishment of the parkway and obtaining a favorable routing. At the earliest mention of the scenic highway, Weede contacted the Advisory Board of the regional Public Works Administration and pledged the aid of western North Carolina and the Asheville Chamber of Commerce in furthering the project. He also suggested that it would be wise to have someone close to the White House present the plan to President Roosevelt as a possible Depression-easing project.[13]

Along with the words of praise, requests for jobs, offers of free rights-of-way, and suggested routings, there came objections. They were usually raised on the grounds that such a road would despoil the few wilderness areas remaining in the East. An editorial in *Nature Magazine* expressed considerable doubt about the wisdom of building such roads, charging that "some of these routes were unwisely opening up sections hitherto not easily accessible, with the result that the natural resources and attractiveness of the areas were being seriously endangered or ruined." [14] The same editorial further objected on the grounds that Americans' outdoor manners were atrocious and that the proposed road would simply make it easier to violate and destroy one of the few remaining unspoiled gardens of nature.

At a meeting of the American Forestry Association, October, 1934, Director of Forestry Robert Marshall vociferously advocated the preservation of the wilderness and the retention of large areas free from the intrusion of skyline highways. He specifically objected to the routing of the proposed parkway through wilderness areas. He was challenged by Cammerer, director of the National Park Service, who defended skyline highways and declared that they were a necessity for modern recreation.[15] Marshall in an earlier letter to Secretary Ickes had argued that there is "one matter connected with this proposed parkway which I consider of far greater moment than the choice between the Carolina and Tennessee routes. That is the neces-

[13] Asheville *Citizen*, January 7, 1962, p. 2.
[14] Vol. XXV (March, 1935), 101.
[15] Thomas W. Conner (quoting Cammerer) to Ickes, October 22, 1934, in National Archives, Department of the Interior, Record Group 48.

sity of keeping the parkway out of the few important primitive areas which are still left in this region." [16] A Tennessean agreed, saying, "A skyline highway not only destroys the finest of the primeval heritage, but in shooting civilization through the middle, halves the pitiful remnants of these pioneer solitudes which have been left us. . . . The fate of one of the few remaining wildernesses lies in the hands of Secretary Ickes." [17] In the end, Cammerer and those of the same mind had their way. The highway was built, but despoliation did not accompany it, thanks to the vigilance of the National Park Service landscape architects, who carefully planned against scarring. Where it was unavoidable, they quickly grassed and replanted with a skillful touch in order to disturb as little as possible the wilderness atmosphere.

An objection of an entirely different nature arose from owners of summer camps, summer homes, and isolated retreats who found themselves in the path of the proposed parkway. Many of them had carefully chosen their particular sites as a deliberate escape, a means of establishing quiet places for rest and recreation, far removed from the odors, noises, and disturbances of automobile traffic, all of which might be wiped out by the coming of a new road. One typically disturbed owner appealed to his congressman, saying, "*We do not want this highway thru this section*, and invoke your aid and assistance in endeavoring to change its course."[18] Many appeals of this nature were presented, and, where possible without detracting from the scenic beauty of the Parkway, these requests were given favorable consideration. Objections, such as those mentioned above, were logical accompaniments of such a grandiose project, but the enthusiasm and tremendous positive action of the parkway boosters and supporters far outweighed those of the objectors. The former, therefore, carried the battle.

16 Marshall to Ickes, August 16, 1934, in *ibid.*
17 Harvey Broome, letter to the editor, *The Nation*, July 11, 1934.
18 Letter, S. H. Ruskin to Zebulon Weaver, in files of North Carolina State Highway and Public Works Commission.

A Godsend for the Needy

ALTHOUGH BY 1890 the great American frontier had in theory disappeared, many of the mountain counties in southwestern Virginia and western North Carolina continued a frontier-like existence well into the twentieth century. As the tide of migration moved westward, much of the Blue Ridge province had become more and more isolated until by 1850 the isolation was nearly complete. This lack of contact with the rest of the world plus soil depletion and population pressure combined to convert what had been the pioneers' promised land into the principal rural slum of the United States.[1] Even prior to 1890 many of the inhabitants had become the object of concern for northern missionary and charitable organizations. By 1920, thirteen or more religious denominations were active among the mountain needy.[2]

For various reasons the people of the Appalachians had failed to keep up with the progress of the rest of the nation and were said to be lagging about a century behind. Their anachronistic existence inspired numerous literary attempts to depict them appropriately. Edgar Allan Poe in 1845 had described them as "fierce and uncouth races of men." [3] The English historian Arnold J. Toynbee was less kind in the 1930's when he asserted that these modern descendants of the original Scotch-Irish were no better than barbarians. He contended that they had retrogressed to such an extent that instead of improving on the Ulsterman they had gone downhill. He charged them with the melancholy crime of losing an inherited civilization.[4] Other writers referred to the same people as "abandoned frontiersmen," "pocketed Americans," "inhabitants of a forgotten frontier," "our contemporary ancestors," "survivals of Elizabethan England," and "twentieth-century

---

[1] C. P. Loomis and L. S. Dodson, *Standards of Living in Four Southern Appalachian Mountain Counties*, U. S. Department of Agriculture Social Research Report No. X (Washington, D. C.: U. S. Department of Agriculture, 1938), 2.

[2] John C. Campbell, *The Southern Highlander and His Homeland* (New York: Russell Sage Foundation, 1921), 323.

[3] Quoted by Horace Kephart, *Our Southern Highlanders: A Narrative of Adventure in the Southern Appalachians and a Study of Life among the Mountaineers* (New York: The Macmillan Co., 1929), 11.

[4] *A Study of History* (D. C. Somervell's abridgement of Volumes I–VI; New York: Oxford University Press, 1947), 149.

pioneers." [5] The Federal Land Planning Committee declared that between 1800 and 1860 the people of the Appalachian mountain region existed under a lower standard of living than that of the average Negro slave. Furthermore, it added, conditions had improved little since the Civil War: thousands of families had less than a $300-a-year cash income.[6]

Some explanation for these tragic economic and social conditions is provided in this statement: "The hill folk are not inferior. They are of Anglo-Saxon and Celtic stock and as intelligent and resourceful as people elsewhere in Anglo-America, but nature denied them nearly all means of making a livelihood except farming." [7] Sadly enough, farming offered them little better than destitution: the North Carolina Tax Commission stated in 1928 that the average cash income for farms in the mountain region was about $86 per year.[8] Lack of arable land, poor farming techniques, and widespread erosion caused at least 100,000 farms in the south Appalachians to be declared unfit for agriculture by 1930.[9] The Department of Agriculture had long warned that much of the land was so poor that it would literally starve to death whoever tried to farm it. Those who ignored the warnings found their lives inevitably robbed of everything except the absolute necessities.[10]

The woes of unprofitable agriculture were compounded by population pressure. The mountain women seemed to be as fertile and prolific as the soil was infertile and nonproductive. North Carolina was rated the most fecund state in the Union, and fear was expressed that the Appalachian mountaineers would have the United States "Chinafied" by the close of the twentieth century if their reproduction ratio continued unabated.[11] For the over-all period 1900–30 the population increase for the region was 55 per cent in contrast to the national aver-

[5] U. S. Federal Land Planning Committee, "Maladjustments in Land Use," 20.
[6] Ibid.
[7] C. Langdon White and Edwin J. Foscue, Regional Geography of Anglo-America (2nd ed. rev.; Englewood Cliffs, N. J.: Prentice-Hall, Inc., 1954), 136.
[8] Asheville Citizen, June 28, 1934, editorial.
[9] J. Wesley Hatcher, "Appalachian America," in W. T. Couch (ed.), Culture in the South (Chapel Hill: University of North Carolina Press, 1934), 377.
[10] Carl C. Taylor et al., Disadvantaged Classes in American Agriculture, U. S. Department of Agriculture Social Research Report No. VIII (Washington, D. C.: U. S. Department of Agriculture, 1938), 5, 8.
[11] Edward A. Ross, "Pocketed Americans," New Republic, XXXVII (January 9, 1924), 171, 225.

age of 33 per cent.[12] Such increases were proportionally much greater than the ability of the soil properly to sustain them; thus, squalor and misery continued to multiply.

To make matters worse, exploitative mining and lumbering had caused extensive damage to the land throughout the region. A journalist traveling through western North Carolina in 1874 had remarked that the area was exceedingly fertile, abounded in minerals, and needed only the "magic wand of the capitalist waved over it to become one of the richest sections of this Union." [13] The capitalists lost no time in waving their wands. They bought thousands of acres of timber and mineral rights for even less than the proverbial song—the selling price all too often ran as low as thirty-five cents an acre. Great band mills and narrow-gauge railroads were brought into the mountains to devour the enormous timber resources. From one end of the Blue Ridge to the other the vicious game of "cut out and get out" was played. In so doing, the exploiters were both greedy and thorough. Typical was a lumber company that began cutting in Avery County, North Carolina, a decade after the Civil War and as late as 1900 was still cutting between 25,000,000 and 30,000,000 board feet of lumber annually.

When the lumber barons had extracted all they deemed profitable, they departed. Behind them remained a cut-over, burned-out, washed-out land. As with timber, so with minerals. Once the cream was gone, so were the exploiters. In their wake they left a destitute people who had depended on them for employment but were left so poor that no funds were available for schools, roads, or similar public improvements, and often none for pressing personal needs.[14] Proof of this is reflected in statistics showing that the total expenditure per child enrolled in elementary and secondary schools for the five most mountainous counties in North Carolina, Tennessee, and Virginia in 1930 was $22 to $26 as contrasted with the national average of $77.[15] Thus,

[12] U.S. Department of Agriculture, *Economic and Social Problems and Conditions of the Southern Appalachians,* U.S. Department of Agriculture Miscellaneous Publication No.205 (Washington,D.C.: U.S. Dept.of Agriculture,1935),5.
[13] Edward King, *The Southern States of North America: A Record of Journeys in Louisiana, Texas, the Indian Territory, Missouri, Arkansas, Mississippi, Alabama, Georgia, Florida, South Carolina, North Carolina, Kentucky, Tennessee, Virginia, West Virginia* (London: Blackie and Son, 1875), 488.
[14] Hatcher, "Appalachian America," 379.
[15] William A. Duerr, *The Economic Problems of Forestry in the Appalachian*

in addition to a deep-seated poverty the area was afflicted with the highest illiteracy rate for white people in the United States.[16]

The mountain people were aware of their straitened circumstances, yet they were reluctant to accept charity. Theirs had long been a depressed economy, but neither social nor political machinery had been devised to alleviate the adverse conditions. It took the innovations of the New Deal to attempt to solve their problems, and the uniqueness of their situation led to an unique approach: the construction of a great national parkway which could provide thousands of needy persons jobs without appearing to be charity.

The idea of building public roads to ease the economic pains of depression was not new. In 1894 the Populist Jacob S. Coxey, who became famous for "Coxey's Army," proposed a $500,000,000 public works relief project of nationwide county road construction to counter the prevailing hard times. Any unemployed person was to be guaranteed work at not less than $1.50 per eight-hour day. Coxey's proposal was ridiculed on the grounds that unemployment was an act of God and hence not within governmental jurisdiction.[17] This attitude continued to prevail until the administration of Franklin D. Roosevelt.

As the 1929 Depression worsened, various projects were considered by which widespread unemployment, in the mountains and elsewhere, might be relieved. Road-building had substantial appeal and seemed ideally suited for relief on a national scale because it possessed the advantage of putting funds to work quickly. The creation of numerous work opportunities within reach of many unemployed persons also made highway construction attractive. Furthermore, the building of new roads would not add to any existing surplus or produce a commodity that had to be bought. The money paid in construction wages would circulate immediately and create a demand for consumer goods that would stimulate the industrial economy.[18]

Region, Harvard Economic Studies, Vol. LXXXIV (Cambridge, Mass.: Harvard University Press, 1949), 90.

16 Vance, *Human Geography of the South,* 32.

17 Samuel Eliot Morison and Henry Steele Commager, *The Growth of the American Republic* (4th ed. rev.; New York: Oxford University Press, 1950), II, 254.

18 Grover C. Dillman, "Roadbuilding as an Agency of Employment during the Depression," *American City,* XLVII (December, 1932), 75–76.

Ickes, in his dual capacity as Secretary of the Interior and Administrator of Public Works, was charged with the responsibility of determining which activities would be suitable for adoption as relief measures. Finding appropriate projects for development—projects which would utilize large numbers of workers and yet produce no commodity to place on an already glutted market—was not simple. Title II of the National Industrial Recovery Act had authorized Ickes to prepare a comprehensive program of public works, including the construction of public highways and parkways.[19] Therefore, when Senator Byrd and others approached him about constructing a parkway linking the Shenandoah and Great Smoky Mountains National Parks, he gave the project favorable attention and eventually approved it as a relief project. Among the arguments advanced for constructing a mountain parkway was that, although the mountain people were economically depressed, they would not leave home for employment. Congressman Doughton, who was born and reared in (and representative for) one of the most poverty-stricken districts of the Blue Ridge, told Ickes, "The only way to help them is to give them employment and the only way to do it is to bring the development to them. You cannot take them to the road, you must bring the road to them." [20] The editor of the Asheville *Citizen* listed a series of reasons why the parkway's construction was absolutely essential if the economic needs of the mountain residents were to be met: the National Industrial Recovery Act would do little for them because they had relatively few industries; the Agricultural Adjustment Act could not offer much aid because their small farms produced no important staple crop; the Tennessee Valley Authority could offer little immediate help, if ever; the creation of the Shenandoah and the Great Smoky Mountains National Parks and a series of national forests had removed much property from the tax books and had halted the timber work which had employed thousands. Thus, a great local construction project, such as road-building, appeared to be their only salvation.[21]

It is highly probable that the features which convinced Ickes to approve the Parkway project were these: several thousand men would be employed for a period of at least two years; the product would be

[19] U. S. *Statutes at Large*, XLVIII, Pt. I, 200.

[20] U. S. Department of the Interior, "Brief of Hearings Relative to Parkway Routing," September 24, 1934, in National Archives, Department of the Interior, Record Group 48.

[21] Asheville *Citizen*, June 28, 1934, p. 4.

permanently useful and would not adversely affect the national economy; and work could begin immediately. The one word which characterized Secretary Ickes' correspondence relative to the Parkway after it was authorized was "expedite." He directed the federal agencies charged with supervision and construction to initiate the work at the earliest possible date.[22] The governor of Virginia was informed, "I will want rapid progress made in the actual construction of this road. You will want this, too, not only to get the road finished but to furnish employment." [23] The governor of North Carolina was also urged to see that no time was lost in beginning construction.[24]

As a means of providing relief for the mountain needy, an initial $4,000,000 appropriation was made on December 5; and thereafter, from time to time, funds were made available for parkway use. Delays in routing and procuring rights-of-way, however, slowed the program to such an extent that nearly two years passed before relief work was started. Among the measures taken was the establishment of four Civilian Conservation Corps camps along the route; each averaging about 150 men. In addition, there were several Emergency Relief Administration projects. At times as many as 1,200 persons were employed in planting and stabilizing the construction slopes, reducing fire hazards, providing erosion control measures, and building fences. Also, three utility areas and seven recreational areas were constructed. These activities provided work for the idle from 1936 until the coming of World War II. And even then the Parkway was not overlooked as a make-work project because the federal government established camps for conscientious objectors and had them doing the same kind of work as had been done by the Civilian Conservation Corps and the Emergency Relief Administration crews.[25] In addition to the standard federal relief agencies, the private contractors who built the road were obligated by law to employ as much local labor as possible. Directly or indirectly, thousands of persons benefited from the millions of dollars made available through the project.

[22] Memorandum, Ickes to Cammerer, November 18, 1933, in National Archives, Department of the Interior, Record Group 48.
[23] Letter, Ickes to Governor George C. Peery of Virginia, November 12, 1934, in *ibid.*
[24] Letter, Ickes to Ehringhaus, November 12, 1934, in Ehringhaus Papers. In spite of Ickes' blandishments, actual construction was not begun for another two years, and thirty years later the Parkway was still unfinished.
[25] Interview with Earl W. Batten, Blue Ridge Parkway engineer, September 5, 1963.

In the words of the superintendent of the Parkway, "The coming of the Parkway was a terrific boost for the local economy." [26] The construction of the Parkway promised relief from sub-subsistence living. New jobs became available the moment the government surveyors began hiring local residents to help survey, cut, and trim the preliminary location lines. Employment opportunities increased when contractors began their local hiring and grew even more when the National Park Service began employing its maintenance and labor force and its rangers. Added to all this were the benefits of expanded markets for local produce and the impact of a newly stimulated tourist industry. Thus, it is not surprising that the coming of the Parkway was considered a godsend by those who were needy and those who were charged with providing help for the poverty-stricken.

[26] Interview with Sam P. Weems, September 5, 1963.

THE SMELL OF SPOILS has long been a potent stimulant in politics. Thus, the news that a lengthy federally financed scenic highway had been proposed and approved set off on the part of interested citizens in Virginia, North Carolina, and Tennessee a landslide of efforts, political and otherwise, to get every possible mile of the road located in their state. Each community through which the Parkway might feasibly pass claimed that its area had the most to offer in scenic beauty and, therefore, was logically the only place to route the road. For example, Craig and Giles counties in Virginia urged that the thoroughfare be routed through that area because it "has been stated by a number of world travelers that this route would afford the most beautiful scenic trail in the eastern part of the United States." [1]

An editorial comment appearing in the Asheville *Citizen* November 13, 1934, illustrated public reaction to the proposed construction: "We do not believe that in the whole history of the mountain counties there has ever been any matter before the people which has excited so eager an interest, or regarding which the people were of so much a unit." Indicative of this was a telegram that the Asheville Hotel Men's Association sent to Governor Ehringhaus:

> WE NEED BIG MEN FAMILIAR WITH MOUNTAINS TO OBTAIN FOR OUR STATE ITS PROPER RECOGNITION AND MATCH THE ABILITY OF VIRGINIA AND TENNESSEE COMMISSIONERS AS EFFORT WILL BE MADE TO DIVERT THIS HIGHWAY FROM OUR SECTION. RELYING ON YOU TO FIGHT THIS THROUGH SUCCESSFULLY. [2]

As the telegram illustrates, the North Carolina boosters were extremely fearful that Tennessee politicians would divert the major portion of the southern end of the parkway away from the Tar Heel state, thereby channeling the tourist trade into Knoxville rather than Asheville. Rivalry between the two was long and bitter, and the new project quickly brought it to life again. The first public news of the enterprise was not published until September 23, 1933, yet less than a

[1] Letter, J. W. Ould to Henry G. Shirley, December 18, 1933, in files of Virginia Highway Department.

[2] McKee Alexander, president, to Ehringhaus, October 13, 1933, in Ehringhaus Papers.

month later the governor of North Carolina had already wired the
chairman of the North Carolina State Highway Commission (who had
been sent to Washington to protect the interests of his state) that:

> IT IS MY CONFIDENTIAL INFORMATION THAT EFFORT WILL BE MADE TO
> DIVERT HIGHWAY TO FOLLOW LEE HIGHWAY THROUGH VIRGINIA THENCE TO
> KNOXVILLE THENCE TO GATLINBURG AND EAST INTO SMOKY MOUNTAIN NA-
> TIONAL PARK AND THUS IGNORE PROPOSED ROUTE FROM WYTHEVILLE
> THROUGH NORTH CAROLINA. THIS FOR YOUR INFORMATION AND TO ENABLE
> YOU TO GOVERN YOURSELF ACCORDINGLY.[3]

Tennessee, in the meantime, was pressing every advantage. She had
no intention of being checkmated by North Carolina. To the director
of the National Park Service, who was to have a considerable voice in
determining the route, came this telegram from the chairman of the
Tennessee State Highway Department:

> THE STATE OF TENNESSEE IS VITALLY INTERESTED IN SEEING THAT AT LEAST
> HALF OF THE MILEAGE OF THE PROPOSED PARK TO PARK ROAD BE LOCATED
> WITHIN THE BOUNDARIES OF TENNESSEE AS REGARDS THAT PORTION SOUTH
> OF THE VIRGINIA LINE. . . . TENNESSEE WILL BE SATISFIED HOWEVER WITH
> HALF OF THE MILEAGE BUT WITH NO LESS.[4]

Such actions reflected a growing awareness of the economic gains
that the new highway would bring. The number of routing recommendations and petitions increased. Everyone seemed to have a suggestion. The Delta Theta Chi sorority of Roanoke informed the authorities that they were "very much interested in having the Sky-Line
Drive come through Roanoke. We are asking that you kindly use
your influence to have this accomplished." [5] Walker's Big Mountain
was highly recommended as the "shortest possible route, and one of
the most Sceneric [sic] routes to be found." [6] Even the 1928 Presiden-
tial election and the prohibition issue entered into the petitions. One
petitioner, evidently still disgruntled over North Carolina's political
leanings and prohibition proclivities, wrote to a Virginia official: "I am
in hopes you will insist on a straight line regardless of what town or
cities it misses. Also insist on its being built in Va. and Tenn. as much

[3] Ehringhaus to Jeffress, October 16, 1933, in *ibid.*

[4] Frank W. Webster to Cammerer, January 4, 1934, in National Archives, National Park Service, Record Group 79.

[5] Letter, Mrs. Aubrey Wallace to Shirley, October 14, 1933, in files of Virginia Highway Department.

[6] Letter, F. R. Newberry to Shirley, November 22, 1933, in *ibid.*

as possible as no tourist wants to tour through a dry state and N. C. has gone against our administration by not voting *wet* and I say let her suffer for her mistakes. D____ poor state anyway."[7]

The official spokesmen for Virginia, North Carolina, and Tennessee also had ideas about where the Parkway should run. Like the private citizens and civic organizations, they began laying plans and placing petitions. When it became evident that competition relative to the routing was likely to become uncontrollable, the highway officials of the three states were asked to reconcile their local interests and submit to the Secretary of the Interior a single recommendation incorporating the route desired. Then, to permit each state an opportunity to present and defend its recommendation, a hearing before a federal committee was arranged for February 5–7, 1934, in Baltimore, Maryland.[8]

With the prospect of millions of dollars of construction money plus continuing millions of tourist dollars whetting enthusiasm, each state prepared diligently for the hearing. The services of the ablest men available, including lawyers, engineers, and politicians, were obtained. Leaders martialed briefs, king-sized photographs, and any other illustrative material that they thought might advance their cause. To hear and judge their recommendations, Secretary Ickes appointed a three-man committee consisting of representatives from the three agencies charged with coordinating and supervising the project: Radcliffe (chairman) from the Public Works Administration, Cammerer from the National Park Service, and MacDonald from the Bureau of Public Roads. Serving as advisors for the committee were members of the District No. 10 Public Works Administration Advisory Board, Straus and Abel Wolman, and landscape architect G. D. Clark. The persons responsible for field supervision of whatever route was chosen, Thomas C. Vint, chief landscape architect of the National Park Service, and Stanley W. Abbott, resident landscape architect, also attended the hearing. From the states there came the highest ranking officials available, including governors, senators, and congressmen, each eager to volunteer his efforts to promote his state's cause.

The Virginia delegation was heard first, on February 5. Its members were generally agreed that their portion should be routed directly

<hr>

[7] H. M. Luck to Shirley, December 10, 1933, in *ibid.*

[8] Fred L. Weede, "Battle for the Blue Ridge Parkway" (unpublished manuscript in Pack Library, Asheville, N. C.), 17.

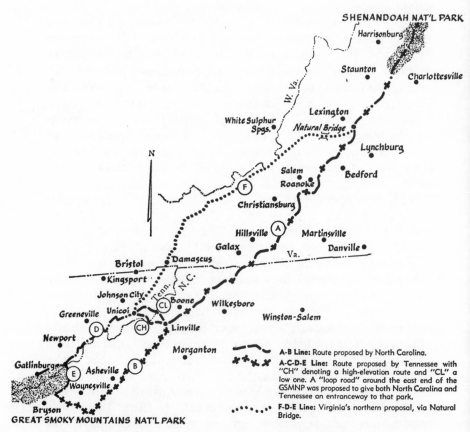

Proposed Shenandoah–Great Smoky Mountains National Parkway. *Based on the original map, courtesy of National Park Service and National Archives.*

from the Shenandoah National Park to the Peaks of Otter in Bedford County; but, beyond this point there was a pronounced difference of opinion. One group, headed by Congressman T. G. Burch, advocated a "southern route" by which the road would continue from the Peaks of Otter into North Carolina through Roanoke, Franklin, Floyd, Carroll, Patrick, and Grayson counties, entering North Carolina near Fancy Gap.[9] A second group, led by Congressman John W. Flannagan, favored a "western" route that would run from the Peaks of Otter through Botetort, Craig, Giles, Pulaski, Bland, Wythe, Smyth, and Grayson counties, and from there make connection with the Tennessee portion of the road.[10] This plan, if adopted, would have completely bypassed North Carolina. It was strongly and successfully opposed.

The North Carolina delegation was heard on February 6, and the Tennessee group on February 7, 1934. Prior to the hearing, North Carolina representatives, sparked by such aggressive civic leaders as Asheville's Weede, had carefully selected a route, appointed a North Carolina Federal Parkway Committee, and commissioned R. Getty Browning, chief locating engineer of the North Carolina Highway Department, to prepare and present the exhibits and materials that would make the most telling impression.[11] To support the Tar Heel presentation, Governor Ehringhaus, United States Senators Bailey and Reynolds, and Congressmen Doughton, Zebulon Weaver, William B. Umstead, A. L. Bulwinkle, and Franklin W. Hancock, Jr., as well as a large group of other prominent Carolinians, went to Baltimore. The basic Carolina proposal was that the Parkway should continue from the Virginia "southern" route on into North Carolina at Low Gap and from there to Roaring Gap, Glendale Springs, Deep Gap, Blowing Rock, Linville Gorge, Little Switzerland, Buck Creek Gap, Balsam Gap, along the Craggies in the vicinity of Asheville, by Pisgah, through the Balsam range to Soco Gap, and into the Great Smoky Mountains National Park—that is, essentially the route followed by the present-day Parkway.[12]

When the Tennessee delegation, headed by Senators Kenneth D. McKellar and Nathan L. Bachman, took the floor, immediate objec-

9 Richmond *Times Dispatch*, February 6, 1934, p. 1.
10 *Ibid.*
11 Weede, "Battle for the Blue Ridge Parkway," 18.
12 Brief presented by North Carolina at the Baltimore hearing, in National Archives, National Park Service, Record Group 70, *passim*.

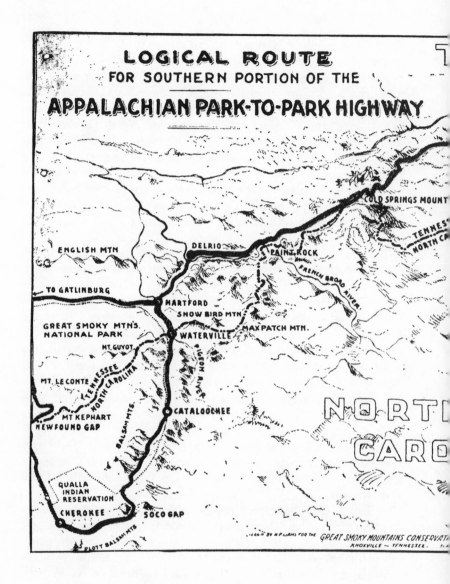

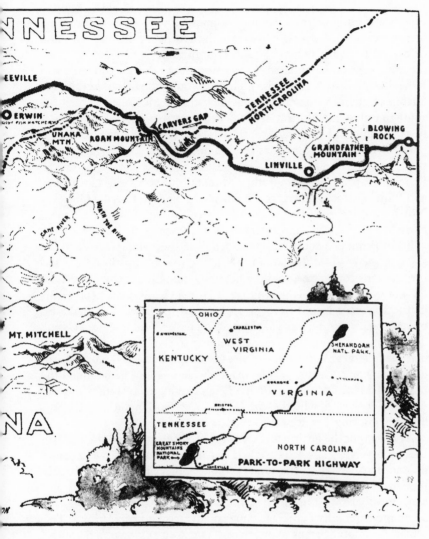

The Maloney Route. *Courtesy of Virginia State Highway Department*

tions were made to the Carolina proposal. An entirely new routing was recommended, giving Tennessee the southern one hundred miles of the route and placing the southern entrance at Gatlinburg. This recommendation heightened the friction between the Knoxville and Asheville interests because the highway would bypass western North Carolina's chief tourist city, Asheville. Senator McKellar wanted the route to follow the North Carolina–Tennessee boundary line as closely as possible, but General Frank Maloney, Knoxville engineer, proposed what became known as the Maloney route. He suggested that the highway run from Low Gap on the Virginia boundary line to Roaring Gap, Little Grandfather Mountain, Horse Gap, Deep Gap, and Blowing Rock, down the Yonahalossee Trail to Linville Gorge in North Carolina, then cross into Tennessee through Carver's Gap and Roan Mountain, with Gatlinburg as the entrance to the Park.[13]

Both Tennessee senators demanded that their state receive a fair share of the road. McKellar, a top-ranking member of the Senate appropriations committee, told the hearing committee that if Tennessee did not get an amount equal to that of North Carolina the proponents of the Parkway would have "a rocky road to travel." To make his point even plainer, he warned them, "You haven't got the money yet." The senator charged that prior to coming to the hearing he had read that the federal government had already decided on an all North Carolina route from Virginia. As he made the accusation, he pounded the table and demanded to know why Tennessee highway authorities had not been consulted, why the experts had been working in North Carolina and ignoring Tennessee.[14]

At this point the chairman, Senator Radcliffe, interrupted to inform the Tennessean, "You are mistaken, Senator, if you think we have any preconceived ideas on the undertaking." To which McKellar tartly replied, "If you have consulted with one side you should have also seen the other side. I'm sure Mr. Ickes would not allot the money for a commercial highway. This is not an advertising proposition." This remark prompted Straus to interject, "You keep talking of a highway. This is a *parkway*." In response, "the Senator had the center of the floor and was speaking loudly. 'I've been sitting up nights working with this thing before you ever thought of it,' he retorted. 'I think

13 Asheville *Citizen*, November 11, 1934, p. 1.
14 Richmond *Times Dispatch*, February 9, 1934, p. 2.

Congress will have something to say about all this. Who is doing this? You or the people who furnished the money?' " [15] Radcliffe broke in again to assure the irate senator that the federal authorities had not decided on an all North Carolina route from Virginia and certainly had not ignored the interests of Tennessee for those of North Carolina. Thereupon Senator Bachman spoke up, "We want a fair decision. We don't want the edge but we don't want them to have the edge." [16]

Senator McKellar's somewhat rude and openly belligerent attitude pained the federal officials, embarrassed his fellow delegates, and certainly did little to put Tennessee in a favored position. The editor of the Knoxville *News-Sentinel* recognized this when he said, "Senator McKellar has hurt, if not the cause of the Tennessee location, the reputation of the state's representatives for fair dealing with our North Carolina neighbors." [17] Cammerer, a member of the hearing committee, was considerably agitated by McKellar's attitude. He posted a letter to the senator immediately after the hearing saying, "I want to keep you fully informed on such [details of the parkway] as you are interested in. I must repeat, however, that the information conveyed to you that Tennessee was being ignored in the location survey is entirely unfounded because I have again verified from my associates in my office that as much time and attention is being given to Tennessee possibilities in location as to the North Carolina side." [18]

One Tennessean who was deeply embarrassed by McKellar's action was Colonel David C. Chapman, president of the Great Smoky Mountains Conservation Association and an active worker in the interests of Tennessee. In a personal letter to the chairman of the North Carolina State Highway Commission, he extended apologies, saying:

> I had hoped to see you after the Tennessee hearing in Baltimore on Feb. 8th but I was rushed away with some of the congressmen who were anxious to get back to Washington.
> What I wish to do is to apologize to you, and through you to all the rest of our friends from North Carolina, for the unseemly conduct of the senior senator from Tennessee. While our respective groups did not agree on the location of the parkway, we could at least scrap it out

[15] Asheville *Citizen*, February 7, 1934, p. 1.
[16] *Ibid.*
[17] Knoxville *News-Sentinel*, March 3, 1934.
[18] Cammerer to McKellar, February 6, 1934, in National Archives, National Park Service, Record Group 79.

like a set of gentlemen. The senator's threats were untimely, uncalled for, and I do not think he could carry them out if he tried.[19]

Partly as a result of McKellar's attitude and partly as a reaction to the great difference in the routes recommended by Tennessee and North Carolina, the hearing committee decided to postpone making a decision until an official reconnaissance party could make an on-the-spot survey of the controversial routes and render an impartial recommendation.[20]

In the interim, those with political influence began applying it. North Carolina's Josephus Daniels, United States Ambassador to Mexico and a close political friend of Secretary Ickes, appealed to him. Daniels was assured that the North Carolina route was being given careful consideration, but he was also cautioned that there were numerous possibilities and many enthusiastic supporters for each.[21] Other North Carolina representatives, too, were making a determined effort to impress the members of the hearing committee and its advisors favorably. They especially concentrated on Radcliffe and Straus, who were invited on bear hunts and fishing trips in the western North Carolina mountains. But to the consternation of the Carolina lobbyists, the office of regional Public Works Administration advisor, held by Radcliffe, was suddenly slated for termination on February 28, 1934. Thus, the influence that had been built up seemed very likely to be lost. With this in mind, a prominent Asheville civic leader told his congressman that it would be necessary to enlist the aid of the highest authority available. "What we want is, if possible, to get this matter up to the President and let the word go out from him that he wants the road through North Carolina." [22]

Thus, Ambassador Daniels wrote to his friend in the White House, President Roosevelt. Daniels declared that he knew perfectly the two routes and was firmly convinced that in grandeur and perfection of beauty the North Carolina proposal was far superior. In closing his appeal, he said, "I do not know exactly the status of the propositions,

[19] Chapman to Jeffress, March 19, 1934, in files of North Carolina State Highway and Public Works Commission.
[20] Abbuehl, "History," 4.
[21] Letter, Ickes to Daniels, March 24, 1934, in National Archives, Department of the Interior, Record Group 48.
[22] Letter, George Stephens to Doughton, February 23, 1934, in Doughton Papers.

but I am writing to you so that when the matter comes up you may have my point of view and give it such weight as you may think it justifies (and on this matter I think I am a good judge)." [23] The weight was considerable, and the pleas of Daniels were to have a favorable influence upon North Carolina's share of the scenic highway.

One of the ablest workers for the North Carolina cause was its senior locating and claims engineer, Browning. He was a native of Maryland but was very familiar with the scenic mountain attractions possessed by North Carolina. He pressed upon the chairman of the hearing committee his view of the reasons for selecting the Tar Heel route: "I would like to call to your attention the fact that nowhere else in the United States, so far as I know, could such an excellent location for a parkway be found, if splendid scenery, high elevations, profusion of beautiful shrubbery, favorable climatic conditions, reasonable construction cost and accessibility for all sections of the country be considered." [24] Browning further informed Radcliffe that the committee would be making no concession to North Carolina by selecting its route; but if the committee overlooked it in favor of another, then "a great injustice would be done, not only to this State, but to all the people of the nation who would be deprived of the opportunity of enjoying what can well be made the most interesting parkway in all the world." [25] Appealing to Radcliffe's political sense, Browning asked him whether the Parkway was to be one that the President could take pride in or one that he would have to apologize for in the years to come: "The building of this Parkway is largely a child of his brain and what more lasting or appropriate monument could he have than an unrivaled National Parkway such as we contemplate." [26]

While this behind-the-scenes lobbying was going on, an inspection party attempted, beginning March 23, 1934, a tour of the terrain through which the proposed routes ran. The group was sizable enough to make necessary the use of fifteen automobiles and trucks. Included were officials from the Bureau of Public Roads, the National Park Service, the Public Works Administration, and the three states and

[23] Daniels to Roosevelt, March 2, 1934, in National Archives, National Park Service, Record Group 79.

[24] Letter, Browning to Radcliffe, June 1, 1934, in files of North Carolina State Highway and Public Works Commission.

[25] Ibid.   [26] Ibid.

other people who turned out to show or be shown the advantages possessed by each route.[27]

The group departed from Roanoke and spent several days on the tour; but sleet, snow, fog, and ice combined to prevent any effective appraisal. Inclement weather continued to delay investigative efforts until April 21, when an aerial survey of the various routes was attempted. It, too, was unsuccessful because of adverse weather. Not until May 18, 1934, was it possible for a suitable reconnaissance to be made.[28] In the course of a five-day outing the reconnoiterers observed the lie of the land and the spectacular scenery along the North Carolina–Tennessee line. They visited such places as Iron Mountain, Cold Spring Mountain, Max Patch Mountain, Gatlinburg, Cherokee, Dillsboro, Waynesville, Mt. Pisgah, Asheville, Mt. Mitchell, Linville Falls, Grandfather Mountain, Blowing Rock, Bellows Gap, Fishers Peak, Galax, White Top Mountain, Walker's Mountain, and Mountain Lake.[29]

The engineer representing Virginia, in making a report of the trip, said, "I am under the impression that the North Carolinians want the entire route in their state, going around by Asheville, whereas the delegation from Tennessee seem to be perfectly willing to take part of it." [30] After giving a detailed description of the Carolina route, he said that it struck him that a compromise line should be utilized, "going from Blowing Rock to Linville and cut over on Roan or Cold Spring Mountain and more or less try to locate the road near the North Carolina–Tennessee line." [31] As he had surmised, the Carolinians did want the entire route and gave no thought to a compromise, as they clearly demonstrated at their first opportunity.

The Roanoke field office of the National Park Service, as an impartial but involved party, had conducted its own investigation. It, too, recommended a compromise route, shifting northwestward from the North Carolina Blue Ridge near Linville, crossing to the Unaka ranges in Tennessee, and going up the valley, entering the Great Smokies via a perimeter or loop road around the northern end of the Park and thereby giving both states an entranceway. The Service believed that

[27] Weede, "Battle for the Blue Ridge Parkway," 21.
[28] Letter, W. W. McClevy to C. S. Mullen, chief engineer, Virginia Department of Highways, June 7, 1934, in files of the department.
[29] Ibid.
[30] Ibid.   [31] Ibid.

such a route would provide a wider variety of scenery and break the monotony of continuous mountain driving.[32]

The Carolinians had been alerted to the possibility that a loop road would be suggested. In planning their battle strategy, however, they declined to propose or support such a road. Congressman Doughton stated their position clearly: "As to the loop . . . I am of course much interested, but fear if we make the suggestion first it might weaken our case; . . . it is my feeling that we should make a straight fight for the road from the Virginia line near Fancy Gap all the way through North Carolina to the Park as certainly our State has claims superior to those in Tennessee." [33]

The "straight-fight" approach proved in the end to be that adopted by North Carolina, and Congressman Doughton, whose home district lay astride the Blue Ridge, became and remained one of the staunchest champions of the Parkway. In the spring of 1934, he told a friend that "this is one matter which I shall *Specialize* on until the final decision is reached." And, indeed, for the remainder of his political life the Parkway was one of his chief interests.[34]

On the lobbying front, a group of Ashevillians found Ambassador Daniels vacationing at Lake Junaluska near Asheville and persuaded him to wire Secretary Ickes, saying, LONG INTEREST AND STUDY OF THE SCENIC PARKWAY . . . PUTS ME IN POSSESSION OF INFORMATION WHICH I THINK YOU WOULD LIKE TO HAVE BEFORE REACHING YOUR FINAL DECISION. He asked the favor of an audience and was given the reply, WILL MAKE NO DECISION RESPECT TO SCENIC PARKWAY UNTIL AFTER CONFERENCE WITH YOU . . . .[35] Not only did Daniels receive the requested appointment, but North Carolina Congressmen Weaver, Doughton, and Bulwinkle also arranged conferences with Ickes. Each, of course, labored to convince him of the superiority of the North Carolina scenery.[36]

It was not until June 8, 1934, that the Ickes-appointed Radcliffe committee composed its recommendation relative to the various road proposals. The report suggested that a compromise route be estab-

---

[32] Interview with Edward H. Abbuehl, resident landscape architect, Blue Ridge Parkway, July 14, 1961.

[33] Letter, Doughton to Jeffress, June 8, 1934, in files of North Carolina State Highway and Public Works Commission.

[34] Letter, Doughton to Jeffress, May 31, 1934, in *ibid.*

[35] Daniels to Ickes, June 21, 1934; Ickes to Daniels, June 21, 1934; in National Archives, Department of the Interior, Record Group 48.

[36] Richmond *Times Dispatch,* June 21, 1934, p. 3.

lished, departing from the Blue Ridge at Linville and making its way to the Smokies via Roan Mountain, Unicoi, Cold Spring Mountain, and Gatlinburg.[37] This was basically the same route proposed by Maloney. If the recommendation were adopted, the three states would have approximately the mileage which had been indicated in Senator Byrd's telegram initiating establishment of the Parkway. It definitely meant that North Carolina's lobbying and superiority argument had partially failed.

The actual contents of the report remained secret for weeks, but the news that a report had been submitted touched off wild speculation about the contents. One North Carolinian, Congressman Weaver, obviously had some premonition because he was publicly quoted as saying that if the recommendation was what he understood it to be it was unfavorable to his state.[38]

Recognizing the delicate political aspects of the case, Secretary Ickes withheld action on it until July 17, 1934, at which time he sent the acting director of the National Park Service a memorandum saying, "Regarding the Shenandoah–Great Smoky Mountains National Parkway, I have approved the route recommended by Messrs. Radcliffe, MacDonald, and Cammerer from the south boundary of the Shenandoah National Park to Blowing Rock, North Carolina. I propose to give further study to the suggested route from Blowing Rock, N. C., to the boundary of the Great Smoky Mountains National Park."[39] He also directed that steps be taken to expedite immediate construction on two sections of the Parkway, one from the southern boundary of the Shenandoah National Park to the James River, and a second extending from near Adney Gap, Virginia, to Blowing Rock, North Carolina: "It is requested that you proceed with all possible speed with this project. I would like if possible to have all funds obligated by February 1, 1935."[40]

Although Ickes had not publicly revealed the routing recommendations made by his committee, certain Ashevillians had foreseen the likelihood that the committee might not suggest placing the Parkway anywhere near their city. In a letter to Senator Bailey, the editor of

[37] Knoxville *Journal,* September 5, 1934, p. 1.
[38] Richmond *Times Dispatch,* June 22, 1934, p. 9.
[39] Memorandum, Ickes to Demaray, July 17, 1934, in National Archives, Department of the Interior, Record Group 48.
[40] *Ibid.*

the Asheville *Citizen* stated that he and others had listened to a speech by the director of the National Park Service and were all convinced that the recommendation would be unfavorable to North Carolina. He offered an explanation: "There is a very strong suspicion in the mind of our people around here that the Tennessee politicians and Senators have been putting over a fine job of lobbying to divert the road from its natural routing." [41] Senator Bailey was urged to go directly to Ickes and use all his tact and diplomacy to persuade the Secretary personally to inspect the entire area prior to approving any further routing. The Senator immediately wrote Ickes, "I am satisfied that you intend that the Scenic Highway to the Smoky Mountains shall be routed with a view to the scenic effects, and not with a view to the political situation. All I ask is that this shall be the governing motive." [42]

Charles A. Webb, Asheville newspaper publisher, was convinced that National Park Service Director Cammerer was the man who had prejudiced the report of the hearing committee against North Carolina. Webb was certain that "he is dead set against us, and I do not believe that any delegation or committee would have any influence with him. I am also satisfied that Mr. Ickes and the President are the only two persons who can help us in securing the location of the Parkway anywhere near Asheville. In my opinion our only hope rests with them." [43] He based his contention upon the belief that Cammerer had been unconsciously influenced by resentment over some unsatisfactory dealings he had had with the governor and General Assembly of North Carolina relative to the Great Smoky Mountains National Park. [44] Whether his surmise is correct is not known, but the National Park Service's recommended route had not favored North Carolina.

Secretary Ickes' announcement that he would give further study to the routing from Blowing Rock to the boundary of the Smokies touched off a new battle between North Carolina and Tennessee. North Carolina was determined to grab all of the mileage from the

[41] Don S. Elias to Josiah W. Bailey, June 16, 1934, copy of letter in National Archives, National Park Service, Record Group 79.

[42] Bailey to Ickes, June 20, 1934, in *ibid.*

[43] Letter, Webb to Jeffress, July 18, 1934, in files of North Carolina State Highway and Public Works Commission.

[44] See Carlos C. Campbell, *Birth of a National Park in the Great Smoky Mountains* (Knoxville: The University of Tennessee Press, 1960), for details of the development of the Great Smoky Mountains National Park.

Virginia line to the Park, and Tennessee was equally determined to obtain a fair share. The battling strength of the Tar Heels centered in Asheville where the Chamber of Commerce had undertaken the task of acquiring an "all North Carolina route" as a means of boosting the income of western North Carolina. The Asheville strategists were no amateurs at lobbying; they realized that support from high places was a prerequisite for success. They decided to appeal directly to the man who would have the greatest weight in deciding the issue, President Roosevelt. Realizing that superior scenery was their strong point, the Asheville men assembled an album of photographs highlighting the beauty of the western North Carolina mountains. To make it more impressive, they had the enlarged photographs bound together within red-morocco covers and FRANKLIN DELANO ROOSEVELT stamped in gold on the front cover. A large delegation, which included Governor Ehringhaus, presented the album to the President. A member of the group described the reaction: "The President commented on the elegance of the book, read the inscription, remarked upon the great beauty of the scenes shown and astonished the group with his familiarity with some of the places pictured. We felt that we had at least got one foot inside the door through this personal contact." [45]

Personal contacts were made whenever possible to win the support of persons strategically placed or in positions to exert influence. Mrs. Harold L. Ickes, a student of Indian affairs, wished to visit the Cherokee Indians in North Carolina. Her husband called upon his old friend Ambassador Daniels to act as her host. Daniels graciously assented and alerted the Asheville Chamber of Commerce, which quickly grasped the opportunity to win further good will. Mrs. Ickes' visit coincided with the annual Rhododendron Ball in Asheville, and the Secretary's lady was given the red carpet treatment during every moment of her stay. As she departed, she let it be known that she had been exceptionally pleased with the treatment accorded her. One of the persons most responsible for arrangements during her visit admitted, "We hoped her husband would be pleased too." [46] Considerably later, when the issue of parkway routing became even more critical, the mayor of Asheville took the liberty of writing to Mrs. Ickes, pleading for her to come to "our assistance by discussing the question with your illustrious husband. . . . I am soliciting your help in getting our case fully

[45] Weede, "Battle for the Blue Ridge Parkway," 25–26.
[46] Ibid., 42.

before your husband. . . . Please forgive me if I have been presumptuous." [47]

The Asheville leaders were at the same time coordinating their many moves with Browning, who had become the generalissimo in charge of North Carolina efforts. He, Weede, and a few others constituted a master planning committee. Browning traveled constantly between Asheville, Raleigh, and Washington, D. C., gleaning information, influencing any and all supporters, and relaying a steady supply of lobbying leads to his associates in Asheville. From Asheville flowed a stream of publicity materials. Every possible agency, from the press to personal friendship, was employed to advance the rendering of a favorable routing through Asheville rather than Gatlinburg. The board of directors of the Asheville Chamber of Commerce composed a resolution setting forth reasons why the all North Carolina route was the only justifiable one. Their basic arguments were: to omit the Carolina scenery would be to omit the most beautiful views in the Southern Appalachians; to divert the route into Tennessee would make Gatlinburg the official entranceway into the Park, to the great damage of North Carolina's tourist industry; and to deflect the Parkway away from western North Carolina would destroy the $50,000,000 economic investment represented by a century-old tourist industry. Every chamber of commerce in the state was urged to petition Ickes with similar resolutions.[48]

Using Knoxville, the rival of Asheville, as their operating base, the Tennesseans conducted activities similar to those in the sister state. They were determined to obtain at least a partial share of the Parkway, regardless of what tactics their opponents might pursue. Renewed lobbying activities in the two states made a new hearing imperative. Secretary Ickes, realizing this, called for a second hearing, to convene in Asheville on September 10, 1934. This action met instant disapproval and criticism from Senator McKellar, who wired Secretary Ickes:

AS WE UNDERSTAND IT ASHEVILLE IS THE PRINCIPAL COMPLAINANT IN THE CASE. . . . ARE YOU GOING TO HAVE ANOTHER HEARING IN TENNESSEE SO THAT THE TENNESSEANS MAY BE HEARD. I TAKE IT THAT YOU WILL NOT REQUIRE

[47] Wickes Wambolt to Mrs. Ickes, July 23, 1934, in National Archives, Department of the Interior, Record Group 48.
[48] Weede, "Battle for the Blue Ridge Parkway," 28.

TENNESSEANS TO GO OVER TO NORTH CAROLINA TO BE HEARD IN THE MATTER.
AS I UNDERSTAND IT THE HEARING WAS TO BE IN *.* . SOME NEUTRAL POINT.[49]

Faced with this irritable and yet perfectly understandable reaction, Ickes changed his plans, canceled the Asheville hearing, and called for a meeting in Washington, D. C., for September 18, 1934. In a telegram to Senator Reynolds he explained that his main purpose for setting the hearing in Asheville had been to give himself an opportunity to inspect personally both routes. Because of the objections, however, he thought it would be wiser to stay away altogether until after the routing decision was made. In that way, he said, he could not be charged with prejudice or with being unduly influenced.[50] Senator McKellar was politically wise in objecting to the Asheville hearing site, as has since been revealed by one of the Asheville leaders. Part of the Tar Heel strategy had been to have in attendance the largest gathering ever assembled in Asheville: "Western North Carolina was on fire and they would have turned out in such numbers it would have overwhelmed Secretary Ickes." [51] To cope with the altered situation, the Ashevillians summoned Senator Reynolds from Washington and very carefully mapped their next moves. It was decided to retain the psychological idea of mass support by arranging for an enormous North Carolina delegation to present itself when the Washington hearing opened.[52]

The Tennesseans had been just as active. According to a report in the Knoxville *Journal*, "East Tennesseans, roused by the danger of losing their share of the scenic highway, prepared to attend in throngs." Congressman J. Will Taylor sounded a call to arms. He emphasized the importance of Tennessee's being well represented at the Washington meetings because North Carolina would try to take every advantage of the situation; "if she succeeds it will mean irreparable injury to Tennessee. All we want is a square deal, and if the location of the highway is determined on the basis of merit, we have no apprehension.... The so-called Maloney route is fair to both sides." [53]

Colonel Chapman, Tennessee's dynamic advocate of the "fair share"

---

[49] McKellar to Ickes, September 1, 1934, in National Archives, Department of the Interior, Record Group 48.
[50] Ickes to Reynolds, September 6, 1934, in *ibid*.
[51] Weede, "Battle for the Blue Ridge Parkway," 31.
[52] *Ibid*.
[53] Knoxville *Journal*, September 5, 1934, p. 1.

policy, urged the Bristol Chamber of Commerce to see that its area was well represented at the Washington meeting. Chapman reminded the Bristolites that if the road were located the way North Carolina desired, it would mean the loss of millions of dollars annually for Tennesseans.[54] The chairman of the Bristol Chamber of Commerce caught the spirit and began sending out material urging the recipients to use every influence they commanded to support the Tennessee route. All were told, "Wire and send a big delegation to Washington, Sept. 18." [55] The chairman of the Tennessee State Highway Commission wrote Radcliffe, asking for information regarding the status of the routing and inquiring about what action Tennessee should take. According to Commissioner Webster, Tennessee had made no official request to have Secretary Ickes examine or investigate any route, nor had Tennessee been advised, except by the press, of which routes were being considered by Ickes. He avowed that Tennesseans did not care to "complicate the situation but you can readily understand that we hardly feel like sitting quietly by and permitting North Carolina to exert all possible influence to securing 100% of this Parkway while we are doing nothing." It was Webster's belief that Tennessee ought to be informed about which recommendations the Secretary was considering so that appropriate action might be taken, "as we certainly do not want to lose this magnificent project by any fault of our own." The commissioner further assured Radcliffe that Tennessee had perfect confidence in the competence of the hearing committee and hence had taken no persuasive action.[56]

That a considerable number of Tennesseans were not willing to place "perfect confidence" in the hearing committee and were determined to take some "persuasive action" was revealed in an article which appeared in the Knoxville *Journal*, September 7, 1934. It stated that 135 Knoxville business and civic leaders would form the bulwark of the defense of Tennessee's claims at the Washington hearing. Each of them had been primed for duty by being told that North Carolina was positive that none of the mileage would be located in Tennessee. All had been reminded that it would be disastrous if Tennessee lost her

[54] Letter, Chapman to chairman of the Bristol Chamber of Commerce, September 6, 1934, in files of Virginia Highway Department.
[55] Mimeographed campaign material in *ibid*.
[56] Webster to Radcliffe, August 3, 1934, in National Archives, National Park Service, Record Group 79.

rightful part of the big highway: "This is a patriotic call, but also one of business. Will we stand idly by and permit Tennessee to lose all the fine publicity and tourist money that this highway will provide?" [57]

Johnson City became, with Knoxville, a center of plan-making. A giant council of war composed of delegates from every town and city in East Tennessee, and also including Governor McAlister as well as representatives from southwest Virginia, gathered in Johnson City on September 15, 1934, to complete plans for presenting the Tennessee defense at the hearing. During a huge banquet, various spokesmen voiced their convictions regarding Tennessee's right to an equal share, and plans were discussed for obtaining that share.[58] Virginia Congressman Flannagan added to the excitement by telling his listeners, "If Tennessee gets anything you've got to fight for it. I'm not exactly charging that a conspiracy has been formed to keep the highway out of Tennessee, but I do think that something is wrong that you people have to put up such a terrific fight to get what is coming to you and is rightfully yours." [59] The secretary of the Knoxville Chamber of Commerce said that what they wanted was very simple: "We want Tennessee to get its share of the highway and we don't want North Carolina to take all of the pie as they are trying to do." [60]

While North Carolina and Tennessee were engaged in lobbying, publicizing their individual claims, and sharpening their battle-axes for the coming Washington hearing, Secretary Ickes had arranged to receive private, neutral information to help him better judge the relative merits of the two proposed routes. At the request of the Secretary of the Interior, Forestry Director Marshall had spent five days examining both the Tennessee and the North Carolina scenery and topography. On August 16, 1934, he informed Ickes that the choice between the North Carolina and the Tennessee routes was so close that he could with perfect propriety choose either and easily justify himself. Marshall showed sympathy for the predicament Ickes was in: "I presume that whichever one you do pick will result in having about twenty-five thousand politicians from the state which loses jumping on your neck." [61] He contrasted the advantages possessed by each state. The

[57] Knoxville *Journal*, September 7, 1934, p. 1.
[58] Kingsport *Times*, September 16, 1934, p. 1.
[59] Johnson City *Chronicle*, September 16, 1934, p. 1.
[60] *Ibid.*
[61] Abstract of memorandum from Marshall to Ickes in a letter from Broome to Weems, November 15, 1960, in files of Superintendent, Blue Ridge Parkway.

A Blue Ridge patriarch
surveys the onslaught of
road-building machinery.
*All photographs in this
section are used by cour-
tesy of the Shenandoah
National Park.*

The Ridge people sprang
from sturdy Scotch-Irish
and German ancestors.

The Parkway offered the proud mountain people work, not charity.

Rocky soils, primitive equipment, and a lack of medical attention were prevalent aspects of life in the Blue Ridge Mountains. Goiters were a common condition.

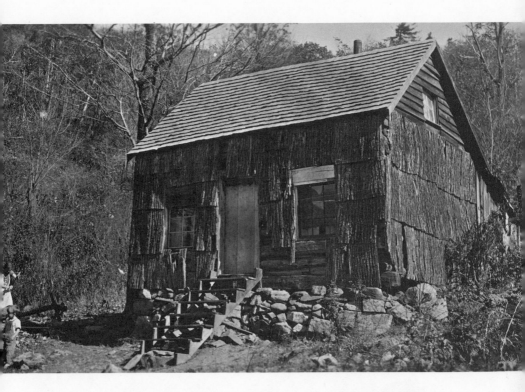

Bark-sided cabins such as this one attested to the unsophisticated building methods of mountain folk. The materials that were most accessible were the ones used.

Most of the mountain houses in the Blue Ridge were improvisations on poverty.

Mountain parents usually had **several mouths** to feed, and marginal existence was common.

Fence styles, like house styles, conformed to the individual's needs and reflected his circumstances as well as his environment.

Carolina way had two important ones: (1) it was more scenic because of the lofty elevations such as provided on the slopes of Mount Mitchell; (2) it would not despoil the wilderness because automobile roads had already been constructed through it and the spruce and balsam had been logged off. Tennessee, on the other hand, was credited with three advantages: (1) its route would be less costly to construct; (2) it would scar the scenery less; (3) it would be less blocked by snow in winter and would have less fog in summer because of the lower elevations followed. Marshall concluded his report with an indirect recommendation: "My own feeling is that the resultant of all these factors would throw the decision in favor of the Carolina route by a hair's breadth, in spite of the fact that the score of individual items is three to two against it." [62]

The publicity agents kept busy in the meanwhile, with boosters for each side citing anything from the Civil War to the Tennessee Valley development project to stimulate support for their cause. In an editorial headed NORTH CAROLINA: RED-HEADED STEPCHILD, the Asheville *Citizen* readers were told how, in a recent speech, Senator McKellar had boasted that the federal government had poured $300 million into Tennessee's development and recovery. Then they were reminded that Tennessee was apparently the favorite child and that Uncle Sam was allowing North Carolina to languish in the role of a red-headed stepchild. Decent treatment for Carolina was demanded, with the plea that "despite the unpleasantness of the Sixties, we are a part of the Union." [63]

The manager of the Asheville Chamber of Commerce was forced to change tactics when the meeting was moved to Washington. He contacted Governor Ehringhaus, informed him of the new plans, and added that he hoped the governor's schedule would not conflict with the hearing. Ehringhaus replied, "Mr. Weede, the Governor of the State of North Carolina would not permit any engagement of any kind to interfere with a meeting which means so much to this State." [64] The Asheville chamber invited all other chambers in the state to join in a "march on Washington" and urged all citizens of the state to attend the hearings. Ambassador Daniels was asked by the Asheville leaders to leave Mexico and come to Washington to make an appeal in

[62] *Ibid.*
[63] Asheville *Citizen*, August 19, 1934.
[64] Weede, "Battle for the Blue Ridge Parkway," 30.

their behalf. He declined, advising that his appearance would very likely do more harm than good: "It would arouse the antagonism of our Tennessee friends and put them on notice of all that I have been trying to do to secure a proper gateway to the Park via Mount Mitchell and Asheville." Daniels told them that he had had a long talk with the President and had conferred several times with Ickes. The Secretary had been very receptive and quite friendly, so much so that the Ambassador assured his friends, "I shall be the most disappointed man that ever lived if he does not grant our request after our conversations." [65] At this distance it is difficult to evaluate exactly the influence Daniels exerted upon Secretary Ickes' final decision, but it may be safely assumed that both Ickes and Roosevelt listened attentively to his pleas and that this pleading, freighted with political and personal influence, greatly affected the final choice of routes. In fact, some of Daniels' arguments were cited by Ickes when he rendered his verdict.

Necessary arrangements had been completed for holding the Washington hearing. The site was an auditorium of the Department of the Interior Building. The hearing was to be conducted in debate fashion, with a total of three hours allowed for oral presentation. Each state was to have an hour and a quarter in which to present its basic evidence, offering proof that its route was truly the superior one. Then, in a fifteen-minute rebuttal, each side was to have an opportunity to refute the opposition's claims and offer final arguments. Ickes designated himself as judge and time-keeper.[66]

With a brass band to send them off, the North Carolina delegation left Asheville on a special train of eighteen Pullman cars. Other cars were picked up en route, including a special carrying Governor Ehringhaus and several state officials. Upon arrival the planners for the Tar Heel delegation provided every supporter with a huge white badge and directed each of them to be present in the auditorium at least an hour prior to the opening of the hearing. According to one of the leaders, this was the scene:

> Soon the white badges began to appear and an hour before the time set every seat was filled with North Carolinians, and many were standing on each side, and in the spaces in the rear. And not a single Tennessee delegate in sight. When at last they did arrive, their faces showed

[65] Daniels to Asheville Chamber of Commerce, September 11, 1934, copy in *ibid.*, appended documents.
[66] Knoxville *Journal*, September 5, 1934, p. 1.

amazement as they edged their way into the packed auditorium or were forced to stand with the white-badged men in the outside hall way.[67]

The participating officials were seated on the stage of the auditorium. A small table and chair had been placed in the center of the stage for Secretary Ickes. On the right were the Governor of North Carolina and his spokesmen; on the left sat the chief executive of Tennessee and his speakers. After shaking hands with the governors, Ickes announced that he would flip a coin to determine which side would speak first and which would close the debate. North Carolina won the toss. Governor Ehringhaus opened the hearing by introducing his speakers, each of whom had been carefully briefed on the subject matter and rehearsed in his timing. They were Senator Reynolds, Congressman Doughton, Frank Page (former North Carolina State Highway Commission chairman), Robert Latham (editor of the Asheville *Citizen*), Senator Bailey, and Browning, who by previous agreement was to have the majority of the allotted time.[68]

In the course of the presentation Browning, using visual aids previously prepared with skill and care (including a beautiful colored diorama of the projected route), stressed the advantages and superiority of the Carolina route. He argued that the Tar Heel parkway would be the more feasible from an engineering standpoint: it crossed only three major streams whereas the Tennessee route crossed seven. Also, approximately sixty miles of the route went through national forests, and right-of-way problems for that portion would be automatically eliminated. It passed through no towns, and the temperature would be twenty degrees lower than in the valleys below because the highway would be built mostly along the top of the mountain range. Finally, the entire route was studded with recreational possibilities, there was unlimited fishing in the area, and it was splendid game country. He told the Secretary and the audience:

> This parkway is so long that a great many people will probably not drive from one end to the other, so we thought that every mile of it ought to be located as carefully as possible because undoubtedly a great many people will drive in from different cities and drive up and down the parkway for a half a day or maybe spend a weekend, but many of them will never go to either end, and it is our belief that this

[67] Weede, "Battle for the Blue Ridge Parkway," 35.
[68] *Ibid.*

entire route would fulfill that requirement of a real parkway. It is
beautiful all the way.[69]

Included in the remarks by Page were these challenging words:

> I just want to bring to your attention, Mr. Secretary, briefly the
> responsibility that lies with you today. You are not locating a road for
> Tennessee or Virginia. You are locating a road for posterity that for
> a hundred years is going to travel it if it is located at the right points.
> If it is not, somebody is going to correct that error sometime between
> now and a hundred years because the whole West, the whole North,
> the whole northeast is going to travel the road that we are putting
> there.[70]

Editor Latham, as planned, stressed the economic aspects of the proposed parkway from the North Carolina viewpoint. He declared that
Carolinians had labored for more than a century to develop a sound
tourist industry in the area through which the projected road would
run. But, he sadly reported, the tourist industry had fallen on hard
times. He hoped that the Parkway's advent would restore prosperity
in tourism, but "our fear is that if this Parkway leaves Asheville out of
the picture, if we are 60, 70 or 40 miles away from it . . . we will be off
the main stream, and instead of our condition being better we feel that
it is going to be made infinitely worse." He emphasized that thousands
of people living in the mountains would be favorably affected by the
coming of the Parkway and pointed out that the mountaineers were
outside all other relief projects and that no machinery had been created to alleviate their pathetic economic condition.[71]

The recording secretary must not have been greatly impressed by
Senator Reynolds' efforts. The stenographic report reads: "*Statement
of Senator Reynolds:* 1. The Senator talked for five minutes." And not
a single remark by him was recorded.[72]

When Tennessee's turn came to present arguments, Governor Mc-
Alister introduced the speakers: Senator McKellar, Frank W. Webster (highway commissioner), General W. T. Kennerly (chairman of
the Citizens Committee of Knoxville, a Parkway booster organiza-

[69] Federal Emergency Administration of Public Works stenographic report
of the hearings, pp. 12–13, in National Archives, National Park Service, Record
Group 79; hereinafter cited as FEA Steno. Rpt.

[70] *Ibid.*, 17.

[71] *Ibid.*, 20, 22.

[72] U. S. Department of the Interior, "Brief of the Hearings," September 24,
1934.

tion), Congressman Taylor, and Senator Bachman.[73] The Tennessee
delegation opened fire with these sentences: "If it is the intention of
this parkway to provide patrons for the hotels of Asheville and vicinity, then we will admit that the route proposed by North Carolina
will admirably answer for this purpose. If, however, as has been announced, the purpose of this parkway is to provide thousands of tourists, who are expected to visit these two parks annually, then we feel
the merits of our claim become axiomatic." [74]

General Kennerly was perturbed by the North Carolina argument
that the scenic road was essential to the Carolina tourist industry,
which had been assiduously built up over a period of one hundred
years. He complained, "Well, that is true, they have had it that long,
but that is no reason, Mr. Secretary, why they should keep it in per-
petuity. . . . our western North Carolina friends . . . claim to have a
monopoly on the land of the sky. Not only do they own the mountains, but they own the sky. We hope they do." [75] He reminded the
Carolinians that seven rivers originating in North Carolina in pre-
historic days found the attractions of Tennessee so tempting that they
cut through the Smokies into Tennessee. Three presidents born in
North Carolina (Andrew Jackson, James K. Polk, and Andrew Johnson) likewise had had the good sense to move to Tennessee, he said.
He added that the people of East Tennessee demonstrated themselves
more patriotic in 1780 than North Carolinians when John Sevier took
a Tennessee mountaineer troop into Carolina to win the Battle of
King's Mountain.[76] What all this had to do with superior scenery or
the routing of a contemporary parkway, he did not indicate. The
North Carolina speakers gleefully pointed this out in rebuttal.

Representative Taylor seemed irked by what the North Carolina
speakers had said about the ancientness of the Asheville tourist industry: "He said they [tourists] were coming to North Carolina hundreds of years ago. My Conscience! They were going to east Tennessee in this mountain section 150 years ago." [77] Senator Bachman, too,
reacted with asperity. He wanted to know, "Are we to be criticized
because the Almighty has cradled more closely together in east Tennessee all of the natural resources of this country, from clay to gold,

[73] FEA Steno. Rpt., 32.
[74] Knoxville *News-Sentinel*, September 18, 1934, p. 1.
[75] FEA Steno. Rpt., 45.
[76] Washington *Post*, September 19, 1934, p. 10.
[77] FEA Steno. Rpt., 51.

than any other place in America? Is it to be held against us and complaint made, that a mighty river, with one fifth of the potential water power in America, flows through that bed, to wake those sleeping resources, and make Tennessee to blossom like a rose?" He said that it ill became the state of North Carolina to try to keep Tennessee from realizing its potential. The Carolinians were charged with unfair action, and he emphatically stated, "We do not want to be treated like a stepchild. All we want and demand is a child's part, and I believe that we are entitled to it." [78] Governor McAlister supported the senator by proposing that a "double road," as he called it, be constructed with one loop leading to the Tennessee side via Gatlinburg and a second loop entering the Park through Cherokee on the North Carolina side.[79]

Senator McKellar opened what amounted to a tirade with this statement: "If a world traveler hasn't had *delirium tremens* he ain't seen nothing yet." To which Senator Bailey from North Carolina later retorted, "If you cut the parkway after running it about 100 miles in North Carolina and then route it into Tennessee, it will be like taking a tourist through purgatory to the gates of heaven and then turning him the other way." [80]

McKellar had been expected to make loud noises, but as he launched into his speech he gave the Tar Heels a tremendous jolt. By some means he had learned the contents of the Radcliffe committee's report to Ickes, and he now demanded from Secretary Ickes confirmation of the recommendations. The committee had unanimously advised the adoption of the Maloney or Tennessee route; and as part of his argument McKellar, to the amazed chagrin of the North Carolinians, read the report and demanded that the committee's recommendation be followed. One of the Tar Heels, who had prided himself on being on top of all the parkway developments, described the feelings of his colleagues and himself: "The announcement was a bombshell for us and no mistake. . . . It was a fine bit of strategy on the part of our opponents and Senator McKellar made the most of it in his fiery and rather ill tempered speech." [81] The Carolinians realized the import of the senator's action and were extremely apprehensive. Most of them felt

[78] *Ibid.*, 51–52.
[79] *Ibid.*, 53.
[80] Washington *Post*, September 19, 1934, p. 8.
[81] Weede, "Battle for the Blue Ridge Parkway," FEA Steno. Rpt., 66.

that they had little chance of winning.[82] Their apprehensions were not eased when Senator McKellar said, "I am perfectly willing, not only willing, but I think it is our duty, to see that North Carolina has half of this parkway. In the same breath I want to say it would be most unfair, under all the circumstances for her to have more than half. . . . I hope, Mr. Secretary, you will follow the recommendation of your committee." [83]

Webster contended that the Tennessee route would be accessible not only to the North Carolina country, such as Blowing Rock, Boone, and Linville, but also to the great fertile East Tennessee valley country including Bristol, Johnson City, Elizabethton, Greeneville, Newport, and Knoxville. He, like Senator McKellar, urged that the route be chosen on the basis of the impartial report submitted by the Radcliffe committee.[84]

Summarizing the North Carolina position, in rebuttal to the flowery Tennessee oratory, Senator Bailey pointed out that his state had tried to advocate a route solely upon its merits, such as directness, economic importance, topography, and scenic advantages. In return, "we were told three Presidents went from North Carolina to Tennessee. We were told John Sevier came back to North Carolina from Tennessee to win the Battle of King's Mountain. These are the old and minimum appeals of attorneys without any cause." [85]

After both sides had presented their arguments, it appeared that the gist of the Carolina case was that its route was scenically superior and to deprive western North Carolina of the parkway would deal a death-blow to the long established tourist industry in that area. The heart of the Tennessee argument was that the original directives and the Radcliffe committee report had intended that the three states, Virginia, North Carolina, and Tennessee, share the road; that the Tennessee route offered a more diversified scenery; and that to deprive Tennessee of a fair share would be unjust and unfair, indeed, would be discriminating against that state in favor of North Carolina.

At the conclusion of the hearing Secretary Ickes complimented both sides on their excellent efforts and assured them that he would try to decide the case strictly on its merits. With a touch of humor he added,

82 Weede, "Battle for the Blue Ridge Parkway," 37.
83 FEA Steno. Rpt., 56, 62.
84 Ibid., 63.
85 Washington Post, September 19, 1934, p. 10.

"I shall take my head between my hands and after wrapping a wet towel around said head shall try to be fair and just. The best cause will win." He also said that he would probably make a trip to inspect the proposed routes for himself. Even then, the decision would not be easy: "If any one here envies my task I'll be glad to resign and let them have the job." [86] The governors were advised that as soon as possible a decision would be made and they would be notified.[87]

While Ickes was pondering the issue, he received a letter from South Carolina's Senator James F. Byrnes, advocating the North Carolina route: "I certainly hope that you may see fit to locate this route via Little Switzerland, Mount Mitchell, the Craggies, thence between Asheville and Black Mountain, and between Asheville and Hendersonville via Mt. Pisgah and to Soco Gap. . . ." [88] From the mayor of Charleston, South Carolina, came this suggestion: "Speaking as an impartial observer from the side lines, it is my opinion that the Park to Park Highway . . . should run through the section possessing the most scenic beauty, and while I hold no brief for either North Carolina or Tennessee, it is my personal opinion, as one deeply interested in the tourist development of the Southeast, that the scenery from Blowing Rock to the Great Smoky Mountains National Park through Western North Carolina, greatly surpasses that of the route decided upon by your committee." [89] The mayor of St. Petersburg, Florida, urged Ickes to take a personal tour of the proposed routes because "many people of this city spend their summers in this beautiful mountainous country and it is in their behalf that I ask close study and attention, and also unbiased judgment in choosing the route that this highway will follow after leaving Blowing Rock, North Carolina." [90] Tampa's mayor told Ickes, "The federal parkway . . . impresses me as a national project for the benefit of the entire United States and not for the benefit of any individual state." Nevertheless, he urged the selection of the North Carolina route in order to give the "great highway the grandeur and beauty it deserves." [91]

Secretary Ickes also received a communication from North Caro-

[86] Asheville *Citizen,* September 19, 1934, p. 1.
[87] Weede, "Battle for the Blue Ridge Parkway," 39.
[88] Byrnes to Ickes, September 21, 1934, in National Archives, Department of the Interior, Record Group 48.
[89] Letter, Burnet R. Maybank to Ickes, October 16, 1934, in *ibid.*
[90] Letter, R. B. Blanc to Ickes, October 11, 1934, in *ibid.*
[91] Letter, R. E. L. Chancey to Ickes, October 11, 1934, in *ibid.*

lina's Governor Ehringhaus reminding him that the project did not belong to Virginia, Tennessee, or North Carolina. The governor stressed the point that the highway was a national project and should be planned in accord with national rather than local desires. He asserted, "The argument which has been put forth by our friends in Tennessee, in all respects, seems to us a division of the spoils argument. . . . With confidence that your decision will be one that will meet with the ultimate verdict of mankind we leave the case in your hands." [92] In reply Ickes assured him, "I shall consider the arguments presented in this letter with other facts and arguments that were offered either at the hearing or that have come to me by way of briefs or in letters. All I can say at this time is that you are in a court of competent jurisdiction in this manner." [93]

The Tennessee campaigners, with considerable justification, seemed to feel that their efforts to obtain an equal portion of the Parkway had been successful and hence believed that when Secretary Ickes made his final decision he would simply approve the recommendations made by his three-man Radcliffe committee. Even so, knowing the determination exhibited by the North Carolina group, the Tennesseans decided to leave as little as possible to chance. Their leaders composed a set of resolutions stating that the original parkway project had been established as a relief measure by President Roosevelt and his advisors with the three states of Virginia, Tennessee, and North Carolina specifically designated to share the mileage, that the Radcliffe committee had recommended the Tennessee route, and that, therefore, it was the wish of the petitioners that Secretary Ickes name as the final route the one recommended by his own committee.[94]

Into the office of Secretary Ickes came sheaves of Tennessee petitions. Among the civic organizations which sent them were the Kiwanis Club, Erwin; the Lions Club, Chamber of Commerce, Rotary Club, Exchange Club, and City Council of Bristol; the Rotary Club and Board of Mayor and Aldermen, Greeneville; the Kiwanis Club, Newport; the Alcoa Civic Club, Alcoa; the Kiwanis Club, City Council, Chamber of Commerce, Hotel Association, Automotive Association, Optimist Club, Civitan Club, and Young Business Men's Club of

[92] Letter, Ehringhaus to Ickes, September 25, 1934, in *ibid.*
[93] Letter, Ickes to Ehringhaus, September 28, 1934, in Ehringhaus Papers.
[94] Mimeographed resolution, November 5, 1934, in National Archives, National Park Service, Record Group 79.

Knoxville.[95] The chairman of the Bristol Chamber of Commerce wrote to the commissioner of Virginia highways optimistically declaring, "We think we have the *battle won in Washington* but another letter from you to Secretary Ickes advocating it as the most scenic, less costly ... [route] will help clinch it—Park Service Engineers have approved and so reported." [96]

The bickering between North Carolina and Tennessee alarmed the Virginia authorities because they feared the controversy might jeopardize the entire project. Highway Commissioner Shirley advised Senator Byrd that North Carolina's determination to have the road come through Asheville or not at all could defeat the whole measure. He added that if the two feuding states could agree to accept the route recommended by Ickes' committee, Senator McKellar had practically guaranteed an appropriation of funds for construction. On the other hand, if the Tar Heels forced the route into Asheville, the senator was determined absolutely to block any appropriations. Senator Byrd replied by asking what should be done in respect to reconciling the differences between the two states. He said that he had kept out of the affair in the belief that it was more diplomatic for Virginia not to become involved in the contest. Regardless of the outcome, he did not believe that McKellar could defeat the entire appropriation.[97] Nevertheless, the Virginia officials were worried, particularly fearing that a prolonged delay might cause the federal government to drop the project and turn to others that could be immediately begun as relief measures. Relative to this Senator Byrd declared, "It is very important to have a contract let even if it is a small one so that the Government may be committed to the construction of the road. . . . I know of nothing more important than to get the first contract awarded." [98]

While the interested states scrambled for every possible advantage, Secretary Ickes delayed making a final decision. It was not until November 10, 1934, that he arrived at his answer and notified the various parties of his choice of routes. On that date he sent identical letters to the governors of North Carolina and Tennessee. For the former the

95 *Ibid.*

96 H. E. Jones to Shirley, stamped "Received 10/8/34," in files of Virginia Highway Department.

97 Letters, Shirley to Byrd, September 25, 1934; Byrd to Shirley, September 28, 1934, in *ibid.*

98 Byrd to Shirley, September 28, 1934, in *ibid.*

letter contained glad tidings; for the latter the tidings were grievous indeed. Ickes wrote:

> After a careful study of various reports on the proposed route of the Shenandoah–Great Smoky Mountains National Highway, as it affects the States of Tennessee and North Carolina; after listening to the arguments presented at the hearings held in the Interior Building, Washington, on September 18, 1934; after studying the maps and reading the briefs offered; and after considering the reports made to me by members of this Department, who, at my instance, made personal inspections of the two routes, I cannot escape the conclusion that the decided weight of evidence is in favor of the so-called North Carolina route. [The parkway should follow] approximately the route suggested by the proponents of the so-called North Carolina route: that is to say, west of Blowing Rock the route will run south of Linville City along the Blue Ridge, and the Mount Mitchell and Craggy Ranges, which lie east of Asheville, thence east into the Mount Pisgah range, bending sharply northwest on a line along that range west of Waynesville, with an entrance into the park at a point where it will connect with the Newfound Gap Highway near Cherokee, North Carolina.[99]

Secretary Ickes also set forth in his letter the grounds upon which he had based his decision. The most influential consideration, he said, was the circumstance that Tennessee already had a recognized and well-established entrance to the Great Smoky Mountains National Park at Gatlinburg, and to give Tennessee the sole entrance to the park would be discriminating against North Carolina. Furthermore, if the Parkway had been routed northeast into Tennessee from Linville, 90 per cent of the tourist traffic would have been channeled into Tennessee. "I can see nothing equitable or fair in such a proposition," Ickes stated. He added that he found the route proposed by North Carolina to be "a more scenic route than the one proposed by Tennessee" and approved of it because it would have the added advantage of lower temperatures during the months of heaviest travel. The fact that the North Carolina route would traverse about sixty miles of the Pisgah National Forest eliminated right-of-way problems for that portion and helped tilt the balance in favor of Carolina as did the knowledge that the Carolina route would require bridging only three fairly large streams whereas the Tennessee proposal would require the crossing of seven rivers. Asheville's arguments regarding the eco-

[99] Ickes to Ehringhaus, November 10, 1934, in National Archives, Department of the Interior, Record Group 48.

nomic aspects of the tourist trade with its life-and-death importance to western North Carolina had evidently scored with the Secretary. He stated that unless there were compelling reasons for so doing, to destroy Asheville's long established tourist industry, ruthlessly and with open eyes, could not be justified because "the tourist trade is the very life blood of this city and a large part of the surrounding country. To adopt the Tennessee route would be cutting an economic artery and this should not be done lightly or without preponderating reasons." [100]

The fact that Tennessee was already receiving millions of dollars of federal funds through the Tennessee Valley development project while North Carolina had nothing comparable to provide employment and benefits for her citizens was also cited as a reason that persuaded the Secretary to award North Carolina the route. Ickes mentioned as well his dreams of a great "scenic highway which would start perhaps in New Hampshire and follow the first definite line of mountains west of the Atlantic Seaboard all the way to Georgia." North Carolina's Blue Ridge route fitted this scheme more acceptably than did the Tennessee proposals. In concluding his lengthy letter, Ickes told the two governors that it was with reluctance that he overruled the findings of a board appointed by himself; but because the state of North Carolina had appealed to him, he had had to decide the issues in accordance with his conscience and best judgment. Therefore, "it is so clear that the equities in this controversy are with North Carolina that my findings must be to that effect. I regret that I cannot concur in the report submitted to me by the committee referred to, and it is hereby overruled." [101]

The North Carolinians were jubilant. Senator Reynolds voiced the general feeling when he said, "It's the best thing that's happened to our section in past political history." [102] The leading western North Carolina newspaper carried huge banner headlines reading, ICKES' DECISION PLACING ROUTE FOR PARKWAY IN N. C. HAILED AS GREAT VICTORY BY ENTIRE STATE.[103] Latham, of the Asheville *Citizen*, expressed his gratification in an editorial entitled "The Parkway Decision." He said that it would be impossible to exaggerate the decision's importance to Asheville and western North Carolina. Construction of the Parkway

[100] *Ibid.*   [101] *Ibid.*
[102] Asheville *Citizen*, November 13, 1934, p. 1.
[103] *Ibid.*

would provide work for thousands of needy men and bring in millions of tourists, which would promote a stable and expanding economy. "Unquestionably this is the greatest stroke of fortune Western North Carolina has ever experienced," he wrote. "The change must be like that effected in a room dimly lighted at one moment by tallow candles and brilliantly illuminated the next by some one's turning a switch and suddenly startling every nook and corner with a flood of electric light." [104]

Innumerable letters and telegrams traveled between North Carolina and Washington, D. C., as well as between Tennessee and Washington during the next few days. From the president of the Asheville Chamber of Commerce went a wire to Ickes reading: YOUR DECISION MARKS BEGINNING OF A NEW EPOCH IN THIS MOUNTAIN REGION AND IS AN INSPIRATION TO ALL OUR PEOPLE.[105] The editor of the Asheville *Citizen* thanked the Secretary for "the understanding manner in which you have dealt with this matter. You have brought new life and new hope to thousands of people in Asheville and the mountain counties round about this city." Ickes was highly complimented for his work in establishing the Parkway, which the editor fully expected to become one of the greatest contributions ever made to the recreational life of the nation.[106] A leading Asheville publicist advised Ickes that his decision had "made us all very, very happy" and that it had put new hope and a new spirit into the breast of all western North Carolinians: "It means a regeneration of this entire area, for we have been in the depths of despair for the past five years, due to the depression, the collapse of a local real estate boom and the failure of forty banks in our section. Now we will pull out of them all." The Secretary was also thanked for having the courage and the intestinal fortitude to do what he considered right. His decision was characterized as being just and right, and his arguments were said to be unanswerable.[107] The mayor of Asheville wired Secretary Ickes that:

THE CITY OF ASHEVILLE IS DEEPLY AND ETERNALLY GRATEFUL TO YOU FOR YOUR SPLENDID AND COURAGEOUS DECISION TO ROUTE THE GREAT PARKWAY THROUGH WESTERN NORTH CAROLINA INTO THE SMOKY MOUNTAINS NATIONAL PARK. WE KNOW THAT YOU WILL NEVER HAVE OCCASION TO REGRET

104 *Ibid.*
105 Ottis Green to Ickes, November 12, 1934, in National Archives, Department of Interior, Record Group 48.
106 Letter, Robert Latham to Ickes, November 13, 1934, in *ibid.*
107 Letter, Webb to Ickes, November 13, 1934, in *ibid.*

THIS DECISION AND THAT CONTINUING DEVELOPMENTS WILL STEADILY EM-
PHASIZE THE WISDOM OF YOUR ACTION. AGAIN MOST GRATEFULLY AND
HEARTILY WE THANK YOU.[108]

Even the North Carolina Republicans had a good word for the Secretary of the Interior:

THE REPUBLICAN CLUB OF BUNCOMBE COUNTY ASSEMBLED IN REGULAR
MONTHLY MEETING CONGRATULATES AND THANKS YOU FOR YOUR IMPAR-
TIAL DECISION ON PARK TO PARK HIGHWAY CONTROVERSY STOP YOU HAVE IN
OUR OPINION ONCE MORE EARNED THE NICKNAME OF HONEST HAROLD.[109]

The women leaders of Asheville demonstrated their gratefulness
and graciousness in a letter assuring Ickes that "with this, and other
Federal aids, before us we feel we will be lifted out of the Slough of
Despond which we have been submerged in for the last several years.
We can now take a new start with a new heart. We know that you
made no mistake in this decision, either for the Old North State, or the
world at large." [110]

While Asheville and the rest of North Carolina were jubilant, Senator McKellar and many other Tennesseans were bitterly disappointed. McKellar quickly protested Ickes' routing decision. He hurried
from San Francisco to appeal personally to President Roosevelt, asking him to review the findings of the Secretary of the Interior and
overrule them.[111] But Senator Reynolds and others in Washington
were successful in blocking any action resulting from McKellar's objections. In this regard, two telegrams sent less than three hours apart
by Senator Reynolds to Weede in Asheville are pertinent. The first
mentioned a conference with the President of the United States, and
the second, in somewhat cryptic language, said:

IN REFERENCE TO MATTER CONCERNING WHICH YOU TALKED TO ME OVER
THE PHONE STOP I HAVE JUST HAD A VERY CONFIDENTIAL CHAT WITH OUR
FRIEND STOP YOU WILL KNOW WHO I AM TALKING ABOUT AND THERE IS AB-
SOLUTELY NO NEED WHATEVER FOR US TO WORRY ABOUT THE MATTER AT
ALL AS IT IS SETTLED FINALLY AND WILL NEVER BE SWITCHED STOP THIS IS
ABSOLUTELY CONFIDENTIAL STOP.[112]

[108] Wamboldt to Ickes, November 13, 1934, in *ibid.*
[109] Ashley B. Leavitt to Ickes, November 13, 1934, in *ibid.*
[110] Business and Professional Women of Asheville, N. C., to Ickes, November
14, 1934, in *ibid.*
[111] Letter, Reynolds to Daniels, November 16, 1934, in *ibid.*
[112] Reynolds to Weede, November 14, 1934, in Weede, "Battle for the Blue
Ridge Parkway," appended documents.

As events were to prove, Senator Reynolds' words of assurance were correct because "our friend," President Roosevelt, did not reverse Ickes' decision, and the matter was truly "settled finally," as the Senator had said.

But many Tennesseans were not content with the decision and wanted it known that they did not consider the affair "settled finally." An editorial in the Johnson City *Press* entitled "An Outrage on Tennessee" lashed out at the adverse ruling. Ickes' decision was denounced as high-handed and arbitrary, reeking with prejudice and favoritism. The Washington hearing was characterized as a farce, and Ickes was charged with making "boobs out of the Tennesseans" by pretending to hold a hearing and make a decision when all the time he had determined to award Asheville the routing. Among the vitriolic statements of the editorial were these: "For sheer arrogance and conceit the decision of Ickes is an outstanding document. . . . It is an unjust, unfair and highhanded piece of business. Tennessee has been robbed by Secretary Ickes of the very minimum consideration to which it was entitled. . . . Tennessee will suffer from the injustice of Ickes' action for a hundred years." [113]

The editor of the Greeneville *Sun* labeled the decision "Unfair and Unjust" and told readers, "This is a decision of favoritism, of prejudice. If a lesser man than a member of the cabinet were concerned, it might be described as a decision inspired by motives of very human spite." [114] The chairman of the Johnson City Chamber of Commerce took up the cry and informed President Roosevelt that "we Tennesseans, who believe in fairness and fair play, are now looking to you to remedy the grave injustice done to us by Mr. Ickes in this matter and feel that you will, certainly, undo this grave wrong." [115] He also wrote to Ickes, apprising him of the reaction to his decision: "To say that we Tennesseans were surprised at your decision in awarding the park-to-park road entirely to North Carolina is expressing it extremely mildly." The Secretary was chided for ignoring the interests of Tennessee and was urged to reconsider his decision.[116]

Tennessee leaders such as Colonel Chapman, Congressman Taylor, and Governor McAlister were reported to be "amazed," "very much

[113] November 14, 1934.
[114] November 14, 1934.
[115] Letter, Jack W. Cummins to Roosevelt, November 14, 1934, in National Archives, National Park Service, Record Group 79.
[116] Cummins to Ickes, November 14, 1934, in *ibid.*

disappointed," and "astounded" by Ickes' decision. Said Chapman, "I am amazed that Mr. Ickes should reverse the decision of his own experts who recommended the Tennessee route after the most exhaustive survey. The merits of the case all lie with the Tennessee route." Congressman Taylor stated, "The action of Secretary Ickes is . . . enough to astound any one familiar with the facts." [117] The Knoxville *News-Sentinel* ran banner headlines declaring: TENNESSEE LOSES PARK-TO-PARK ROAD: ICKES DITCHES OWN COMMITTEE'S RECOMMENDATION.[118]

But not all of Tennessee took a belligerent attitude. Marshall McNeil, editor of the Knoxville *News-Sentinel,* sent Ickes a telegram telling him that WE ARE NOT ENDEAVORING TO QUARREL EITHER WITH YOUR DECISION OR YOUR RIGHT TO MAKE IT. But McNeil suggested that it would be only fitting if another public works project were launched which would build a loop road around the northern end of the Great Smoky Mountains National Park as had been previously proposed.[119] Ickes, in a tactful manner, replied that for the time being the government was "committed to as big a program as is justified in undertaking the big parkway itself." [120] This, to all extents and purposes, officially ended the controversy between North Carolina and Tennessee regarding the actual routing of the Parkway; but the two states continued to quarrel over related matters for many years thereafter.

[117] Knoxville *News-Sentinel,* November 12, 1934, p. 1.
[118] *Ibid.*
[119] Telegram, McNeil to Ickes, November 15, 1934, in National Archives, Department of the Interior, Record Group 48.
[120] Telegram, Ickes to McNeil, November 20, 1934, in *ibid.* However, the present-day Foothills Parkway is the result of a project in the southern Great Smokies, similar to the one proposed by McNeil.

In September, 1935, the first rocks were blasted from the mountains to begin construction of the Blue Ridge Parkway. A 12.5-mile strip extending south from the Virginia-North Carolina border was built first because North Carolina had been able to obtain right-of-way clearances without difficulty. *Courtesy Blue Ridge Parkway*

The 9.4-mile section of Parkway from Humpback Rocks (Mile 5.8) to Love, Va., was generally acknowledged by workers to be one of the roughest of the early construction jobs. The contractor used 35,000 drills and estimated that some 100,000 cubic feet of solid rock were drilled and blasted on this section alone. *Courtesy Bureau of Public Roads*

Mountains were moved carefully to avoid cluttering the countryside
with chunks of rocks. *Courtesy Bureau of Public Roads*

Native laborers were employed often to afford relief from the Depression. *Courtesy Blue Ridge Parkway and Bureau of Public Roads*

Rock crushers were strategically located to transform the native stone into road materials. *Courtesy Bureau of Public Roads*

Tunnel construction on the Parkway in the 1930's and 1960's utilized the "jumbo" method. A truck with two platforms was backed up the side of a mountain where drillers, standing on the platforms and using sledge hammers, bits, and muscle, bored several lines of 10-foot horizontal holes back into the rock. Other holes bored in a circular pattern near the center of the tunnel area were drilled diagonally and dynamited first to allow space for the crumbling rock discharged in the remaining blasts. Then the sides and roof were shored up, and the process was repeated until the tunnel was complete. *Courtesy Bureau of Public Roads*

By the 1960's tunnel construction had undergone slight modifications
although the method was virtually the same as that of the 1930's. The
difference was mainly in materials and equipment used. Steel was used
in place of wood to brace the walls, and air hammers and drills replaced the sledge hammers and muscle. *Courtesy Bureau of Public
Roads*

In 1969, some thirty years after the beginning of construction, the Blue Ridge Parkway was nearing completion. A section near Asheville had recently been finished, and only construction of a short segment near Grandfather Mountain (Mile 306.6) remained. A right-of-way controversy that was not resolved until 1968 delayed building the Parkway section near Grandfather Mountain. *Courtesy Asheville Chamber of Commerce*

One Little Indian  8

NORTH CAROLINA HAD WON a major victory over Tennessee and had thereby cleared the biggest hurdle in getting the Parkway routed on her own terms. But the Tar Heel state quickly and most unexpectedly ran into a routing obstacle which caused headaches for the authorities for several years. The problem was how to obtain a right-of-way through the Cherokee Indian reservation in order to make the final link-up between the Shenandoah and Great Smoky Mountains National Parks. The North Carolina officials had assumed that the Indians would gladly cooperate for the sake of acquiring a new highway into their relatively isolated land, especially because the leading right-of-way officials were on friendly terms with the chief of the Cherokees, Jarrett Blythe.

At a congressional hearing held in Washington, D. C., in July, 1939, North Carolina's Browning, as senior engineer and claims adjustor for the state, set forth the reasoning which had guided Carolina dealings with the Indians relative to Parkway right-of-way. He testified that originally the plan was to route the Parkway through Soco Gap and west down Soco Creek into the town of Cherokee. The Indians were expected to welcome this plan because it would lead millions of tourists directly to the doors of their crafts shops. With that assumption in mind, state highway officials had acquired the necessary right-of-way. But when Park Service officials made preliminary Parkway surveys, they objected to the location on the grounds that it was not as straight as desired, was not sufficiently broad, and was too steep for Parkway purposes. The Service then recommended changing the right-of-way from sixty feet to one thousand feet and specifying that the road would be a parkway with restricted uses.[1] Years later Chief Jarrett Blythe declared, "The Indians were at first in favor of the Parkway but they quickly changed their minds. Why? Because," pointing his aged hand toward the Indians' tiny bottomlands, "if the State had

[1] House of Representatives, Committee on the Public Lands, *Hearings on House Resolution 6668, A Bill to Grant the State of North Carolina a Right of Way for the Blue Ridge Parkway across the Cherokee Indian Reservation in North Carolina*, 76th Cong., 1st Sess., 1939, pp. 21–22; hereinafter cited as *Hearings on H.R. 6668*.

taken the amount of right-of-way demanded by the Park Service every one of these bottom fields would have been ruined." [2]

Under the leadership of a vice-chief, opposition to the routing of the Parkway through Indian lands became so adamant that for five years no satisfactory arrangement could be concluded between the state of North Carolina and the Cherokee Indian Council, which was charged with administering the affairs of the tribe. Among the objections raised by the Indians were these: (1) the Parkway "would establish the Government in the tourist business in competition with the taxpayers, and eventually will largely exclude the taxpayers from the tourist trade in the vicinity of the Parkway. . . . The Park Service will supply tourist accommodations to meet the demand of every taste and purse"; (2) the abutting property owners would have no access privileges; (3) the abutting property owners would have no right to establish stores, gasoline stations, or signboards along the Parkway; (4) the Parkway, if routed over Indian lands, would deprive the tribe of from twelve to fifteen miles of potential development property; (5) the Parkway, if permitted, would bisect the Indian boundary, thereby setting precedent and laying the foundation for further alienation of Indian lands for park purposes.[3]

In short, what was desired was the opportunity to convert the Parkway into an ordinary highway permitting catering to the expected influx of tourists. The leaders of the Indian opposition had keen enough economic and political sagacity to realize that the proposed Parkway with its scenic easement restrictions would prevent this. According to an observer:

> One member of the Tribal Council owned some land along or near the old wagon road from Soco to Cherokee, and he wanted to build a motel and profit from the travel. All sorts of false rumors had been circulated among the Indians. The State Highway Department was accused of trying to rob the Indians. It was the old, old story of white man's injustice to the red man. The leader of the opposition was keen and clever. His wife was smart and she aided him.
>
> This knotty problem caused us many headaches. . . . The fact that we were dealing with wards of the Federal government presented complications. Reasoning was ineffective against ancient hatreds. . . . Pressures that might have been used against our own race were not tenable under the circumstances . . . .[4]

[2] Interview with Chief Blythe, May 19, 1963.
[3] Hearings on H.R. 6668, p. 56.
[4] Weede, "Battle for the Blue Ridge Parkway," 48.

An interesting and unique legal situation added complications. The Eastern Band of Cherokee Indians was a corporation, chartered by the state of North Carolina in 1889. In this charter the state had confirmed for the Indians their ownership of lands purchased previously by them. These lands were thereafter held in common. The charter provided for local self-government in which a council and chief would be elected every two years and would be charged with conducting the affairs of the tribe. Normally, such a state grant carried with it the inherent right of eminent domain, but by a deed dated July 21, 1925, title to the Indian land was vested in the United States government, to be held in trust for the tribe, with the Secretary of the Interior designated as agent of the United States and guardian of the Indians. Thus, without favorable action of the tribal council and the guardian or, failing that, congressional legislation, the state of North Carolina could not enter condemnation proceedings against the Indian lands in either state or federal courts. Hence, the state could easily be stymied in its efforts to obtain the desired right-of-way.[5]

When the question of right-of-way approval was introduced in the Indian council, it was defeated by a vote of 7 to 4. The superintendent of the Cherokee Indian Agency wrote to the commissioner of Indian Affairs explaining the vote: "The result was brought about by a persistent misrepresentation of the real facts by a small group of Indians, largely of light degree of Indian blood, who have persistently opposed every move for improvement here since we voted ourselves under the Wheeler-Howard Act." [6] Later he confided to the commissioner that he was convinced that a large majority of the Indians were and always had been in favor of the Parkway. He charged that an Indian minority, by means of intimidation and threats of bodily harm, had blocked every attempt by the tribal council to pass a favorable resolution.[7]

As it became increasingly obvious that acquiring a right-of-way down Soco Valley would be difficult, if not impossible, a compromise proposal was advanced whereby the Parkway would avoid the valley and skirt the eastern edge of the reservation. This route would have bypassed the village of Cherokee, and several council members objected. One councilman listed his reasons. In the first place, he said, the

[5] *Hearings on H.R. 6668*, pp. 8, 37.
[6] C. M. Blair to John Collier, December 14, 1935, in files of Superintendent, Cherokee Indian Agency, Cherokee, N. C.
[7] Letter, Blair to Collier, January 30, 1936, in *ibid.*

Cherokees were already favorably located at the entrance to the Park, and tourists were as interested in seeing Indians as they were in visiting the Park. Approval of a right-of-way for a road on the back side of the reservation would ruin this situation and cause the loss of thousands of dollars annually. Secondly, the Indians were enjoying their best season in years: "Their crafts are selling as fast as they can make them; their leases and rentals are turning money badly needed by them into their treasury, and I for one, as their Councilman, will never sell out their interests to white people and move the gate of the Great Smoky Mountains National Park from Cherokee to Waynesville or Asheville, N. C. So the answer . . . to the proposition is NO." [8] And regardless of whether there was any validity in such reasoning, the answer was NO for years.

A western North Carolina white man who had labored to obtain an acceptable agreement that would give final clearance for the right-of-way wrote in exasperation to his congressman, "It is embarrassing to contemplate a situation in which the combined talent of the State and Federal governments shall not prove adequate to cope with one Redskin." [9] Another frustrated white citizen wrote to Congressman Doughton, telling him:

> I think Congressman Weaver, or the Park Service investigators, or the Indian Service investigators have explained to you that the opposition to this measure has been, all along, a matter of spite work on the part of one man, who has influenced a small group with untruthful accusations.
>
> We folk in Western North Carolina have endeavored to iron this matter out, but this disturber will not listen to any reasonable suggestion of any kind . . . .[10]

Secretary Ickes was caught between two obligations—his obligation to the National Park Service, as chief of that agency, to procure for it the most suitable route for a parkway, and his obligation, as guardian of the Cherokee Indians, to protect their interests. After much thought

[8] Typewritten copy, "Comments of the Chiefs and Councilmen of the Eastern Band of Cherokees with Reference to the Proposition Submitted by State Highway Commission for Parkway Across the Reservation," in *ibid.*

[9] Personal letter [name withheld] to Weaver, February 2, 1938, in files of North Carolina Park, Parkway, and Forests Development Commission, Waynesville.

[10] Weede to Doughton, July 6, 1939, in files of North Carolina Park, Parkway, and Forests Development Commission.

he composed a letter and sent it to the tribe. He said plainly that he would not coerce the Indians: "If you do not want the road to be built where the National Park Service desires it to go, it will not be built." But he encouraged them to consider well the benefits to be derived before rejecting the Parkway. He pointed out that great benefits would result from the large number of visitors who would be brought by the new road. To protect the Indians' interests, he guaranteed that no concessions, hotels, or service stations would be built by the Parkway authorities within the reservation. He frankly admitted that the "greatest value of this road will be to white people living all over the country, who will be made happy by seeing the beauty of the Cherokee Reservation. If the Cherokees decide to permit the construction of this parkway they will be befriending many white people living all over the United States." But the Indians were also advised that if they did not approve current proposals for the Parkway, either a new route avoiding the reservation would have to be found or else the road would have to terminate at Soco Gap.[11]

The leaders of the Indian opposition were politically adept, and they did not hesitate to take advantage of Secretary Ickes' dilemma. They played heavily on the theme that, as usual, the white man was trying to take advantage of the Indian and push him off land rightfully belonging to the Indian, as the white man had done for centuries. In appealing to Ickes they avowed that there was a conspiracy to defraud the Cherokees of their lands for Parkway purposes: "The Eastern Band of Cherokee Indians appreciate your interest, solicit your sympathetic understanding, and request your continued cooperation in securing us the rights of men and the full protection of the United States Constitution to the end that Cherokee history shall not repeat through the alienation of Indian lands for the Blue Ridge Parkway." [12]

And thus it went. The efforts of North Carolina representatives, National Park Service officials, Indian agency authorities, and Secretary Ickes himself were not sufficient to conclude an agreement with the council of the Cherokee Indians, largely because of the determined resistance of a small minority. Charges and counter-charges were

[11] Ickes to Cherokee Indian Tribe, May 20, 1935, in files of Superintendent, Cherokee Indian Agency.

[12] Letter, Fred B. Bauer to Ickes, September 3, 1938, in National Archives, National Park Service, Record Group 79.

hurled. On the heels of the charges came investigations by various state and federal agencies. And always, there were more delays, delays which prevented the acquisition of the desired right-of-way. In desperation, various actions were taken to bypass the council as a means of obtaining the necessary land. Congressional hearings and bills seeking congressional authorization for condemnation proceedings were proposed. Typical of the bills was House Resolution 6668, presented by Congressman Weaver of North Carolina, which called for a "Bill to Grant the State of North Carolina a Right-of-Way for the Blue Ridge Parkway Across the Cherokee Indian Reservation . . . ." [13]

When the opposition leaders learned of the proposed legislation, they immediately drafted a letter of protest and sent a copy to all members of the Seventy-Sixth Congress. Included in the letter was a plea for congressional protection: "Today, we who are without franchise, without representation in Congress, appeal to Congress for the full protection of guardianship over our property. We . . . appeal to you, our guardians, to oppose every effort to obtain authority of law from the 76th Congress to alienate our lands to others, or to appropriate them to Government uses, for the Blue Ridge Parkway or for other purposes." [14] The appeal stressed the fact that the Cherokees, although they were wards of the federal government, were self-supporting and received no annuities or rations from the government. But, they said, the Parkway posed a serious threat to their economic well being and would nullify opportunities for self-support. Therefore, they implored Congress to protect their rights and lands.

To counter the Indian action, the chairman of the Western North Carolina Advisory Committee dispatched a letter to the chairman of the Public Lands committee, House of Representatives, setting forth basic reasons for making the right-of-way bill, House Resolution 6668, law. He contended that the passage of the measure was most desirable from the viewpoint of western North Carolina and could not work injury upon anyone. Moreover, he believed that its passage was necessary in order that the Parkway might follow the routing originally selected, the only satisfactory routing available. The rights of the Indians were safeguarded in every respect, and the Parkway would prove greatly beneficial to the Cherokees. A decision was urgently

13 *Hearings on H.R. 6668*, p. 1.
14 Bauer to all members of the 76th Congress, December 31, 1938, copy in files of North Carolina Park, Parkway, and Forests Development Commission.

needed because the delay was preventing construction not only of the Parkway but also of state highways and other roads in the area, to the detriment of thousands of residents and tourists.[15]

When House Resolution 6668 reached the House Committee on Public Lands, representatives from the Cherokee tribe, the state of North Carolina, the National Park Service, the Indian Agency, and others were present. The leader of the Indian opposition, which had effectively blocked the granting of Parkway right-of-way, testified, "Now, we are trying to protect our property, our homes, our bread and beans. If they bring the parkway through here, it will kill the country for any further development. . . . It will kill the property that it goes through." Then he leveled charges against the Indian Agency officials, declaring that they were the real obstructionists and were supported by a group within the Park Service who wanted to maintain the eastern end of the Park as a wilderness area and were therefore opposed to the building of any road there. He averred that the agency was trying to set up a model soviet community with so-called cooperatives on the Parkway. Furthermore, if House Resolution 6668 became law, a precedent would be set making it possible for all of the Indians' land to be taken from them. If such came to pass, and it would, he said, then "only the full bloods, who will have been reduced to acting showmen for the necessities of life, will be allowed to remain for the entertainment of the rubber-necked tourists." This opponent of the Parkway appealed to the congressional sense of justice to protect the land for which the Indians had sacrificed both blood and money to gain more than a century before. Again he said, "We are making this fight against this bill solely to protect our bread and beans. . . . By keeping the parkway out . . . we will be in position to develop tourist accommodations and a revenue which will be of great aid to us." [16]

The appeal was apparently effective because the best efforts of the pro-Parkway group, including both Indians and whites, failed to score a victory. As was reported in the New York *Times:*

> The ghost of Old Tsali, a Cherokee Indian martyr, has again foiled white men who are driving a $35,000,000 pleasure boulevard across 500 miles of mountain country in Virginia and North Carolina. . . . A short section of the proposed road passed through the Qualla Indian Reser-

15 Charles E. Ray, Jr., to Rene L. DeRousen, July 4, 1939, in *ibid.*
16 *Hearings on H.R. 6668*, pp. 54, 73–75.

vation west of Asheville, and the tribesmen of old Tsali refuse to grant, trade or sell a right-of-way. . . . Once too often, the Indians say, they have received a deal from the bottom of the deck by the Federal Government. . . .[17]

Finally, after years of debate, futile solicitations, and frequent beatings of the political tom-toms, the United States Congress, on June 11, 1940, solved the impasse by authorizing the Secretary of the Interior to convey to the state of North Carolina the portions of the Cherokee land necessary for the Parkway construction. In reality, the state of North Carolina had provided the solution by working through the superintendent of the Cherokee Indian Agency and Chief Blythe, with Browning being the prime mover representing North Carolina. After much haggling, the three had decided to abandon the original proposal to go down Soco Creek Valley with the Parkway. Instead, the scenic road was to be routed along the ridges northwest of the Reservation, thereby bypassing the town of Cherokee and entering the Park a short distance north of Cherokee.

To accomplish the compromise had required considerable finesse. A conference had been arranged between Chief Blythe, Browning, and Clyde M. Blair, superintendent of the Cherokee Indian Agency. Blair had repeatedly tried to obtain an agreement which was satisfactory and just to both parties but had failed. This time, "He suggested $40,000.00. Mr. Browning did not bat an eye. Chief Blythe nearly fainted." [18] Browning told Blythe that if he could get the council to pass a resolution offering the right-of-way at that price he would present it to the state for acceptance or rejection. At Blythe's request the council did pass the resolution and also agreed to deed the land to North Carolina, if the agreement was accepted. The state concurred, and this removed the last obstacle in procuring the Cherokee right-of-way. But at a price. Not only was the state of North Carolina to compensate the Indians for their "loss" by paying them the sum of $40,000 or $30 per acre, whichever amount was larger, but it was also to build (and did), without expense to either the Indians or the federal government, a "suitable State Highway between Soco Gap and Cherokee Village." [19]

With this settlement the National Park Service was able to an-

[17] August 27, 1939, p. L–23.
[18] Weede, "Battle for the Blue Ridge Parkway," 49.
[19] U. S. Statutes at Large, LIV, Pt. 1, 1941, pp. 299–301.

nounce that "the pipe of peace was figuratively passed around the offices of the United States Department of Interior today when a five year old controversy over the location of a parkway site through a North Carolina Indian Reservation ended in an amicable settlement that assures satisfactory completion of the nation's longest parkway." [20] This "amicable settlement" completed, for the moment, the major right-of-way and route selection problems and cleared the way for decisions about the legal and engineering steps that necessarily preceded construction.

[20] Department of the Interior, Information Release Service, January 7, 1941, National Archives, National Park Service, Record Group 79.

ALONG WITH THE PROBLEMS of authorization, financing, and routing a question arose that has become standard: "What is a *parkway*, and what is the difference between it and an ordinary expressway or a highway?" The National Park Service, which is charged with the administration of the Blue Ridge Parkway, has defined this type of road as a development of the highway but differing from the usual highway in that it (1) is designated for noncommercial, recreational use; (2) seeks to avoid unsightly buildings and other roadside developments that mar the ordinary highway; (3) is built within a much wider right-of-way in order to provide an insulating strip of park land between the roadway and the abutting private property; (4) eliminates frontage and access rights and preserves the natural scenic values; (5) preferably takes a new location, bypassing built up communities and avoiding congestion; (6) aims to make accessible the best scenery in the country it traverses; hence the shortest or most direct route is not necessarily a primary consideration; (7) eliminates major grade crossings; and (8) has entrance and exit points spaced at distant intervals to reduce interruptions to the main traffic stream.[1] The ordinary road is built primarily to be commercially useful, and the pleasure of the traveler is secondary. A parkway, however, is a special kind of road designed and constructed primarily for the pleasure of the people who use it. The average highway is built within the confines of narrow right-of-way, but a parkway is built through the middle of a park; hence it is sometimes called a "parklet." As one authority appropriately said, "The parkway seeks to marry Beauty and Usefulness."[2]

Two other terms that frequently appeared in reference to parkway construction were *right-of-way* and *scenic easement*. Generally speaking, a right-of-way is a strip of land, obtained by process of purchase or condemnation, over which a road is built and in which legal title resides in the hands of the grantee. Scenic easement, on the other hand, refers to an acquired privilege in which the grantee enjoys full and absolute control over the use to which a piece of land is put, but legal

[1] Definition offered by Demaray at Congressional Hearings on House Resolution 8838, in *Congressional Record*, 75th Cong., 3rd Sess., 1938, LXXI, Pt. 1, p. 481.
[2] *Blue Ridge Parkway News*, I, No. 4 (1937), 1.

title rests in the grantor's hands. In the case of the Parkway, the National Park Service insisted on obtaining a right-of-way of one hundred acres per mile in fee simple, plus fifty acres per mile of scenic easement control. The average width of the right-of-way strip was set at one thousand feet, with no portion to be less than two hundred feet in width. The variation of width was dependent upon topographical and other natural conditions, requirements of design, and cost of acquisition.

Scenic easements were sought for the purpose of protecting the natural setting, and owners were expected to continue the customary use of the land. No commercial buildings, power poles, or other industrial structures were to be erected on the land. No trees or shrubs were to be removed except by express permit of the grantee, but cultivated crops could be planted and maintained and harvested in accordance with good farming practices. No unsightly or offensive material, such as sawdust, ashes, trash, or junk, was to be placed on the land. No commercial sign, bill, or advertisement was to be displayed.[3] In short, scenic easement restrictions meant that the land so affected was placed under the very rigid guardianship of the National Park Service to prevent the erection of a maze of roadside signs, jerry-built hot dog stands, or anything else that might mar the scenic grandeur of the Parkway.

The term right-of-way was a rather common and fairly well understood phrase, even as it applied to the newly authorized Parkway, but "scenic easement" was almost unknown or even entirely foreign to the average person's vocabulary. Many persons, eager to get their share of Parkway frontage, gladly agreed to relinquish scenic easement rights but completely failed to realize what an enormous amount of control they were granting to the federal government. Scenic easement was thus one of the most difficult aspects of the Parkway for the public to understand. Both the unlettered farmer who had granted the scenic easement in the first place and the congressman called upon to vote for Parkway appropriations or to provide legislation relative to the project had difficulty in comprehending what was meant by the term.

Right-of-way acquisition proved to be much more difficult than had been originally expected. One of the authorities on the history of the Blue Ridge Parkway was moved to say, "It is very doubtful if the top officials gave any consideration as to what a parkway implies as to

3 *Congressional Record*, 75th Cong., 3rd Sess., 1938, LXXXI, Pt. 1, pp. 481–82.

right-of-way and limitage of frontage rights. There is no doubt but that some of the State officials thought of this project as simply another road." He also pointed out that the states had hoped, even had been promised, that much of the right-of-way would be given free, "but little did they reckon with the free and independent peoples of Floyd, Franklin, Carroll, and Patrick Counties." Within a short time the state of Virginia was being asked to pay not only for right-of-way but also for scenic easement privileges.[4]

The concerned states and the federal government had agreed in the beginning that the former would procure, by purchase or other means, such land as was required for Parkway purposes, including both right-of-way and scenic easement. Once acquired, the land would be deeded to the federal government, whose obligation it was to construct a scenic highway thereon. To fulfill their obligations, both Virginia and North Carolina utilized existing laws and enacted such additional legislation as was necessary. The General Assembly of North Carolina ratified on January 23, 1935, a special act in which the State Highway and Public Works Commission was authorized to acquire all right-of-way and easement for the construction of federal parkways in North Carolina. One portion of that act clearly demonstrated the state's power of eminent domain. It stated "that the right-of-way acquired or appropriated may, at the option of the Commission, be a fee simple title, and the nature and extent of the right-of-way and easements so acquired or appropriated shall be designated upon a map showing the location across each county, and when adopted by the Commission, shall be filed with the Registrar of Deeds in each county, and upon the filing of said map, such title shall vest in the State Highway and Public Works Commission."[5]

When translated into the language of the man on the ridge, what North Carolina's General Assembly had provided was that by the simple and traditional process of posting a map on a wall at the county courthouse, designating the desired right-of-way, the state automatically became possessor of that land. The original owner was left with two choices. He could accept the state's offer of compensation or file suit for damages. And, of course, in the meanwhile the state was au-

[4] Abbuehl, "History," 3.
[5] North Carolina, *Public Laws and Resolutions*, 1935 Session of the General Assembly, Ch. 2, pp. 1–2.

thorized to proceed with construction. For example, on June 7, 1935, the state of North Carolina filed with the registrar of deeds, Surry County, a map showing in detail the land proposed for acquisition for the first section of approximately twelve miles of the Parkway as it entered North Carolina. The map contained on its title sheet the following declaration:

North Carolina
State Highway and Public Works Commission

APPALACHIAN PARKWAY
COURTHOUSE MAPS
PROJECT 2 SECTION A
COUNTIES: Alleghany & Surry
TO WHOM IT MAY CONCERN:
The State Highway and Public Works Commission has this day appropriated for use as a Federal Parkway the land described in this set of maps. All persons who claim an interest in said lands are requested to file at once with the State Highway and Public Works Commission a statement of their interests and such compensation as they claim to be entitled to. All claims which are not satisfactorily adjusted may be prosecuted in the Superior Court of the county in a special proceeding commenced before the Clerk, provided such proceeding is instituted within six months from the completion of the construction of the roadway involved in this particular project . . . .[6]

In Virginia, to obtain the desired right-of-way, the General Assembly simply passed an act giving the State Highway Commission authority to procure the land as it would for any state road:

Be it enacted by the General Assembly of Virginia that, in addition to its other powers and duties, the State Highway Commission be, and is hereby authorized and empowered to add to the State Highway system a route from a point at or near Jarman's Gap running generally in a southwesterly direction . . . to the North Carolina or Tennessee line, the widths and grades, and the alignment between places designated by the State Highway Commission, to be determined by the State Highway Commission.[7]

[6] "Memorandum Regarding Legal Aspects of Deed from the State of North Carolina to the United States Government Covering Right-of-Way of the Shenandoah–Great Smoky Mountains National Parkway," undated, in Ehringhaus Papers.

[7] Virginia, *Acts of the General Assembly*, 1933 Extra Session, 38.

The same act granted the commission authority to transfer the property acquired to the federal government provided the latter agreed to construct a roadway thereon. Thus, although the approach by the two states was different, the result was the same.

During this period it became necessary for the federal agencies charged with supervision of the Parkway to lay plans for coordinating and implementing the authorized construction. The Bureau of Public Roads and the National Park Service officials met and defined the operating procedure. There was to be a division of labor and a linking series of actions, as follows. (1) The work in general was to be handled as were other major National Park projects in accordance with an inter-bureau agreement between the National Park Service and the Bureau of Public Roads. (2) The engineer of the Bureau of Public Roads and the landscape architect of the Park Service were to make the necessary reconnaissances and establish "flagged lines," that is, lay out the tentative path of the road. (3) The state highway departments were to follow up the flagged lines with survey parties, which would run preliminary location lines and measure the various levels, thereby indicating the amount of fill or cut to be expected. (4) On the preliminary lines the Bureau of Public Roads was to project the proposed center line and thereby "locate" the highway, which is to say, the bureau would take the information provided by the survey parties and incorporate it into a map. (5) The located lines were to be marked in the field by the engineers of the bureau; cross sections were to be taken and maps furnished to the state highway departments showing the lands necessary to be acquired for right-of-way or development purposes. (6) The state highway departments would then proceed to obtain the desired right-of-way from private owners plus options on such additional areas as might be sought for future park use. (7) While the states were obtaining the right-of-way, the bureau would complete the design of the project and prepare the contract plan and specification requirements for construction, with the approval of the Park Service. (8) As soon as the states had obtained the right-of-way, they were to convey property deeds to the federal government. (9) Upon acquisition, transfer, and acceptance of right-of-way property, and upon approval by the Park Service, the Bureau of Public Roads would advertise for bids and thereafter supervise the construction of the Parkway in the same manner as any other major park road. (10) All survey, design, and construction work was to be done under the direction of the Bureau of Public Roads, and the Park Service was to exercise landscape and architectural supervision and determine the sufficiency and satisfactory character of right-of-way agreements, releases, and deeds.[8]

This procedure was followed in order to correlate the activities of the many agencies involved in planning and constructing the Parkway. For the sake of convenience, relative to survey, design, construction, and letting of contracts, the Bureau of Public Roads divided the Parkway into numbered sections. The Virginia portion was designated Section 1, with alphabetical subdivisions running from 1-A through 1-W, omitting 1-I and 1-O to prevent errors in reading blueprints. Section 1-A, for example, ran some 8.497 miles from Jarman's Gap to Rockfish Gap, Virginia, and Section 1-W ran 10.778 miles from Piper Gap to the Virginia–North Carolina boundary. North Carolina's share was designated Section 2, with similar alphabetical subdivisions 2-A through 2-Z, omitting also sections 2-I and 2-O. Thus, Section 2-A ran from the Virginia–North Carolina boundary to the junction with United States Highway 21, 12.695 miles; and Section 2-Z ran from Big Witch Gap to Ravensford, 7.465 miles. In addition, for convenience of supervision, the Bureau of Public Roads divided the Parkway into several projects and appointed an engineer with a convenient field office location, to be in charge of each. It was also agreed that the Park Service would designate a landscape architect who would be present in the field to represent the National Park Service. An acting superintendent was to be named by the Service, and he was to be charged with handling all questions of right-of-way.[9]

Even before these technical details were decided, Virginia had begun survey work for extending the Parkway south from the Skyline Drive. According to news reports, a group of six Virginia highway engineers had begun surveying shortly prior to September 22, 1933, weeks before official initiation of the project by federal and state authorities.[10] A measure of the progress made by the Virginia survey

[8] Mimeographed Inter-Bureau Agreement between National Park Service and the Bureau of Public Roads, December 2, 1933, in National Archives, National Park Service, Record Group 79.

[9] Ibid.

[10] Waynesboro News-Virginian, September 19, 1933, p. 1.

parties is given in a November, 1933, communication from Highway
Commissioner Shirley to Senator Byrd: "I am starting ten parties out
to make survey of the Sky Line Drive [extension]. . . . We have about
30 miles of preliminary lines already." [11]

As flagging and reconnaissance continued in Virginia, the possibility of routing the road adjacent to the famed Natural Bridge of
Virginia was given serious consideration. It was thought that the
bridge itself might be included as a wayside park and that the routing
of the road by the bridge would provide a relief from continuous
mountain driving. The proposed route would have left the Blue Ridge
near the Tye River Gap, thirty-five miles south of Jarman's Gap,
passed by the Natural Bridge, and come back to the Blue Ridge at
Powell's Gap, some five miles west of the Peaks of Otter. But objections quickly arose, especially from Senator Carter Glass of Lynchburg, Virginia, who protested any deviation from the crest of the Blue
Ridge route originally scheduled. As a result of the protests, Secretary
Ickes ruled that the initial routing would be adhered to.[12]

The task of location reconnaissance proved interesting and challenging. The supervisory landscape architect reported that the problem of determining the final location was far from simple and was
aggravated by the lack of good maps. No geological survey maps
existed for at least one section being reconnoitered, and a sketch made
by the Appalachian Trail Club was occasionally the only map available.[13] The survey parties found themselves cutting swaths through a
country so isolated that it still presented a frontier-like atmosphere.
Getting to the survey site itself was an adventure that carried the survey crews from modern cities and transportation into a mountain
wilderness where the terrain was extremely rugged and the obstacles
to a man on foot were quite numerous. Of this, the acting superintendent of the Parkway, Stanley W. Abbott, said, "Work of the Bureau of Public Roads under H. J. Spelman, William M. Austin, Colonel W. I. Lee, and their locator and survey crews, who breasted all
manner of weather, snakes, chiggers, frostbite, and whatever, was ab-

[11] Letter, Shirley to Byrd, November 27, 1933, in files of Virginia Highway Department.
[12] Historical report to the chief architect, National Park Service, by the
resident landscape architect, January 10, 1937, p. 6, in files of Superintendent, Blue
Ridge Parkway.
[13] Abbuehl, "History," 2.

Cuts made during construction have exposed the rocks and curious faults that are indigenous to the Blue Ridge Mountains. Geologists say that compared to the Blue Ridge the Himalayas are in their swaddling clothes and the Rockies have barely reached middle age. Visitors to the Parkway are especially attracted to greenstone Humpback Rocks (Mile 5.8), the quartzite Grandfather Mountain (Mile 306.6), and the granite Looking Glass Rock (Mile 417.05). *Courtesy Blue Ridge Parkway*

Peaks of Otter visitor center features exhibits on mountain wildlife (top, Mile 86). A pioneer farm may be seen at Humpback Rocks visitor center (bottom, Mile 5.8). *Courtesy Blue Ridge Parkway*

Building in the Blue Ridge Mountains was often crude. Logs were
hewn for floors and walls with a broad-axe (6) and dressed with an
adz (5). Builders used the frow (1) and mallet (2) to split logs and
make finishing boards and shakes (shingles); they shaved the shakes to
a proper thickness with a drawknife (8). Hardwood pegs (4) were
forerunners of nails, and holes for the pegs were drilled with the auger
(7). The scriber (3) was used for marking dimensions on wood.
Courtesy Blue Ridge Parkway

One of the highest peaks along the 469 miles of Parkway is Waterrock Knob in North Carolina's Great Balsam Mountains. The scenic overlook is 5,280 feet above sea level and commands views of the Great Smokies, the Nantahalas, the Cowees, the Pisgahs, and other ranges west of Asheville in "The Land of the Sky." Rhododendron (left) bloom along the Parkway in masses of deep red from mid-May through June. *Waterrock Knob picture courtesy N.C. Dept. of Conservation and Development; flower courtesy Stella Anderson, Skyland (N.C.) Post*

The Museum of North Carolina Minerals (top, Mile 331.0) exhibits native stone such as mica, feldspar, kaolin, and tungsten. One of the larger visitor facilities is at Doughton Park (bottom, Mile 241.1). *Courtesy Blue Ridge Parkway*

Flame azalea (top) grows in abundance throughout the Parkway. One of its spectacular colors is a flaming red, but white, yellow, and other shades of red are also common. The plant blooms from mid-May to mid-June. The lady's slipper (bottom) is really a wild orchid that has acquired a common name from the shape of its flower. Both pink and yellow varieties are found along the Parkway but are relatively rare. They bloom in May. *Courtesy Blue Ridge Parkway*

This eerie photograph was taken at Buck Creek Gap. *Courtesy Asheville Chamber of Commerce*

solutely heroic and fully as romantic as any engineer work in the early railroad days." [14]

One of the buyers charged with purchasing land for the project, in reminiscing about the early days of the Parkway, recalled, "Some of that country was so isolated that I had to pack my own supplies and camp out many nights in order to reach the areas we wanted to buy." [15] He repeatedly found that the ridge country was so remote that the radio had not yet made its way there. Often, when he stopped his car to inquire for information, or to take a lunch break, he would leave the car radio on so that the mountain people could listen to it. The rarity of the radio was underscored by the youngster who stood with wide eyes and eager ears listening to the music and news and then asked, "Mister, will you wait here until I can go git Gran'pappy and bring him? He ain't never heerd one of them things." Consent to wait was given, Gran'pappy was brought, and he "heerd" the amazing "thing" his grandson had "fotched" him to hear.[16]

These people were indeed isolated, but the isolation had not dulled the keenness of their wit. A member of the early survey remembered: "On one occasion we were having a lunch break, sitting around chatting, when one of the old timers, a mountain man who had been cutting survey paths for us, made a most enlightened remark. With a smile on his wrinkled old face he said, 'Well, sir, I've looked at this ole Blue Ridge many a time and racked my brain trying to figure out what it was good fur and now, by golly, I know. It's good fur a road!' " [17]

The surveys were launched as quickly as possible. One purpose of the haste was to clear the way for construction that might help relieve the unemployment created by the Depression. But to her embarrassment and financial loss, Virginia encountered unexpected problems that delayed construction for many months. One delay stemmed from a difference of opinion between the Virginia officials and the National Park Service representatives concerning scenic easement. The original directive from Secretary Ickes had specified that the states would be expected to acquire and deed to the United States a two-hundred-foot right-of-way. This in itself was enough to create dissension because

[14] Letter, Abbott to the director of the National Park Service, September 11, 1953, in National Archives, National Park Service, Record Group 79.
[15] Interview with Weems, September 5, 1963.
[16] Ibid.
[17] Interview with Abbuehl, July 16, 1962.

the amount was far beyond the quantity of footage ordinarily required for state highway rights-of-way. Later the Park Service, with the approval of the Secretary of the Interior, issued a memorandum requiring, in addition to the two hundred feet of right-of-way originally asked for, another eight hundred feet, four hundred on either side of the center line, for scenic easement purposes. For a parkway expected to extend some five hundred miles, the additional scenic easement meant that the two states would be saddled with an extra burden of acquisition. This would require expenditure of considerable sums of money.

Virginia Highway Commissioner Shirley did not feel that Virginia was justified in spending state funds to purchase such scenic easement. He said that Virginia would purchase the specified two hundred feet of right-of-way but would procure the scenic easement portion only if the state could obtain it free of charge, which very quickly proved an impossibility. Shirley remained adamant on this point to the chagrin of the National Park Service officials. A. E. Demaray, associate director of the Park Service, hoping to force Shirley to comply, urged Secretary Ickes to announce that the Parkway would not be built unless minimum right-of-way was donated by the states.[18] One of Shirley's political friends advised him, "It has not been my pleasure to know Secretary Ickes personally, but from the set of his lower jaw as indicated by his pictures, I am inclined to think that we should not antagonize him too much, and therefore I would suggest that he be reasoned with on this question and assured if necessary that we will give him the thousand foot right-of-way where ever it is practical and can be done with a reasonable amount of expense." [19] Shortly thereafter Secretary Ickes informed Senator Byrd that "the matter of the thousand foot scenic easement is very important to the proper development of the parkway and I trust that it can be concluded satisfactorily." [20]

To provide ample room for the cuts and fills on the steep slopes of the scenic highway, the Park Service and the Bureau of Public Roads decided to ask the two states to procure a fee simple right-of-way that

[18] Letter, Demaray to Ickes, September 17, 1934, in National Archives, National Park Service, Record Group 79.

[19] Letter, Miller to Shirley, September 22, 1934, in files of Virginia Highway Department.

[20] Letter, Ickes to Byrd, October 10, 1934, in National Archives, Department of the Interior, Record Group 48.

would average one hundred acres per mile and an additional fifty acres per mile of scenic easement. North Carolina readily accepted the proposal, but Virginia was reluctant to do so because of previous difficulty experienced in obtaining scenic easement. As late as 1948, the supervisory landscape architect for the Parkway was reporting that "Virginia has never officially accepted the 100 acres per mile in fee simple. There was a gentleman's agreement between the Governor and the Secretary [of the Interior] that the State would acquire 400 feet of scenic easement on either side in addition to the 200 foot right-of-way." [21] The gentleman's agreement obviously did not solve the problem satisfactorily: "North Carolina has always been most cooperative and generous in trying to acquire all the right-of-way requested. In Virginia the attitude has been quite different. . . . They never accepted the 100 acres per mile standard. . . . At times the impression has almost been that official Richmond was doing the Government a big favor by allowing the Parkway to be built through the State." [22]

To add to the delays occasioned by the scenic easement issue, questions arose about whether the state of Virginia would be able to collect gasoline taxes from sales made on the Parkway and whether she would have any control over the sales of alcoholic beverages in establishments along the route. Virginia insisted that the deeds conveying the right-of-way to the federal government should specifically reserve to the state jurisdiction over the land for purposes of regulating liquor sales and collecting gasoline taxes. The National Park Service, through its legal office, asserted that such reservations would be useless unless ratified by the state legislature and, furthermore, because the state and federal governments would have concurrent jurisdiction, Virginia could impose its usual legal regulations on private enterprise in the area without specific provisions relative to the Parkway.[23]

To further complicate matters for Virginia, the Public Works Administration funds appropriated for Parkway construction were obligated for expenditure not later than December, 1935. Thus Virginia faced the distinct possibility of losing her share of those funds unless she quickly made satisfactory decisions. The necessity of immediate action greatly expedited the state's attention to the matter. On the advice of Virginia's attorney general, a general warranty deed conveying the necessary lands from Virginia to the federal government

---

[21] Abbuehl, "History," 4.   [22] *Ibid.*
[23] Waynesboro *News-Virginian*, October 17, 1935, pp. 1, 8.

was placed in escrow with the First and Merchants Bank of Richmond, Virginia, to be delivered to the federal government upon enactment of Virginia legislation safeguarding the state's rights. Then an appeal was made to the commonwealth's General Assembly to enact the required legislation.[24]

Pressed by necessity, the General Assembly passed the required legislation on February 3, 1936. Thus, Virginia ceded to the United States the power and jurisdiction over the lands embraced in the deed being held in escrow and over any other lands appertaining to the Parkway. The legislation authorized the federal government to "regulate traffic thereon, to protect the said land and property thereon belonging to the United States from damage, depredation, and/or destruction, and to operate and administer the said land and property of the United States embraced in said parkway as a National Parkway." [25] But Virginia reserved the right to tax all motor vehicle fuels and lubricants or their sale on the Parkway; to tax, license, regulate, or prohibit the sale of any intoxicating beverages on any land conveyed; to tax all non-federal property erected; to require licenses and impose license taxes upon any business conducted; and to exercise exclusive governmental, judicial, executive, and legislative powers and jurisdiction in all civil matters except where these powers might conflict with those of the United States.[26] With this legal action completed, it was finally possible to deed the lands, advertise, open bids, and award contracts for Parkway construction in Virginia. Even so, it was not until February 29, 1936, that the first contracted grading work in Virginia, covering 8.127 miles between Adney Gap and Pine Spur Gap, immediately south of Roanoke, began.[27]

While Virginia was experiencing a series of delays in clearing the way for the letting of construction bids, North Carolina, in order to hasten the beginning of relief work, condemned the entire right-of-way on Section 2-A of the route—the extreme northern portion of the Parkway in North Carolina. The land was then deeded to the United States without reservations.[28] Flagging operations started in Carolina in the fall of 1934; and on August 24, 1935, the Secretary of the Interior announced the letting of the first contract on the Parkway,

[24] Virginia, *Acts of the General Assembly*, 1936 Session, pp. 4–7.
[25] *Ibid.*   [26] *Ibid.*
[27] Letter, Tolson to Alexander, September 22, 1953, in National Archives, National Park Service, Record Group 79.
[28] Abbuehl, "History," 5.

covering about twelve and one-half miles of construction extending from the Virginia border to North Carolina State Highway 266, at a cost of $363,847.50.[29] On this project, as on all others, the work to be done was publicly advertised via government bid schedules, which contractors seeking the job completed and filed as bids on the particular project.

Each bid schedule contained a listing of the characteristic types of work. On an average project the work and variety of materials included the following: clearing and grubbing, selective removal of trees and snags (6-inch, 10-inch, 18-inch, and 30-inch sizes), stripping and storing of top soil, unclassified excavation, unclassified excavation for structures, station yards overhaul, borrow for topping, foundation fill, stone or gravel sheathing, replacing topsoil, porous material for tree root protection, furrow ditches, crushed gravel or crushed stone base course, concrete, reinforcing steel, dry rubble masonry, rough-cut stone, reinforced concrete culvert pipe, loose rip-rap, corrugated galvanized steel metal pipe underdrains, drop inlets of various sizes, reinforced concrete inlet covers, bituminous gutter, stone curb, rock-paved gutter, damp-proofing, unit seeding, and, eventually, asphalt paving.[30] To insure that maximum financial benefits would accrue to the American economy, the bidder was required to pay a specified minimum wage and to utilize to the fullest extent possible manufactured articles, materials, and supplies produced or manufactured in the United States.[31]

Thus, little by little, the obstacles and the unavoidable red-tape preliminaries were disposed of, and the way was made clear to initiate at least a portion of the construction. A local newspaper gave this account of the first actual construction: "More than 100 men started work on the Parkway at the Carolina-Virginia line above Low Gap Monday morning, this being the first 12 mile section of the Parkway which was recently awarded by the Federal Bureau of Roads to Nello Teer. . . . The men were secured from the relief and unemployment rolls of Alleghany County, with a representative of the unemployment office of Winston-Salem on hand personally Monday to see that the contract was provided with sufficient labor from the proper

[29] Asheville *Citizen,* August 25, 1935, p. 1.
[30] Bid Schedule, Project 1-N-2, pp. 1–2 ff, in files of Superintendent, Blue Ridge Parkway.
[31] *Ibid.,* E-8.

source." [32] The term "proper source" referred to the Parkway's relief provision, which stated that the labor force was to be recruited
from the relief and unemployment rolls of the county or political
division in which the construction project was located. According to
one project superintendent, "About 90% of the hand labor came from
the nearby creeks and coves. Only the skilled labor was brought in
from the outside." [33]

This construction was in Section 2-A, beginning on the Virginia–
North Carolina boundary and extending southward 12.695 miles. The
contract was awarded in August, 1935, and actual work began in
September. Grading contracts were gradually let for the following
projects, in the order named: 2-B, 2-C, 2-D, 1-A, 1-P, 1-Q, 1-R, 1-S,
1-T, 2-E, second half of 2-M, first half of 2-N, and second half of
2-P. By January 1, 1937, a total of 133.47 miles was under construction.[34]

The road-building was not pursued on a contiguous section basis;
rather, it was scattered along the entire route. Furthermore, the idea
was used deliberately. One of the men responsible was North Carolina's Governor Ehringhaus, who suggested to Secretary Ickes that
instead of section by section construction, priority should be given to
those projects which would most easily open scenic areas for public
use and which would provide employment in the portions of the state
where relief needs were greatest and unemployment the most pronounced. Secretary Ickes responded, "I appreciate your suggestions
. . . and I am glad to inform you that they coincide with the program
for construction which has been prepared by this department." [35]

Difficulties relative to obtaining rights-of-way were also elemental
in promoting piecemeal construction. A report submitted by the
senior claims adjustor of North Carolina mentioned a series of cases
that were delaying right-of-way proceedings. One property owner
refused to make a settlement until easement restrictions were legally
interpreted for him. Another, with poor pasture land worth not more
than fifteen dollars per acre, was holding out for forty dollars. A farmer had requested a cattle lane across Parkway lands and refused to
settle when Park Service representatives denied the request. An owner

---

[32] Mount Airy *News*, September 19, p. 1.
[33] Interview with Mathis, September 3, 1963.
[34] Parkway Progress Chart, in office of Superintendent, Blue Ridge Parkway.
[35] Letters, Ehringhaus to Ickes, June 11, 1935; Ickes to Ehringhaus, June 21,
1935, in Ehringhaus Papers.

was bringing suit challenging the constitutionality of the appropriating act. A property holder had agreed to move his tenant house outside the construction area and tear down his barn but was quoted as being "unreasonable as to settlement, and insists we cannot take the full right-of-way." [36]

As a rule the owners of property in the path of the Parkway were anxious to sell because the Depression had made money so scarce that any source of income was welcome. There were, however, those who for sentimental or economic reasons refused to relinquish their holdings. For example, Ashe County, North Carolina, was then one of the poorest of the mountain counties, but at one period there were forty suits in court relative to right-of-way.[37] It is said that one penurious farmer was "so concerned" about an old hen and her setting of eggs on the projected right-of-way that he refused to grant clearance until he was given one dollar allowance for the value of the setting of eggs that had been "disturbed." Informants recalled another case of a man who would not agree to move his barn because only a small corner of it projected over onto the right-of-way. The problem was neatly solved by a Solomon-like slicing: the corner of the barn was cut off. The farmer had what the local people called a "catty-cornered" barn, and the Park Service had the desired right-of-way. One claims adjustor reportedly encountered a widow whose romantic sentimentalism blocked the acquisition of a right-of-way. Her husband had brought the lady as a young bride to the house, which now stood directly athwart the desired right-of-way. She had never spent a night away from that house since her husband carried her over the threshold, and she was not inclined to break family tradition merely for a right-of-way. Ingenuity came to the rescue of both the lady and the claims adjustor: the house was sawed in half. The state moved one half of the cabin and let the widow sleep in the other half that night; the next day the remaining half was moved, and tradition was maintained.

An infinite amount of patience and tact was required in dealing with recalcitrant owners. Sometimes the adjustors were forced to make repeated visits and plead with the property holder, using a catalog of

[36] Letters, J. P. Dodge to Browning, May 12, May 13, 1937, in files of North Carolina State Highway and Public Works Commission.
[37] Interview with J. Gordon Gibbs, North Carolina claims adjustor, Raleigh, July 5, 1963.

approaches. At other times the solution was found by bargaining, frequently by appeal to civic pride, again by holding forth the promise of future economic gain, and, as a last resort, by introducing the possibility of a law suit. Often a man's reputation determined whether he would become involved in legal proceedings. If the person was respected, he stood an excellent chance of getting a favorable decision; if, however, his reputation was not the best, he frequently preferred to settle out of court, holding out for all he could squeeze from the state.

But, there were those for whom neither reason nor pleas were sufficient. One man took his shotgun, double-barreled and loaded, stood at the edge of his property, dared a construction bull-dozer operator to "trespass," and thereby successfully temporarily halted construction. To a few old timers, sentimentally attached to their ancient log cabins, exceptions were made, and they were granted life-tenure leases on their homes. Caroline Brinegar was such a person. Her cabin still stands and is now richly utilized by the Park Service to "tell" the story of the mountain people. As might be surmised, most of the right-of-way headaches came not from the mountain natives but from absentee owners who had purchased slices of the Blue Ridge country to use as summer retreats, either for private cabins or as commercial summer resorts. Some of these "outlanders" were reluctant to relinquish enough property to permit Parkway passage through their holdings. They plagued the officials with petitions asking that the scenic highway be routed around them, and they frequently asked for exorbitant compensation and were occasionally powerful enough to get either the high price or an alteration of the routing.[38] Even so, some of the right-of-way problems seemed insoluble; and one of them, relative to the routing via Grandfather Mountain, continued to block the construction of a vital link in the scenic highway until 1968.[39]

[38] This portion has been based on numerous interviews with men who were involved in adjusting claims or procuring rights-of-way, especially J. Gordon Gibbs, claims adjustor for North Carolina; Sam P. Weems, ex-superintendent of the Parkway; and Edward H. Abbuehl, former Parkway landscape architect.
[39] The controversy hinged upon a difference of opinion about what constituted a proper route around Grandfather Mountain. National Park Service authorities wanted a "high road" offering scenic beauty comparable to other portions of the Parkway. Local landowners, especially those involved in developing Grandfather Mountain as a tourist attraction, were adamant in holding out for "low

Once construction was under way, the contractors and the supervising authorities had to call upon their ingenuity to accomplish the assigned task of constructing a parkway along the crest of the mountains. There were few precedents to guide them in building such a lengthy road, designed solely for scenic views and pleasure driving; so the project became something of a gigantic laboratory, experimenting with anything from blasting through huge mountains of rock to landscaping the scars of such construction in an attempt to preserve the wayside scenery.

One of the first problems the contractors encountered was that of getting to the job. More often than not they found the projects completely inaccessible and were forced to build access roads prior to beginning Parkway construction. Many of the mountain roads were little more than ruts and were usually inadequate for accommodating the heavy loads of material and equipment required for the Parkway. Such roads were reworked before they were used; sometimes the county responsible for their maintenance aided in the rehabilitation, but more frequently no help was forthcoming.

The huge rock formations that were a part of the proposed route also created problems. Construction workers quickly found that trying to cut cleanly the folded and faulted masses of stone was extremely difficult. If the road had been an ordinary highway, there would have been no problem. The rocks could have been drilled, filled with explosives, and simply blown asunder. Because this was to be a scenic parkway, however, controlling both the size of the cut and the size of the blast was vital lest there be an ugly scar or else a wholesale scattering of huge boulders which would destroy nearby trees and shrubbery or otherwise mar the natural scenery. Even with care an occasional miscalculation regarding the structure of the rocks and the amount of explosive required for the shot resulted in a much larger unheaval than had been anticipated. One construction superintendent, with a rueful grin of recollection, told of such an instance. So much material was

road" and blocked the right-of-way acquisition. Proposal and counterproposal during the years merely emphasized the stalemate, and the state of North Carolina remained reluctant to exercise its option of eminent domain. Finally, however, a satisfactory right-of-way agreement was reached, and the land was officially deeded to the federal government, October 22, 1968, thereby permitting the letting of contracts for construction of what had become the final link in the Parkway.

blasted loose and spread over such a wide area that it was deemed more suitable to convert the over-blast into a parking overlook rather than try to clean it up and cart it away.[40]

Drilling in rock formations along the crest of the Blue Ridge required skilled labor and great expenditures. Section 1-C, from Humpback Rocks to Love, 9.387 miles, was conceded to be one of the roughest of the early Parkway projects because of the excessive amount of rock encountered. The contractor bought 35,000 drill bits and drilled some 100,000 feet of solid rock to accomplish his basic job, according to the construction superintendent. The blasting holes were often drilled as deeply as thirty feet into solid rock at the rate of about three holes per driller per day, depending on the type of rock encountered and the skill of the worker. The rate of construction was determined by the rapidity with which the drillers bored their holes, and hence the entire crew was quite conscious of the drillers' performance record. And as construction crews have done for centuries, they made a sport of the job. Occasionally a drill would stick in a hole and thus botch the driller's work, delaying construction. It became the practice to hold a kangaroo court at the end of the work day for the drillers and their helpers whose drills had become stuck. As a penalty for an "offense" the guilty party had to bend over and receive a sharp whack across the rump, one whack for every foot of drill stuck. On one occasion, a Negro helper, with cause, became alarmed when his driller stuck three drills in one day, totaling about sixty feet of drill. Fearing the consequences in the coming evening's kangaroo court, the helper went to the foreman, who was an expert driller, and said, "Mr. Charley, please come and see if you can't get these drills unstuck. If you can't them boys is going to ruin my setter tonight." [41]

Because most of the labor was recruited locally from the ranks of the unemployed, the contractors were faced with the problem of determining what each prospective employee was qualified to do. "It was amazing how many of them wanted to be truck drivers," said one of those in charge of hiring. When asked what kind of workers they made, he replied, "As a rule they were good workers, inexperienced but intelligent and willing to labor. We had very little absenteeism and very little shirking on the job. Most of them were delighted to

[40] Interview with Mathis, September 3, 1963.
[41] Ibid.

have a job that brought in a little ready cash and the 30 cents per hour minimum was more than most of them could earn anywhere." When questioned about the honesty of the mountain workers, that is, about whether they were prone to carry off tools, the answer was, "As such things go they were quite trustworthy. About the only thing we missed in any serious quantity were the doublebitted axes that were used in cutting right-of-way. As you know, the mountain people used wood for both cooking and heating purposes. Those new double-bitted axes made it so much easier for their wives to cut fire wood that the men just couldn't resist taking them as one of their fringe benefits." [42]

As early as October, 1934, plans for the Parkway had matured sufficiently for the designers to be considering recreation and service areas that could add considerably to the visitors' enjoyment. Plans were drawn to include eighteen of these areas: Humpback Rocks, Norwall Flats, Lick Log Spring, Peaks of Otter, Pine Spur, Smart View, Rocky Knob, Fishers Peak—all in Virginia—and Cumberland Knob, the Bluffs, Thompkins Knob, Linville Gorge, Crabtree Creek, Mount Mitchell, Craggy Gardens, Pigeon River Falls, Tennessee Bald, and Richland Balsams in North Carolina. Provisions were made for either picnicking, camping, hiking, lodging, eating, or automobile service, or a combination of these. In April, 1936, development work began on the Cumberland Knob recreation area in North Carolina, financed by federal resettlement funds. In May, 1936, similar work began on the Rocky Knob recreation area in Virginia. Additional areas were made available for active development in June, 1936: Pine Spur and Smart View in Virginia plus the Bluffs in North Carolina. All of these, and later ones, were incorporated into the recreational resources of the Parkway, and in the beginning they were instrumental in employing sixty to seventy men per development area and fulfilled the relief needs for which the project had been originally initiated. [43]

Something of the magnitude of the over-all undertaking and the multiplicity of the problems that were encountered in the early con-

---

[42] *Ibid.*

[43] Historical report to the chief architect, National Park Service, by the resident landscape architect, Roanoke, Va., January 10, 1937, pp. 14–16; in National Archives, National Park Service, Record Group 79.

struction of the Parkway is evident when one recalls that the project was plotted on paper and officially launched in September, 1933, as an *emergency* relief measure. Yet, actual work did not begin until September, 1935—two years later. The interim was filled with a multitude of correspondence, routing controversy, and efforts to obtain the necessary right-of-way. One of the men who labored to make the project a reality said, "It was not always smooth sailing; there were many dark days and the wonder is that a project with such a nebulous beginning did not fall because of its magnitude and complexities." [44]

Among the complexities he had in mind were the large number of agencies involved in the undertaking. The Park Service had Roanoke, Richmond, and Washington, D. C., offices actively participating; the Bureau of Public Roads had a Washington office and two field offices; there were three divisions of the Forestry Service to deal with; and other federal agencies included the Cherokee Indian Agency, Veterans Administration, Civilian Conservation Corps, Public Works Administration, and Civilian Public Service Administration. The highway departments of Virginia and North Carolina were closely involved at the state level as well as several civic and local groups of semi-official standing.

With the large number of officials and agencies engaged in the work, it is a wonder that customary red tape did not strangle the project. One of the officials who did much to make the undertaking prosper gave this explanation: "The fact that it has survived and become established is a tribute to many things—to the few people who believed in its merits and were willing to fight for a high standard and to the cooperation that prevailed between the various agencies." [45] With actual construction finally started on both the North Carolina and Virginia sides in the mid-1930's, the Parkway became an actuality, at least in part; and slowly, section by section, construction has continued, except in the war years.

More than a full generation has passed since the birth of the Parkway, and parts of it are still under construction. But the undertaking has produced what has become known as the most "scenic and heavily traveled recreational thoroughfare in America." [46] Today the Blue

---

[44] Abbuehl, "History," 9.
[45] *Ibid.*
[46] Asheville *Citizen*, August 19, 1961, p. 1.

Ridge Parkway forms an integral part of the National Park system, comprising the following acreage:

Fee Simple Acreage: in Virginia:	28,102.66
in North Carolina:	41,222.02
TOTAL:	69,324.68
Scenic Easement Acreage: in Virginia:	385.34
in North Carolina:	917.41
TOTAL:	1,302.75.[47]

The total mileage of the Parkway will be 477 miles, including approach roads, with Virginia having 225 miles and the remainder belonging to North Carolina. As it now stands, the motor road is complete, except for the section around Grandfather Mountain.[48] The states of Virginia and North Carolina have each expended not less than two million dollars on right-of-way and scenic easement acquisition.[49] It has been estimated that the Parkway will have cost "approximately 96 million dollars when complete. This amounts to about two cents a year per taxpayer for each of the past 25 years." [50]

[47] Letter, Abbuehl to S. Herbert Evison, January 19, 1962, in files of Superintendent, Blue Ridge Parkway.

[48] Asheville *Citizen*, July 3, 1961, p. 1.

[49] Edward H. Abbuehl, "A Road Built for Pleasure," *Landscape Architecture*, LI (July, 1961), 233.

[50] Letter, Weems to Evison, July 31, 1962, in files of Superintendent, Blue Ridge Parkway. Inflation, of course, will considerably boost this estimate. Another fascinating development will also alter the above mileage and acreage figures— Congress recently approved a 180-mile extension of the Parkway, terminating in the low ridge country north of Atlanta.

ALTHOUGH THE ROUTE had been selected and even construction itself had begun, controversy continued to threaten the future of the road along the mountaintops. This time the debate was centered in Congress. It arose from the desire to incorporate the highway into the federal recreational system and thus place responsibility for its maintenance and administration in the hands of a permanent agency of the government. Temporarily, the Parkway, as a relief project, was under the jurisdiction of the federal Public Works Administration, funds of which were used for construction and which would continue for only a relatively short time.

On July 14, 1934, Secretary Ickes' administrative assistant, E. K. Burlew, had notified National Park Service officials that the Secretary of the Interior wanted the scenic highway handled as a Park Service road and asked that they obtain an opinion from the solicitor's office concerning the legality of such a procedure.[1] Demaray, acting director of the National Park Service, drafted the inquiry: "The Secretary desires that this highway be operated as a *Parkway* and under the supervision of the National Park Service when completed. The question has arisen whether the National Park Service has the authority to operate the Parkway after it is completed and turned over to the United States by the respective States." [2]

From the solicitor, months later, came the opinion that there was authority under Title II of the National Industrial Recovery Act, as extended by Section 12 of the Emergency Relief Appropriations Act of 1935, to construct the proposed Parkway. The Department of the Interior was authorized by the same statutes and by the executive order of June 7, 1935, to exercise jurisdiction over the construction of the road. But legal complications required that Congress pass an act designating the federal agency responsible for the maintenance and administration of the road.[3] With the approval of the Bureau of the

[1] Letter, Burlew to Demaray, July 14, 1934, in National Archives, National Park Service, Record Group 79.

[2] Letter, Demaray to First Assistant Secretary, Department of the Interior, July 18, 1934, in National Archives, National Park Service, Record Group 79.

[3] Letter, Attorney General to Ickes, June 20, 1935, in *ibid.*

Budget and the Secretary of the Interior, Congressman Doughton introduced on April 24, 1936, House Resolution 12455, "To Provide for the Administration and Maintenance of the Blue Ridge Parkway in the States of Virginia and North Carolina by the Secretary of the Interior, and for other purposes." [4]

Upon introduction by Doughton, the resolution was referred to the Committee of the Whole House with the recommendation that it be called for and debated. An objection by Congressman Jesse P. Wolcott (R., Mich.) barred further debate temporarily. Wolcott complained that the costs would run to more than $25 million and was dissatisfied because the Parkway had been authorized by executive order rather than by Congress: "It is the President's responsibility for doing it without the consent of Congress. Two wrongs do not make a right. For that reason, Mr. Speaker, I object." [5] The resolution was called again on June 15, 1936, but met objections by numerous Republicans from the North.[6] Congressman Doughton was experienced in legislative finesse, and as the Parkway was dear to him and to his constituents, he had no intention of dropping the issue. On June 20, 1936, the day that the second session of the Seventy-fourth Congress was scheduled to adjourn, he moved that the rules be suspended and the bill be passed. Nevertheless, under the leadership of Representative Wolcott even this move was defeated.

A sample of the congressional debate will indicate the tenor of the objections and the answers given. Congressman Robert F. Rich (R., Pa.) raised the question, "Now why should the taxpayers of this country be asked to keep up a road 477 miles in length between the park in Virginia and the park in North Carolina, when the people of these two States will get the benefit of it?" Congressman Doughton fielded the question by asking another, "Why should the taxpayers keep up the national parks and recreational grounds anywhere?" To which Rich complained, "Why put them all down there in Virginia and North Carolina? You have already had the lion's share!" At this point Congressman Taylor from Tennessee became curious. "Is this the same parkway that was formerly known as the Sky Line Highway a year or so ago?" Doughton replied, "Yes, it has been changed to the Blue Ridge Parkway." Taylor's next words, "Which you North Carolinians took away from us Tennesseans," revealed that Tennes-

---

[4] *Congressional Record,* 74th Cong., 2nd Sess., 1936, LXXX, Pt. 8, p. 8577.
[5] *Ibid.*   [6] *Ibid.*

seans had not forgotten their defeat. Doughton rejoined, "We are proud of it, and if Tennessee had been as fair as she is beautiful she would not have opposed North Carolina in the locating of the trail."

Representative Wolcott took the floor and denounced the Parkway with these words: "Mr. Speaker, I think that this is the most ridiculous undertaking that has ever been presented to the Congress of the United States." He then pointed out that he and his colleagues had fought the measure ever since it had come from the Consent Calendar. Vigorously he protested against the strategy of presenting the proposal to Congress under the suspension of the rules within hours of the scheduled adjourning time. Warming up, he declared, "I charge, and I charge it without fear of successful contradiction, that this is a movement to get the Congress of the United States to put its stamp of approval on one of the most colossal steals that has ever been perpetrated upon this House." He stated that the purpose of the act was to build a free highway through Virginia and North Carolina, and perhaps Tennessee, without those states contributing a single donation. He warned his fellow legislators that "this is the most visionary thing that has ever been presented to the Congress since the days of the Passamaquoddy and the Florida Ship Canal, and I entreat the House to consider this bill with the same logic and the same reasoning that it considered these two visionary projects."

Representative Willis Robertson from Virginia reminded the House that very seldom in his years of service had a sectional issue been injected into a legislative matter and that he hoped it would not be now. He assured his colleagues that the bill involved no appropriations and that construction would go ahead whether or not Congress passed the bill. But he also declared, "We are not trying to get something free. . . . We want this park for you, for our friends from every state to come and enjoy." Representative Wolcott rebutted that sectionalism was not the issue; "we want you to build your highways on the same basis that the State of Michigan . . . or any other State in this Nation has to build their highways." [7]

When the debate ceased and the motion to suspend the rules and pass the bill, as proposed by Congressman Doughton, was put to a vote, it failed to carry. Had the opposition been dealing with an ordinary legislator, they might have had reason to feel that the third defeat

[7] *Congressional Record*, 74th Cong., 2nd Sess., 1936, LXXX, Pt. 10, pp. 10583–87.

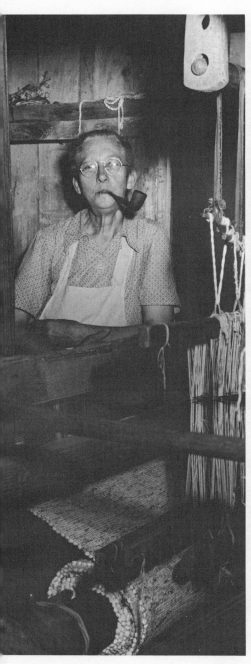

Weaving is demonstrated at Brinegar Cabin (Mile 238.5) and black-smithing at Mabry Mill (Mile 176.2). *Courtesy Blue Ridge Parkway*

Mabry Mill preserves an almost dying craft—gristmilling. The young miller adjusts the flow of grain. *Courtesy Blue Ridge Parkway*

Puckett Cabin (Mile 189.9) was the home of a mountain midwife, Orlean Puckett, from 1865 to 1939. Her skill served the region until medical facilities came to the mountains. *Courtesy Blue Ridge Parkway*

The Asheville North Fork Reservoir is seen from Craggy Pinnacle.
Courtesy Asheville Chamber of Commerce

The United States National Park Service is charged with the care of the Blue Ridge Parkway. In addition to watching over the forests and wildlife, the Parkway rangers offer numerous services including guided nature walks, informal and informative talks around camp-fires, and assistance to all who seek it. *Courtesy Asheville Chamber of Commerce*

The Parkway's many picnic areas, like this one at Craggy Gardens, attract visitors from every state in the Union and from many foreign countries. More than half the nation's population is within driving range of the Blue Ridge.

Another mountain craft, molasses making, is demonstrated at this mill just off the Parkway in Bull Creek Valley (Mile 373). *Courtesy Blue Ridge Parkway*

in a row had dealt a *coup de grâce* to House Resolution 12455. Such was not the case at all. Doughton had powerful and influential supporters. In less than an hour after the bill had been defeated, it was back before the House. Representative John J. O'Connor from New York, by direction of the Committee on Rules, submitted a privileged report asking that House Resolution 12455 be considered as having been engrossed and read for the third time and that the House immediately proceed to vote upon the passage of the bill without any intervening motion except a motion to recommit, with or without instruction.[8]

Immediately, there was an outcry of objections. New York Republican Bertrand H. Snell charged that the Committee on Rules had gone beyond all limits in bringing in this rule: "The bill is the rankest operation of the Rules Committee I have ever known in the House of Representatives." Congressman Earl C. Michener (R., Mich.) labeled it "the gaggiest gag rule ever presented to this body." Wolcott reiterated his objections and urged his colleagues to vote against the measure. He claimed that the amount of money being asked for Parkway use was one tenth of that appropriated in the previous year for all relief purposes. He called attention to the millions of needy persons who were without proper nourishment, clothing, and roofs over their heads and entreated his fellow congressmen to "use some common sense in consideration of this bill and vote it down as you have on three different occasions. Let us not go home from this Congress without voting for at least one measure which is in the interests of the taxpayers, the merchants, the industrialists, and the agriculturists of this Nation."

Representative Thomas A. Jenkins, (R., Ohio) was just as condemnatory: "So long as the Republic stands, our successors will be appropriating money to maintain this show place. . . . We can with as much propriety build a parkway from Niagara Falls, a showplace in the East, to Yellowstone Park, a showplace in the West." Finally, after many more similar objections, Representative Arthur H. Greenwood (D., Ind.) accused his opposition friends of having a case of jitters. He pointed out that there was nothing in the bill about appropriations and that finance was not the issue: "That has already been provided for. It is simply a question of the maintenance and management of the Parkway in one Government department, whereas now two departments are administering this project." [9] The congressman was proper-

8 *Ibid.*, 10611–14.   9 *Ibid.*

ly informed. There was nothing in the bill about appropriations, simply the provision that the Parkway would be administered and maintained by the National Park Service, Department of the Interior. The opponents refused to recognize that it was a *national* parkway. All that they were willing to see was that it was being constructed with federal funds for the immediate benefit of Virginia and North Carolina.

When the bill was put to the final vote, it barely squeaked through, 145 voting yea, 131 voting no, and 147 not voting. A motion, the last desperate effort of the opposition, was made to reconsider the bill, but the motion was tabled. The bill was signed on June 20, 1936, by the Speaker of the House and was passed on to the Senate, where it was also approved.[10] It was presented to President Roosevelt on June 22, 1936. With his signature, what had been House Resolution 12455 became Public Law No. 848. The new law specified that all lands and easements conveyed or to be conveyed by Virginia and North Carolina to the United States for the right-of-way and recreational areas of the Parkway between the Shenandoah and Great Smoky Mountains National Parks "shall be known as the Blue Ridge Parkway, and shall be administered and maintained by the Secretary of the Interior through the National Park Service." [11]

In addition to consolidating the administration of Parkway affairs within a single federal agency, Public Law 848 finally gave the highway a name, designating it as the "Blue Ridge Parkway." Typical of the uncertainty that had marked other aspects of its history, the road until this time had lacked an agreed-upon title. It had borne a variety of tentative names, such as Skyline Drive, Skyland Drive, Park-to-Park Highway, Scenic Parkway, Shenandoah National Park to Great Smoky Mountains National Parkway, and Shenandoah National Park to Great Smoky Mountains National Park Parkway. The last two were used most frequently in the early days, but they were too long to be written easily in correspondence and on blueprints and consequently were not popular. Many persons became concerned about finding a more appropriate title, and as early as November 17, 1933, Secretary Ickes began to receive letters suggesting such designations as "Appalachian Scenic Highway," "Appalachian National Parkway," "Southern Appalachian National Parkway," and "Southern Appalachian

10 *Ibid.*
11 U. S. *Statutes at Large*, XLIX, Pt. 1, 1936, p. 2041.

Parkway." [12] The Radcliffe committee itself, when it recommended the route to be taken by the Parkway, had a suggestion: "It would seem that a suitable name for this Parkway, as now recommended, would be the Appalachian Parkway and we would so recommend." [13]

Even earlier, Demaray had informed Secretary Ickes that the Regional Public Works Committee recommended that the project be called "The Shenandoah–Great Smoky Mountains National Parks Parkway and Stabilization Project." By way of explanation Demaray added, "The recommendation that the word *Stabilization* be introduced into the title of the project is based on the fact that stabilization represents an important phase of the project." [14] That is, the Parkway was expected to stabilize the economy of the mountain people in the area touched by the road. Ickes vetoed the suggestion, saying, "I do not approve of this suggested name and I wish some shorter and characteristic name could be proposed. I especially object to the word *stabilization*." [15]

Other suggestions continued to arrive. Among them was one from Senator Byrd, proposing that the Parkway be named "The Ickes Highway." This proffered honor was graciously declined by the Secretary of the Interior despite the senator's assurance that "as a matter of fact you nearly alone deserve the credit for this great undertaking." [16] Even at this early date President Roosevelt had begun to acquire a near demigod image, and it was to be expected that his name should be suggested in connection with the project. An Asheville, North Carolina, citizen requested that Ickes carefully consider the possibility and the political practicality of calling the road "The Roosevelt Parkway." [17]

Desirous of finding a characteristic and descriptive name, Secretary Ickes suggested that Demaray consult the Division of Geographic Names about the suitability of the tentative title, "The Appalachian

[12] C. A. Raysor to Ickes, November 17, 1933; Charles E. Peterson to director of National Park Service, November 18, 1933; Conrad L. Wirth to Cammerer, December 5, 1933, all in National Archives, National Park Service, Record Group 79.

[13] Report of the Radcliffe Committee, June 8, 1934, in National Archives, National Park Service, Record Group 79.

[14] Letter, Demaray to Ickes, February 10, 1934, in National Archives, National Park Service, Record Group 79.

[15] Memorandum, Ickes to Demaray, February 12, 1934, in *ibid.*

[16] Letter, Byrd to Ickes, September 11, 1934, in *ibid.*

[17] Letter, George Coggins to Ickes, November 20, 1933, in *ibid.*

Parkway." [18] The executive secretary of the Division of Geographic Names replied that the majority of the Executive Committee on Geographic Names had authorized him to say that they saw no reason why "Appalachian Parkway" should not be recommended to Secretary Ickes. But, it was his personal opinion that the name was too broad for the project. If the road were not extended beyond its current limits, it seemed that "Southern Appalachian Parkway" or "Blue Ridge Parkway" would provide a more accurate description. He hoped that by using the name "Southern Appalachian Parkway" attention would be called to the fact that there was no "Northern Appalachian Parkway," which might in turn produce a special effort to have the highway extended northward. He closed his recommendation with this comment: "I should prefer to see *Blue Ridge Parkway* adopted unless it be felt that the adoption of the broader name will further the broader project. I suggest *Blue Ridge Parkway* because the parkway lies upon the Blue Ridge throughout most of the length of both the parkway and the ridge. It is, geographically, a most appropriate name." [19]

These suggestions were forwarded to Secretary Ickes by Demaray, who remarked, "You will note that the Board prefers *Blue Ridge Parkway* and also suggests *Southern Appalachian Parkway*. Will you please indicate your preference as to name?" [20] About a month later the Department of the Interior disclosed the Secretary's choice: *"Blue Ridge Parkway* is the name selected by Secretary of the Interior Harold L. Ickes to designate the parkway connecting the Shenandoah and the Great Smoky Mountains National Parks." [21]

Thus Ickes found an appropriate name, and Congress approved when it passed Public Law No. 848 in the summer of 1936, making the Blue Ridge Parkway part of the National Park System. Under the legislation creating the National Park Service, the Service was required to (1) conserve the scenery and the natural and "historic objects and the wildlife there and (2) provide for the enjoyment of the same in such a manner and means as shall leave them unimpaired for the enjoyment of future generations." [22] Over the years these have

[18] Memorandum, Ickes to Demaray, January 14, 1936, in *ibid*.
[19] Letter, George C. Martin to Demaray, January 14, 1936, in *ibid*.
[20] Memorandum, Demaray to Ickes, January 14, 1936, in *ibid*.
[21] Department of the Interior, Press Release, February 18, 1936, in *ibid*.
[22] Statement by Director Wirth of the National Park Service to the North Carolina State Highway Commission, May 31, 1962, in files of Superintendent, Blue Ridge Parkway.

been the basic guiding principles of the National Park Service as it has worked to fulfill its own five-fold mission for the Parkway: (1) to link the Shenandoah and Great Smoky Mountains National Parks through the mountains of western Virginia and North Carolina, (2) to provide quiet leisurely motoring, free from the distractions and dangers of the ordinary speed highway, (3) to give the visitor an insight into the beauty, history, and culture of the Southern Highlands, (4) to afford the best type of recreational and inspirational travel, and (5) to protect and preserve the natural scenery, history, and wildlife within the Parkway confines.[23]

23 *Ibid.*

Fulfilling the Promise

LONG BEFORE THE POLITICIANS and the numerous other interest groups came to an agreement regarding the precise location of the proposed scenic highway, many minds were at work seeking means of best developing this pioneer recreational unit. The problem facing the planners was most complex. Constructing a road would have posed no major difficulty, but this was more than just a road. It was to be a scenic parkway—so constructed as to open windows and doors to both nature's scenery and man's highland civilization in the best National Park Service tradition of "share, yet preserve."

Lessons learned from the recently established Shenandoah National Park were of great help. There, a ridgetop highway called the Skyline Drive had been constructed to open up a mountain wilderness and provide inspiring scenic views. In the process, however, all of the people residing within the park area had been evacuated and their cabins razed. Thus, nothing remained of mountain culture in its original setting for later generations of visitors to see. Park Service officials were determined that this mistake would not be repeated along the Blue Ridge Parkway. When reconnaissance teams began their surveys, they were reminded to be constantly alert to any handiwork of man worthy of preservation as physical evidence of a pioneer way of life. As a result, the Parkway now offers a wide variety of historical attractions, as well as those provided by nature. Among the historic buildings preserved, for instance, are an old tavern (Polly Woods' Ordinary, Milepost 85.5), a remarkably well-built cabin (Matthews Cabin, Milepost 176.1), a grist mill that is still operating (Mabry Mill, Milepost 176.2), the home of a mountain midwife whose own twenty-four children never lived beyond infancy (Orlena Puckett Cabin, Milepost 189.9), and a pioneer log church with a rib-pole roof (Cool Spring Baptist Church, Milepost 272.0).

In fact, the total and continuing developmental program along the entire length of the Parkway is a rewarding study in the utilization of a variety of skills and services. Park Service officials have labored constantly in behalf of the program, calling upon the skills of the highway engineer, landscape architect, land management specialist, naturalist, historian, and even the philanthropist. Perhaps the most obvious of these is the skill of the engineer, for the road itself is the evidence. Its surface is smoothly paved, and the route is superbly engineered. To the pleasant surprise of the traveler, especially one who is pulling a camper trailer, the road winds its way with a deceptive ease. The curves are properly elevated, and the grades are gentle enough to allow negotiation by even the largest trailer, without undue labor on the part of the towing automobile. Engineers also strived to provide the widest variety of scenery possible. Realizing that some visitors would prefer to see the Parkway piecemeal, the planners made provisions for relatively frequent interchanges. In addition, numerous roadside parking areas, called overlooks, were built, allowing the motorist to pull safely off the Parkway to enjoy the breath-taking panoramas. And, capitalizing on a unique opportunity, the engineers routed the road through a vast mountain wilderness, opening to the general traveler many previously inaccessible places—places with such romantic names as Ravens Roost (Milepost 10.7), Twenty-Minute Cliff (Milepost 19.0), Terrapin Mountain (Milepost 72.6), Thunder Ridge (Milepost 74.7), Purgatory Mountain (Milepost 92.2), Sweet Annie Hollow (Milepost 138.5), Frying Pan Gap (Milepost 409.6), Devils Courthouse (Milepost 422.4), Rough Butt Bald (Milepost 427.1), and Big Witch Gap (Milepost 461.6).

Working very closely with the engineer was the landscape architect. He determined which trees would be sacrificed, which stone cliff would be blasted, where the overlooks would go, what could be done to hide the scars made by the construction crews, where a retaining rail would be located, and whether roadside fences would be stone or rail. In short, any question of an aesthetic nature came within the province of this specialist, whose guiding principle over the years has been to promote to the fullest the Parkway's natural beauty.

The large number of persons whose land adjoined the road's right-of-way created the need for a land management specialist, a man who could convince these neighbors that what was good for the Parkway was also good for them. The nature of the work demanded a rare combination of skills—the gregariousness of a county agent and the tact of a diplomat—because the goal was to enlist the landholders in a joint effort to present to the motoring public an eye-appealing rural scene. Those tilling the soil, especially the persons to whom the Park Service granted leases for land use, were prevailed upon to practice scientific farming. Those with livestock were urged to construct rail fences, with the Service providing free rails. Those with grain crops, such as corn and wheat, were asked to leave their harvested crops in neat shocks along the roadside. The remarkable success of the land management program is not as evident as that of the engineer for the simple reason that the scenes along the Parkway, whether they incorporate a rail fence, a field with neat rows of corn shocks, a field of cabbage, or a field of tobacco, are so "natural" that the passerby little dreams of the great amount of effort exerted to make that scene possible and to keep it, or its equivalent, available for future generations.

One of the greatest challenges imaginable was the task assigned to the naturalist division of the Parkway—developing a program that would best interpret the physical and cultural aspects of a 469-mile swath of Americana. All plans had to be made with "authentic," "natural," "intriguing," and "simple" as guidelines. The basic belief was that the Parkway would become a great national greenbelt—a haven for urbanites seeking relief from the heat and pressures of city life.

As a first step toward accommodating the needs of such visitors, several recreational areas were laid out, with the first one, Cumberland Knob (Milepost 217.55), opening in 1937. Eighteen areas, varying in size from 250 to 6,000 acres, will be made available for visitor services and accommodations. Sixteen were in use by 1969, seven in Virginia and nine in North Carolina:

Virginia	*Milepost*	*North Carolina*	*Milepost*
Humpback Rocks	8.5	Cumberland Knob	217.55
Whetstone Ridge	29.0	Doughton Park	239.3 & 241.1
Otter Creek	60.8	E. B. Jeffress Park	271.8
Peaks of Otter	85.9	Cone Memorial Park	294.0
Roanoke Mountain	120.5	Price Memorial Park	296.5 & 297.15
Smart View	154.5	Linville Falls	316.4 & 316.5
Rocky Knob	167.1 & 169.0	Crabtree Meadows	339.5 & 340.5
		Craggy Gardens	364.4 & 367.6
Others to be developed:		Mount Pisgah	407.8 & 408.8

Virginia	*Milepost*
Pine Spur	143.2 & 144.1
Fishers Peak	213.3

In addition, six visitor centers were established, as follows:

At Humpback Rocks (Milepost 5.8) a pioneer mountain farm has been reconstructed, complete with cabin, chickenhouse, root cellar, barn, pigpen, and spring house, all equipped as they might have been originally. Nearby, an attractive native stone visitor center serves as a

combination information station and wayside museum, utilizing artifacts and photographs to interpret the home and farm life of mountain
people.

At James River (Milepost 63.6) a visitor center-museum imparts a
colorful story of early transportation history, featuring the James
River Canal. Restored portions of the locks and well-illustrated, colorful interpretive panels describe one type of travel of the past.

The Peaks of Otter Center (Milepost 85.9), facing Sharp Top's
towering peak, stresses plant and animal ecology. Animals such as the
fox, skunk, beaver, bobcat, and otter are represented by carefully preserved specimens. Interpretive panels and audiovisual aids help the
visitor understand the delicate relationship between plants and animals
in the natural history of the Parkway.

Easily one of the most popular centers of the entire Parkway is Mabry
Mill (Milepost 176.2) and its allied attractions. Park naturalists reconstructed the old grist and sawmill of Ed Mabry in order that the visitor
might see a live exhibit—a real mill and a working miller who demon-
strates the milling process. Incorporated into the mill area are other
interpretive media, all designed to tell about mountain industry. In the
Matthews Cabin—itself an outstanding example of mountain architecture and workmanship—artifacts and interpretive devices provide
an intriguing look into the tanning and shoemaking crafts as illustrated
by the work of Simon Scott, a pioneer tanner. Other exhibits include a
whiskey still (very much a part of mountain industry), a mint still, a
sorghum mill, and a blacksmith shop with bellows and anvil busily
working. Here, too, in the last days of autumn, usually most of October, local people make apple butter and sorghum molasses the way
their forefathers did. The aromas of hot apple butter and cooking molasses, coupled with visitor participation in the stirring, help make these
annual demonstrations so popular that parking space is usually at a
premium.

The largest center on the Parkway, the Museum of North Carolina
Minerals (Milepost 331.0), caters to one of the nation's most avid hob-
byists, the rock hound. In a manner understandable to the average lay-
man, numerous exhibits describe the varied North Carolina minerals,
from precious stones to ordinary mica. Included for both the student
and serious collector is a well-selected study collection of rocks and
minerals native to the Parkway area. Ranger-naturalists schooled in
geology are on duty to answer questions and give assistance to those
seeking information, whether it be the location of a ruby mine or the
identification of a puzzling bit of stone.

In the heart of the Craggy Gardens (Milepost 364.4) a small wayside
museum exhibits the vegetation of the high Craggies and similar peaks
along the Parkway. Specimens of flowers native to the area are avail-

able for identification purposes. Included in the displays are remarkable wax reproductions of the laurel, azalea, and rhododendron, so realistic that the flowers appear to have just burst into bloom.

To supplement these facilities, park naturalists have established trails to provide for nature study as well as relaxation for the traveler. A number of these are self-guiding: Greenstone Trail (Milepost 8.8), Trail of the Trees (Milepost 63.6), Elk Run Trail (Milepost 86.0), and Craftsman's Trail (Milepost 294.0). Each is a twenty- to thirty-minute nature walk, with either fixed labels along the trail or well-illustrated booklets available at the trail's beginning to show the way. Most of the campgrounds have guided nature walks, too, which are led daily in the summer by ranger-naturalists who present natural history highlights and interpret pertinent aspects of nature encountered along the trails.

Because the naturalists were aware that many visitors would have neither the time nor the desire to hike nature trails, other provisions were made for those who preferred to stay near their cars and the overlook areas. Thus, there are numerous wayside exhibits, each with a story to tell. These are of three types: signs, easels, and orientation devices. The signs have letters routed out in native wood, each carrying a brief interpretive story, usually in less than a hundred words. For example, the Coiner's Deadnin' sign at Humpback Gap (Milepost 6.0) tells of the methods pioneers used to clear land; the Bull Creek Valley overlook sign (Milepost 373.8) deals with the death of the last buffalo sighted in the Blue Ridge Mountains in 1799. The easel exhibits, both versatile and attractive, are glass-enclosed, using either vari-colored drawings or photographs to present their particular stories. At Boston Knob (Milepost 38.8), for instance, there is an easel showing the migratory pattern of birds frequenting the Parkway; at Big Witch (Milepost 461.6), an easel deals with the legend of Big Witch, last of the eagle killers. The orientation devices are brass directional markers mounted in native stone, used to point out to the viewer, by line of sight, specific features such as distant mountain peaks. The approach to all of the roadside exhibits is signaled by an appropriate emblem—the mountain squirrel rifle and powder horn—mounted so that the rifle points toward the item being featured.

At amphitheater and campfire circles, the summer visitor encounters yet another facet of the naturalists' interpretive efforts—the evening talks. Each evening, usually from early June through Labor Day,

campers and their guests are invited to gather around a blazing campfire or assemble in a picturesque open-air amphitheater. There, after
get-acquainted preliminaries which might include anything from
ghost tales to group singing, a park ranger speaks on such topics as
"Pioneer History," "Exploring the Parkway," "Parkway Animal
Life," and "Parkway Plants." The physical setting, the glow of the
campfire, the attention of the audience, and the enthusiasm of the
ranger create a feeling of camaraderie that few other occasions provide.

Supplementing the work of the naturalists has been the research of
historians, both professional and amateur. Among the wayside exhibits
that reflect their contributions are Yankee Horse Logging Exhibit
(Milepost 34.4), Story of Mountain Weaving (Milepost 238.5), Daniel Boone's Wilderness Road (Milepost 285.1), Route of the King's
Mountain Men (Milepost 331.0), Indian Lore (Milepost 422.4), and
Route of the Rutherford Expedition (Milepost 441.9).

The philanthropist, too, has been important to the Parkway. From
the fortune of the "Denim King," Moses H. Cone, came the 1937 donation of a 3,600-acre recreation area now known as the Moses H.
Cone Memorial Park (Milepost 294.0). The Parkway Craft Center,
offering products from members of the Southern Highland Handicraft Guild, was originally the summer mansion of the Cone family.
In compliance with Mrs. Cone's wishes, the Park Service has developed the area as a public "pleasure ground," including carriage roads,
trails, fish lakes, and handicraft demonstrations.

Another philanthropy helped provide one of the Parkway's most
popular campgrounds, the one at Julian Price Memorial Park (Milepost 296.7). The 3,900-acre park stands on land donated by the Jefferson Standard Life Insurance Company of Greensboro, North Carolina, as a permanent memorial to the president and founder of the
company, Julian Price, who died in an automobile accident.

The 440-acre Linville Falls recreation area (Milepost 316.4) was
acquired with the help of John D. Rockefeller, Jr. The National Park
Service has built an attractive campground on the shores of the Linville River and, in addition, has constructed a trail along the walls of
the deep gorge, exposing to view the spectacular waterfalls, framed
by grotesque water-carved rocks—a sight that previously was restricted to the most experienced hikers.

Thus, from its very beginning, the Parkway has benefited from the helping hands and imagination of countless people, each making a contribution toward the common goal of establishing a unique recreational highway. They were all aware that man had devastated mountain wilderness before, and they resolved that man could do better. Instead of ugly scars and rubble, they left a road for pleasure, one that emphasized the work of nature while de-emphasizing the work of man. It was an innovative enterprise, initiated because of a vision, pursued in spite of controversy, and pushed to completion with a liberal contribution of American ingenuity.

Things to see and do along the Blue Ridge Parkway

The Blue Ridge Parkway begins at Rockfish Gap, Virginia (Milepost 0.0), and extends in a generally southwesterly direction to the Oconaluftee River in North Carolina (Milepost 469.1). Only the section around Grandfather Mountain in North Carolina (Milepost 298.6 to 305.1) was not complete in 1970. There is, however, a route around this area. The more prominent places of interest along the Parkway are listed below for quick reference.[1]

VISITOR CENTERS

Milepost	Features[2]
5.8	HUMPBACK ROCKS. Information center-museum. Reconstructed pioneer homestead and history of the mountain people. Self-guiding trail.
63.6	JAMES RIVER. Information center-museum. Reconstructed locks of James River Canal. Illustrated panels of local canal history. Campfire program. Conducted walks. Self-guiding trail.
85.9	PEAKS OF OTTER. Information center-museum. Story of plant and animal ecology. Conducted walks. Self-guiding trails. Evening talks (illustrated).
176.2	MABRY MILL. Information center-museum. The art and technique of mountain industry: gristmilling, tanning, distilling, blacksmithing. Self-guiding trail.
331.0	MUSEUM OF NORTH CAROLINA MINERALS. Information center-museum. The industrial minerals of the region plus a study collection of native rocks and minerals.
364.4	CRAGGY GARDENS. Information center-museum. Vegetation of the high Craggies. Self-guiding trail.

LOG CABINS

Milepost		Milepost	
85.5	Polly Woods' Ordinary	146.5	Bell Spring House

[1] This portion was derived, in the main, from *Seasonal Interpreters Guide* (Roanoke, Va.: Blue Ridge Parkway, 1967).
[2] See Chapter 11 for more information about these centers.

Milepost   *Milepost*
150.8   Kelly Spring House   241.1   Caudill Cabin
154.5   Trail's Cabin   253.0   Sheets Cabin
176.1   Matthews Cabin   272.0   Preacher Brown Cabin
189.9   Puckett Cabin   272.0   Pole Spring House
238.5   Brinegar Cabin   272.0   Cool Spring Baptist
                                            Church

SELF-GUIDING TRAILS

Milepost

5.8   MOUNTAIN FARM TRAIL. A twenty-minute walk, featuring a pioneer homestead of a hundred years ago. Reconstructed buildings equipped with furniture and implements. Guide booklet. Labeled trail aids.

8.8   GREENSTONE TRAIL. Winding twenty-minute trail through an oak-hickory forest. Crosses remnants of slave-built, stone hog-fences. View of Shenandoah Valley. Labeled trail aids.

63.6   TRAIL OF THE TREES. One of the few riverside Parkway trails, twenty minutes long. Offers the most varied low-land forest life of the entire route. Good bird-watching. Labeled trail aids.

86.0   ELK RUN TRAIL. Plant and animal ecology. A thirty-minute trail. Guide booklet (adults and children).

168.0   ROCKY KNOB TRAIL. Hardwood trees and plant life. A thirty-minute trail. Guide booklet.

176.0   PIONEER INDUSTRY TRAIL. Operating grist mill and blacksmith shop, tanning exhibit, mountain still, and sorghum mill. Labeled trail aids.

271.9   CASCADES TRAIL. Heavy forest and a plummeting waterfall. A thirty-minute trail. Labeled trail aids.

308.3   FLAT ROCK TRAIL. Loops through forest for forty-five minutes. View of Grandfather Mountain and Linville Valley. Guide Booklet.

316.4   LINVILLE FALLS TRAIL. A trail through rare virgin forest. No specific time length. Balcony views of the Falls and the grotesquely carved gorge. Labeled trail aids.

364.6   CRAGGY GARDENS TRAIL. Twenty minutes through the rhododendron "gardens." Guide booklet.

ROADSIDE EXHIBITS

S: Interpretive sign   OD: Orientation Device   E: Easel display

Milepost	Type	Content
0.0	S	History of Rockfish Gap
2.9	E	Geography of Great Valley
6.0	S	Methods of land-clearing
8.8	S	Origin and use of stone fences
10.4	E	Story of Catoctin greenstone
10.7	OD	View orientation, Raven's Roost
17.6	E	The story of hickory trees
19.0	S	Origin of place name: "Twenty-Minute Cliff"
34.4	S	Early logging history
38.8	E	Birds on the Parkway
44.4	E	The Pines
52.8	S	The Public Forest
72.6	E	Natural history of the box turtle
76.5	S	Apple Orchard Mountain
81.9	E	Story of the Tulip Tree
85.9	S	Peaks of Otter area
85.9	S	Story of the Big Spring
90.0	E	Oak trees
99.6	S	Geographical story of the Great Valley of Virginia
129.6	E	Story of Roanoke Valley
143.9	E	Blue Ridge drainage
154.5	S	Trail's Cabin
162.4	S	Origin and use of mill pond
168.0	S	View orientation coupled with local history
176.2	S	Story of Mabry Mill
188.8	S	Rail fences, types and origins
189.8	S	Story of Orlena Puckett, mountain midwife
202.8	S	Story of Mt. Airy Granite and Quarry
218.6	S	Origin of place name: "Fox Hunters Paradise"
230.1	E	Pond and swamp biology
232.5	S	Geology of Stone Mountain
238.5	S	Story of Brinegar Cabin and home weaving
241.1	S	Story of a mountain farm
274.3	E	Roadside flowers

Milepost	Type	Content
285.1	E	Daniel Boone and Wilderness Road
294.0	S	Information about Moses H. Cone Memorial Park
296.7	S	Information concerning Julian Price Park
308.3	S	Pisgah, the First National Forest
310.0	E	Origin of Brown Mountain Lights
318.4	S	Geology and minerals of the area
323.1	OD	View orientation, Bear Den
328.6	S	Story of the railroad loops
329.7	E	Story of Table Rock
331.0	S	King's Mountain Men's Crossing
337.2	E	Groundhogs
342.2	E	The Black Mountains
344.1	S	Story of Singecat Fire and conservation
349.2	S	Timber Wildlife Study Area
349.9	E	Story of Mount Mitchell
355.3	E	Parkway leaving Blue Ridge
361.2	S	Story of Asheville watershed
373.8	S	Death of last buffalo in these mountains
393.8	S	French Broad River
398.3	E	Story of disappearance of American chestnut
415.7	E	Migration of monarch butterfly
417.0	S	Geology of Looking Glass Rock
418.8	S	Origin of place name: "Graveyard Fields"
422.4	S	Indian lore of the area
428.5	E	Bears
441.9	S	Indian trail and route of Rutherford Expedition
451.2	E	View orientation, Waterrock Knob
457.9	S	The Plott Balsams and local lore
458.2	S	Great Smoky Mountains National Park
458.6	S	Entrance orientation
459.5	S	Cherokee Reservation
461.9	E	Big Witch, last of the eagle killers

CAMPGROUNDS

Campgrounds[3] are open from May through October on a first-come, first-served basis. Sites are available for both trailers and

[3] See Chapter 11 for more information.

tents. Each campground has comfort stations and convenient drinking water but no provisions for electrical hook-ups, showers, or laundry. There is a nominal admission fee.

Milepost		*Milepost*	
60.8	Otter Creek	296.7 & 297.15	Julian Price
85.9	Peaks of Otter		Memorial Park
120.5	Roanoke Mountain	316.4	Linville Falls
167.1	Rocky Knob	339.5	Crabtree Meadows
239.3 & 239.4	Doughton Park	408.8	Mount Pisgah

PICNIC AREAS

The twelve picnic grounds contain parking spaces, tables with seats, grilled fireplaces, litter disposals, drinking water, and comfort stations. In addition, numerous single tables are located in overlooks marked with the "picnic table" sign. There is no admission fee for the picnicker.

Milepost		*Milepost*	
8.5	Humpback Rocks	296.5	Julian Price
85.9	Peaks of Otter		Memorial Park
154.5	Smart View	316.5	Linville Falls
169.0	Rocky Knob	340.5	Crabtree Meadows
188.8	Groundhog Mountain	364.6	Craggy Gardens
217.55	Cumberland Knob	407.8	Mount Pisgah
241.1	Doughton Park		

CONCESSIONS

To accommodate the traveler, the National Park Service has granted a few concessionaires the privilege of catering to the public in remote areas not likely to be serviced by local enterprise.

Milepost	
29.0	Whetstone Ridge. Food, gas, crafts, telephone.
60.8	Otter Creek. Food, gas, crafts, telephone.
85.9	Peaks of Otter. Food, gas, crafts, telephone, bus service for hikers, lodging.
169.0	Rocky Knob. Gas, picnic supplies.
174.0	Rocky Knob. Housekeeping cabins, telephone.

Milepost
176.1   Mabry Mill. Food, crafts, telephone.
241.1   Doughton Park. Food, lodging, gas, crafts, telephone.
257.0   Cherry Hill. Food, gas, crafts.
258.6   Northwest Trading Post. Mountain produce, crafts.
339.5   Crabtree Meadows. Food, gas, crafts.
408.6   Mount Pisgah. Food, lodging, gas, crafts, telephone.

DEMONSTRATIONS

Milepost
176.2   MABRY MILL. Gristmilling and blacksmithing. *Open all season.* Apple butter- and sorghum-making, *late September and most of October.* All products for sale.
238.5   BRINEGAR CABIN. Weaving on oldtime loom. Basket-making. Handcrafted textile goods for sale. *Open all season.*
294.0   PARKWAY CRAFT CENTER. Weaving, gem-cutting, rug-making, wood-carving by members of the Southern Highland Handicraft Guild. Wide range of authentic handicraft articles for sale. *Open all season on an "as available" basis.*

Blue Ridge Parkway Log

The attractions noted in *Italics* have been described in the text. The directions "left" and "right" are relative when a traveler is driving south on the Parkway.

S—interpretive sign. E—lift-top easel. OD—orientation device

Milepost

0.0   Rockfish Gap, Virginia. U. S. 250 access. Right 4 mi. to Waynesboro; left 16 mi. to Charlottesville. S. Howard Johnson Restaurant (off Parkway)

0.2   Afton overlook, elev. 1898

2.9   Shenandoah Valley parking overlook, elev. 2354. E.

4.4   Va. 609, right to Sherando; left to Martin's store

5.8   *Humpback Rocks visitor center.* Pioneer exhibit, self-guiding trail

6.0   Humpback Gap parking area, elev. 2360. S.

8.5   *Humpback Rocks picnic area.* 91 sites, 2 comfort stations

8.8   *Greenstone* parking overlook, elev. 3007. Self-guiding trail. S.

9.2   Laurel Springs Gap, elev. 2878

9.6   Dripping Rocks parking widening

10.4   Rockpoint parking overlook, elev. 3113. E.

10.7   *Ravens Roost* parking overlook. OD.

11.7   Hickory Spring parking widening. Fountain

13.1   Three Ridges parking overlook, elev. 2697

Milepost

13.7   Reeds Gap, elev. 2637. Va. 664, right to Va. 814; left to Roseland and Amherst

15.4   Love Gap

16.0   Va. 814, left to Massie's Mill

17.6   The Priest parking overlook, elev. 2695. E.

18.5   White Rock Gap, elev. 2549

19.0   *Twenty-Minute Cliff* parking overlook, elev. 2715. S.

19.9   The Slacks parking overlook, elev. 2800. S.

22.1   Bald Mountain parking widening, elev. 3250. U.S.F.S. road to Bald Mountain Tower

23.0   Fork Mountain parking overlook, elev. 3294

23.4   Highest point north of the James River, elev. 3333.7

24.3   Left, road to FAA Aircraft Direction Finder Station

25.6   Spy Run Gap, elev. 3033

26.4   Parking overlook

27.2   Tye River Gap, elev. 2969. Va. 56, right 4 mi. to Vesuvius, 6.5 mi. to Steeles Tavern; left .75 mi. to Montebello

29.0   *Whetstone Ridge.* Sandwich shop, gift shop, service station

Milepost

29.5 Va. 603; no access. Cemetery

31.4 Still-house Hollow parking widening. Fountain

31.9 Va. 886; left, unimproved road to Montebello

33.0 Yankee Fence exhibit

34.4 Yankee Horse parking area, elev. 3140. Logging Railroad exhibit. S.

34.8 Yankee Horse Ridge

37.4 Irish Gap, elev. 2279

37.5 Va. 605, right to Irish Creek and Buena Vista; left to Va. 60 and Amherst

38.8 Boston Knob parking area, elev. 2508. E.

39.9 Clark Mountain public road

40.0 Clarkes Gap, elev. 2177

42.4 Irish Creek Valley parking widening, elev. 2665

44.4 Whites Gap parking overlook, elev. 2567. E.

44.9 Chimney Rock Mountain parking widening, elev. 2485

45.6 Humphreys Gap, elev. 2312. Buena Vista overlook. U.S. 60, right 5 mi. to Buena Vista, 11 mi. to Lexington; left 23 mi. to Amherst

46.9 Indian Gap. Public crossing; no access

48.9 Licklog Springs Gap, elev. 2481

49.3 House Mountain parking overlook, elev. 2498

50.1 Robinson Gap, elev. 2412

50.5 Va. 607; no access

51.1 U.S.F.S. road to Bluff Mountain Tower (gated)

52.8 Bluff Mountain parking overlook, elev. 1850. S.

Milepost

53.1 Bluff Mountain Tunnel, 630 ft. long

53.6 Rice Mountain parking overlook, elev. 1755

54.1 Browns Creek, elev. 1560

55.1 White Oak Flats parking overlook, elev. 1460

55.2 Otter Creek, elev. 1458

55.9 Dancing Creek parking overlook, elev. 1300

57.6 Upper Otter Creek overlook

58.2 Otter Creek Flats parking overlook, elev. 1055

59.7 Otter Creek parking overlook

60.4 The Riffles parking overlook, elev. 825

60.8 Otter Creek. Campground, 42 tent sites, 25 trailer sites, campfire circle, coffee shop, gift shop, service station

61.4 Terrapin Hill parking overlook, elev. 760

61.6 Otter Creek Bridge. Va. 130, right 2 mi. to U.S. 501, 8 mi. to Glasgow; left 12 mi. to Elon, 20 mi. to Lynchburg

62.5 Lower Otter Creek parking overlook, elev. 685

63.1 Otter Lake parking overlook, elev. 655

63.6 James River overlook. Visitor center, self-guiding trail, footbridge and trail to Kanawha Canal lock exhibit

63.65 Cemetery

63.7 James River Bridge. U.S. 501, right 9 mi. to Glasgow; left 2 mi. to Big Island, 22 mi. to Lynchburg

67.1 Falling Rock Creek

Milepost

68.6 Trail to Marble Spring Lean-to (AT Club)

69.1 James River Valley parking overlook, elev. 1874

71.0 Petites Gap, elev. 2361

72.6 *Terrapin Mountain* parking widening, elev. 2884. E.

74.7 *Thunder Ridge* parking area, elev. 3485

74.8 Thunder Hill, elev. 3510

75.5 Arnold Valley parking widening

76.2 U.S. Air Force road

76.5 Apple Orchard parking widening, elev. 3933. S.

76.6 U.S. Air Force access road to Bedford radar installation on Apple Orchard Mountain

76.7 Highest point on Parkway in Virginia, elev. 3950

78.4 U.S.F.S. road 35. Right to Welch; left to Methodist Church camp. Sunset Field overlook

79.7 Onion Mountain parking overlook, elev. 3145

80.0 Black Rock Hill parking widening

81.9 Headforemost parking widening, elev. 2861. Fountain. E.

83.5 Wilkinson Gap, elev. 2511

83.6 Flat Top Mountain Trail parking area, elev. 2610. Trail to Flat Top Mountain, elev. 4001

85.5 *Polly Woods' Ordinary*

85.65 *Peaks of Otter concession area*, elev. 2525. Lodge (56 rooms), restaurant, grill, gift shop, 24-acre lake

85.89 Cemetery

85.9 *Peaks of Otter visitor cen-*

Milepost

ter (right). Ranger office, service station, amphitheatre, self-guiding Elk Run Trail and trail to Hearkening Hill, trail to Johnson farm group
Peaks of Otter, elev. 2535 (left). Camp store; restrooms; bus station for trips up Sharp Top Mountain (elev. 3875); trail to Sharp Top Mountain, Va. 43; campground, 80 tent sites, 62 trailer sites; Little Stony picnic area, 62 sites. S.

89.1 Powell's Gap, elev. 1916

89.4 Upper Goose Creek parking overlook, elev. 1925

90.0 Porters Mountain parking overlook, elev. 2102. E.

90.9 Bearwallow Gap, elev. 2258. Va. 695, left to U.S. 460. Va. 43, right 5 mi. to Buchanan

91.8 Mills Gap parking widening, elev. 2432

91.9 Mills Gap, elev. 2425

92.2 *Purgatory Mountain* parking widening, elev. 2415

92.6 Sharp Top parking widening, elev. 2415

93.1 Bobblets Gap parking overlook, elev. 2418. Bobblet Cemetery

93.2 Bobblets Gap. Va. 617; no access

94.1 U.S.F.S. Hammond Trail

95.2 Pine Trees parking overlook, elev. 2490

95.3 Harveys Knob parking overlook, elev. 2524

95.9 Montvale parking overlook, elev. 2441

96.6 Iron Mine Hollow parking

widening, elev. 2365
96.9   Taylor Mountain parking
        overlook, elev. 2340
97.6   Black Horse Gap, elev.
        2402
99.6   Great Valley parking over-
        look, elev. 2493. S.
100.9   The Quarry parking over-
        look, elev. 2170
101.5   Curry Gap, elev. 1985
104.4   Va. 652; no access
104.8   Va. 657; no access
105.0   U.S. 460, accommodation
        folder rack. Leaflets and
        bulletins
105.8   U.S. 460, right 9 mi. to
        Roanoke; left 20 mi. to
        Bedford
107.5   Va. 738; no access
107.6   Glade Creek
107.7   Va. 685; no access
108.4   Va. 604; no access
110.6   Stewarts Knob parking
        overlook, elev. 1275. S.
111.6   Va. 651; no access
112.2   Va. 24, right 5 mi. to Roan-
        oke; left 4 mi. to Stewarts-
        ville
113.6   Va. 634; no access
114.8   Roanoke River Bridge, riv-
        er elev. 825
115.3   Va. 618; no access
116.2   Dundee
116.4   Va. 658; no access
117.2   Va. 617; no access
117.6   Cemetery
117.65 Va. 116; no access
118.6   Va. 666; no access
119.2   Va. 668; no access
119.8   Yellow Mountain loop exit
120.3   Yellow Mountain loop en-
        trance
120.5   *Mill Mountain Spur. Roan-*
          oke Mountain camp-
          ground, 60 campsites, 40

trailer sites, campfire circle, trail
121.5   U.S. 220, accommodation
        folder rack. Leaflets and
        bulletins. Right 5 mi. to
        Roanoke; left 21 mi. to
        Rocky Mount
122.4   Va. 679; no access
123.2   Buck Mountain parking
        overlook, elev. 1465
124.15 Va. 613; no access
124.4   Back Creek, elev. 1160
124.45 Va. 615; no access
126.1   Va. 688; no access
126.2   Masons Knob parking
        overlook, elev. 1425
127.6   Va. 691; no access
128.7   Metz Run parking over-
        look, elev. 1875
128.8   Va. 690; no access
129.3   Poages Mill parking over-
        look, elev. 2032
129.6   Roanoke Valley parking
        overlook, elev. 2125. E.
129.7   Viaduct
129.9   Lost Mountain parking
        overlook, elev. 2200
131.0   Va. 690; no access
132.0   Dividing Springs, elev.
        2800
133.0   Slings Gap parking over-
        look, elev. 2860
133.1   Slings Gap, elev. 2825. Va.
        612; no access
133.6   Bull Run Knob parking
        overlook, elev. 2890
134.3   Lancaster Gap, elev. 2786
135.6   Cemetery
135.9   U.S. 221, right 19 mi. to
        Roanoke
136.0   Adney Gap, elev. 2690. Va.
        602; no access
136.1   Cemeteries. Access to Va.
        602

U. S. Department of Agriculture Social Research Report No. VIII. Washington, D. C.: U. S. Department of Agriculture, 1938.

U. S. Department of Agriculture. *Climate and Man. 1941 Yearbook of Agriculture.*

_____. *Economic and Social Problems and Conditions of the Southern Appalachians.* U. S. Department of Agriculture Miscellaneous Publication No. 205. Washington, D. C.: U. S. Department of Agriculture, 1935.

U. S. Federal Land Committee. "Public Works and Rural Land Use," *Report of the Land Committee to the National Resources Planning Board.* Washington, D. C.: Government Printing Office, 1942.

U. S. Federal Land Planning Committee. "Maladjustments in Land Use in the United States," *Supplementary Report of the Land Planning Committee to the National Resources Board,* Pt. VI. Washington, D. C.: Government Printing Office, 1935.

U. S. National Resources Board. *Report on National Planning and Public Works in Relation to Natural Resources Including Land Use and Water Resources with Findings and Recommendations.* Washington, D. C.: Government Printing Office, 1934.

U. S. *Statutes at Large.* Vols. XLVIII, XLIX, LIV.

Virginia. *Acts of the General Assembly,* 1933, 1936.

Unpublished Material and Interviews

Abbuehl, Edward H. "History of the Blue Ridge Parkway." Paper read before Blue Ridge Parkway Rangers' Conference, Roanoke, Va., February 8, 1948. Manuscript in the files of Superintendent, Blue Ridge Parkway, Roanoke, Va.

Abbuehl, Edward H., Parkway supervisory landscape architect. Personal interview, July 16, 1962, Roanoke, Va.

Batten, Earl W., Parkway engineer. Personal interview, September 3, 1963, Roanoke, Va.

Blue Ridge Parkway. Historical Files, Office of Superintendent, Roanoke, Va.

Blythe, Jarrett, chief, Eastern Band of Cherokee Indians. Personal interview, May 19, 1962, Cherokee, N. C.

Byrd, Harry F., United States senator. Personal interview, June 3, 1962, Waynesboro, Va.

Cherokee Indian Agency. Historical Files, Office of Superintendent, Cherokee, N. C.

Milepost

175.9   Va. 603, Rocky Knob cabins

176.1   Matthews Cabin

176.2   Mabry Mill, elev. 2855. Visitor center, coffee shop, gift shop, water-powered sawmill, carpenter shop, and working grist mill. Self-guiding pioneer industry trail, including blacksmith and wheelwright shop exhibit, mint still, whiskey still. Molasses- and apple butter-making exhibit in season. S.

177.7   Meadows of Dan, elev. 2960. U.S. 58, right 21 mi. to Hillsville; left 16 mi. to Stuart

178.3   Cemetery

178.8   Va. 744

179.3   Round Meadow parking overlook. Trail

179.4   Round Meadow Viaduct, elev. 2800. Round Meadow Creek, elev. 2690

180.1   Maybery Presbyterian Church and Cemetery. Va. 600

180.5   Va. 634, Yeatts store contiguous on right

180.6   Mabry Gap

180.7   Maybery Creek, elev. 2775

181.4   Cemetery. Access to Va. 602 left

183.4   Pinnacles of Dan, elev. 2875

183.9   Access to Va. C-614

184.2   Cemetery. Access to old Va. 614

185.0   Va. C-638; no access

186.4   Cemetery. Access to Va. C-608

186.5   Cemetery and parking area at private road crossing, 186.4

Milepost

186.7   Va. C-631, right to Laurel Fork

187.7   Va. 639

188.8   Groundhog Mountain parking overlook, elev. 3025. Picnic area, 26 sites and 1 comfort station, trail from parking area to observation tower, cemetery in parking area island. S.

188.9   Va. 608; Va. C-608, no access

189.1   Pilot Mountain parking overlook, elev. 2950

189.9   Puckett Cabin parking area, elev. 2848. Historic building. S.

190.6   Va. 608

191.4   Va. 608

191.9   Bluemont Presbyterian Church and Cemetery at private road crossing

192.3   Va. C-648, left to Mt. Airy; left on Va. C-771 to Willis Gap

193.2   Volunteer Gap, elev. 2706

193.7   Orchard Gap, elev. 2675. Va. 691, right to Hillsville; left to Mt. Airy

194.7   Va. 608

195.5   Wards Gap, elev. 2750. Va. 608; no access

196.45 Va. 682

198.4   Va. 685, left to Va. C-608

199.0   Va. 608

199.1   Turnoff connects with U.S. 52

199.4   Fancy Gap, elev. 2925. U.S. 52, left 14 mi. to Mt. Airy

199.9   Va. C-778

202.25 Va. 608

202.8   Granite Quarry parking overlook, elev. 3015. S.

203.9   Piedmont overlook

204.85 Va. 700

Milepost

205.75 Va. 608

206.1   Piper Gap, elev. 2759. Va. 620; no access

206.35 Va. 608, right to Va. 620 and 97

206.9   Mt. Carroll Methodist Church and Cemetery

207.75 Va. 608

208.25 Blue Ridge Church and Cemetery; access to Va. C-608

209.35 Va. 715, right to Galax

209.85 Va. 716

209.9   Hanks Branch

211.1   Va. 612

212.2   Hanks Branch

213.1   E. Fork Chestnut Creek

213.3   Va. C-612

215.15 W. Fork Chestnut Creek

215.3   Va. 799

215.7   W. Fork Chestnut Creek

215.85 Va. 89, right 7 mi. to Galax; left 22 mi. to Mt. Airy

216.0   W. Fork Chestnut Creek

216.25 W. Fork Chestnut Creek

216.9   State Line, Virginia and North Carolina

217.3   Road connects with N.C. 18; right 15 mi. to Sparta; left 22 mi. to Mt. Airy

217.55 Cumberland Knob, spur to left. Parking, picnic area, 25 sites, comfort stations, shelter, cemetery. Bully Creek and Cumberland Knob loop trail

218.6   Fox Hunters Paradise parking overlook, elev. 2805. Trail to High Piney Spur. S.

220.4   Secondary road, N.C. 1460

221.8   Saddle Mountain Church, elev. 2755. Secondary road crossing

225.2   Hare Mill Pond, elev. 2590. Secondary road crossing

Milepost

226.2   Secondary road crossing

227.6   Secondary road crossing

229.2   Public road crossing

229.6   U.S. 21, elev. 2700. Right 7 mi. to Sparta; left 25 mi. to Elkin

230.1   Little Glade Mill Pond parking overlook, elev. 2709. E.

230.9   Public road crossing, left to Cherry Lane, right to Sparta

231.5   Public road crossing

231.8   Public road access

232.5   Stone Mountain parking overlook. S.

233.7   Parking widening, elev. 3200

234.0   Public road access

234.1   Bullhead Gap, elev. 3193; public road crossing

235.0   Mahogany Rock parking overlook, elev. 3436

235.7   Devil's Garden parking overlook, elev. 3428

236.9   Air Bellows Gap parking overlook, elev. 3744

237.15 Air Bellows Gap, elev. 3729. Overpass; public road access

238.5   Brinegar Cabin parking overlook, elev. 3508. S. *Enter Doughton Park;* Brinegar Cabin, weaving exhibits, and gift shop

239.3   Camping area, 96 campsites, 3 comfort stations, campfire circle

239.4   Trailer area, 28 trailer sites, 1 comfort station

239.9   Low Notch, elev. 3482

241.1   Doughton Park. Right to coffee shop, service station; left to lodge (75 cap.), picnic area, 56 sites. S.

Milepost

242.4   Alligator Back parking overlook, elev. 3388
243.4   Bluffs View parking overlook, elev. 3334
243.8   Grassy Gap, elev. 3218
243.95 Grassy Gap road (locked)
244.5   Cemetery
244.7   Basin Cove parking overlook, elev. 3312
246.1   Public road access, right to N.C. 18
246.92 Public road crossing
247.26 Public road crossing (unimproved)
248.1   N.C. 18, right 2 mi. to 2 motels, restaurant, gasoline, Laurel Springs; left 24 mi. to N. Wilkesboro
249.3   Public road crossing
250.0   Public road
250.8   Peak Creek. Public road crossing, right to Upper Mountain experiment station
251.5   Alder Gap, elev. 3047. Public road access right
252.4   Public road crossing
252.8   Sheets Gap parking overlook, elev. 3342. Public road exit on left
254.1   Rattlesnake Mountain and public road crossing
255.1   Public road crossing
256.5   Public road crossing
256.9   Cherry Hill coffee shop, gift shop, service station
257.7   Public road crossing
258.6   Public road crossing (old N.C. 16), Glendale Springs on right. Northwest Trading Post, gift shop
259.25 Public road crossing. Cemetery on left
259.85 Public road crossing

Milepost

260.3   Jumpin-Off Rocks parking area, elev. 3165
261.2   Horse Gap, elev. 3108. N.C. 16, right 12 mi. to W. Jefferson; left 22 mi. to N. Wilkesboro
262.25 Daniel Gap, elev. 3167
263.15 Joint crossing
263.7   Gilliam Gap, elev. 3238. Private crossing
264.45 The Lump parking overlook, elev. 3465
265.15 Calloway Gap, elev. 3439. Public road crossing
266.3   Radio relay tower, Watson's Dome
266.9   Mount Jefferson parking overlook. S.
267.65 Public road crossing, Blue Ridge Baptist Church and Cemetery
268.0   Benge, elev. 3330. Public road crossing
269.8   Phillips Gap, elev. 3221. Public road crossing; private minerals museum
270.2   Lewis Fork parking overlook, elev. 3290
271.8   Right to E. B. Jeffress Park
271.9   Cascades parking overlook, elev. 3570. Picnic area, self-guiding trail to Cascades pedestrian overlook (Falls Creek), trail to historic building, picnic area
272.0   *Cool Spring Baptist Church*
272.5   Thompkins Knob parking area; trail to historic buildings
273.6   Thompkins Knob, elev. 3914
274.3   Elk Mountain parking overlook, elev. 3789. E.
274.5   Joint crossing
276.4   Deep Gap, elev. 3142. U.S.

Milepost

421, right 12 mi. to Boone; left 26 mi. to N. Wilkesboro

277.1   Stoney Fork Valley parking overlook, elev. 3405

277.7   Osborne Mountain View parking overlook, elev. 3500

278.1   Carroll Gap parking overlook, elev. 3430

279.2   Public road crossing

280.1   Public road; no access

280.8   Access to U.S. 421 & 221, right 4 mi. to Deep Gap, 7 mi. to Boone; picnic area adjacent to U.S. 421

281.75   Grandview parking overlook, elev. 3240

285.1   Daniel Boone's Wilderness Road. E.

285.55   Bamboo, elev. 3262. Access road to Boone on right

288.1   Public road crossing

288.55   Cemetery

288.8   Public road

289.1   Yadkin Valley parking overlook, elev. 3830

289.6   Raven Rocks parking overlook

290.5   Thunder Hill parking overlook, elev. 3776

290.7   Cemetery

290.75   Public road (Green Hill Road)

291.9   U.S. 321 & 221, right 7 mi. to Boone; left 2 mi. to Blowing Rock

292.7   Enter Cone Memorial Park

293.5   Moses Cone parking overlook, elev. 3865

294.0   Moses Cone Memorial Park Craft Center. Southern Highland Handicraft Guild handicraft shop, visitor center, and self-guid-

Milepost

ing trail; Cone family cemetery. S.

294.6   Sandy Flat Gap. U.S. 221, left 2 mi. to Blowing Rock, 13 mi . to Beacon Heights; right to Shulls Mills Road, Flannery Fork Road, and Trout Lake

295.0   Leave Cone Memorial Park, enter *Price Memorial Park*

295.4   Sims Creek Viaduct, 85 ft. high, 385 ft. span

295.9   Sims Pond parking overlook, elev. 3447

296.5   Picnic area, 100 sites, 2 comfort stations

296.7   Price Lake parking overlook, elev. 3393
Left to campground; 29 tent sites; 6 trailer sites, 1 comfort station. S.

297.15   Right to campground; 99 tent sites, 62 trailer sites, 5 comfort stations

297.2   Parking overlook, elev. 3410. Amphitheatre and boat launching ramp

298.6   Holloway Mountain Road; temporary end Parkway, access to U.S. 221 south, left.

Gap "X" Proposed Construction Travel via Holloway Mountain Road and U.S. 221 (Yonalossee Trail) to Beacon Heights

305.1   U.S. 221, Beacon Heights. Leave U.S. 221 and resume Parkway south. Right 3 mi. to Linville

305.25   Beacon Heights parking area, elev. 4212

306.2   Grandmother Mountain Gap, elev. 4051

Milepost

306.6   Grandfather Mountain parking overlook, elev. 4154

307.4   Grandmother Mountain parking area, elev. 4063

307.6   Parking widening, elev. 4015

307.9   Public road, right 2 mi. to Linville; left to Roseboro

308.3   Flat Rock parking area, elev. 3987. Self-guiding trail. S.

310.0   Lost Cove Cliffs parking overlook, elev. 3812. E.

312.25   N.C. 181, right 2 mi. to Pineola; left 32 mi. to Morganton

315.6   Camp Creek parking overlook, elev. 3442

316.4   *Linville Falls.* Campground, 55 campsites, 20 trailer sites, campfire circle, parking area, and self-guiding trails to Linville Falls overlooks

316.5   *Linville River* parking area, elev. 3250. Picnic area, 100 sites, 3 comfort stations

316.6   Linville River Bridge, elev. 3257

317.55   U.S. 221, right 6 mi. to Spruce Pine; left ¼ mi. to Linville Falls community, 24 mi. to Marion

318.4   North Toe Valley parking overlook, elev. 3540. S.

319.8   Humpback Mountain Viaduct

320.8   Chestoa View parking area, elev. 4090

323.1   Bear Den parking overlook, elev. 3359. OD.

325.9   Heffner Gap parking overlook, elev. 3067

327.3   North Cove parking overlook, elev. 2815

Milepost

327.5   McKinney Gap, elev. 2790. Public crossing, right 5 mi. to Spruce Pine; left 10 mi. to U.S. 221

328.6   Apple Orchard parking overlook, elev. 2980. S.

329.4   Swafford Gap, elev. 2852

329.7   Table Rock parking overlook, elev. 2870. E.

330.9   Gillespie Gap, elev. 2819. N.C. 226, right to *Museum of North Carolina Minerals*, Spruce Pine, 6 mi.; Marion, 14 mi.; N.C. 226A, Little Switzerland, 3 mi

332.6   Lynn Gap, elev. 3109

333.4   Little Switzerland Tunnel, 547 ft. long

333.9   McCall Gap public road, elev. 3490. Left to Little Switzerland

335.4   Bearwallow Gap and Crabtree public road (no access), elev. 3482

336.3   Gooch Gap, elev. 3360. Wildacres public road

336.8   Wildacres Tunnel, 249 ft. long

337.2   Deer Lick Gap parking overlook, elev. 3452. E.

338.8   Three Knobs parking overlook, elev. 3880

339.5   *Crabtree Meadows.* Restaurant, gift shop, service station, campground, 71 campsites, 22 trailer sites, 3 comfort stations, amphitheatre

340.5   *Picnic area,* 82 sites, 1 comfort station

342.25   Black Mountains parking overlook, elev. 3892. E.

344.1   Buck Creek Gap parking overlook, elev. 3373. N.C. 80, right 14 mi. to Mica-

Milepost

ville; left 6 mi. to Marion. S.

344.56 Twin Tunnel, 240 ft. long

344.7 Twin Tunnel, 401 ft. long

345.3 Singecat Ridge parking overlook, elev. 3406

347.6 Big Laurel Gap and U.S.F.S. road, elev. 4048

348.8 Curtis Valley parking overlook, elev. 4460

349.0 Rough Ridge Tunnel, 245 ft. long

349.2 Licklog Ridge parking overlook, elev. 4602

349.9 Mount Mitchell parking overlook, elev. 4821. E.

350.4 Green Knob parking overlook, elev. 4761

351.9 Deep Gap, elev. 4284. U.S.F.S. road right (gated)

352.6 Big Pine Bear Stand, elev. 4479

353.9 Cherry Log Ridge, elev. 4925

354.8 Toe River Gap, elev. 5168. U.S.F.S. road (Old Perely Toll Road) left.

355.0 Game warden's cabin, right

355.3 Black Mountain Gap, elev. 5160. Ridge Junction parking overlook, elev. 5160. E. N.C. 128, right 4.8 mi. to Mount Mitchell; NPS and commercial radio antennas

355.4 Enter Asheville watershed

358.5 Highest point on Parkway north of Asheville, elev. 5676.5

359.8 Balsam Gap parking overlook, elev. 5320

361.1 Cotton Tree Gap, elev. 5141

361.2 Glassmine Falls parking overlook, elev. 5197. S.

Milepost

363.4 Bullhead Gap. Graybeard Mountain parking overlook, elev. 5592

364.1 Craggy Dome parking overlook, elev. 5640

364.35 Craggy Pinnacle Tunnel, 176 ft. long

364.4 Craggy Gardens visitor center, elev. 5497. Self-guiding trail

365.5 Craggy Flats Tunnel, 335 ft. long

367.6 Bee Tree Gap, elev. 4900. Right 1.38 mi. to *Bear Pen (Craggy Gardens)* picnic area, elev. 5220

368.2 Potato Field Gap, elev. 4600 (south end Asheville watershed)

372.1 Lanes Pinnacle parking overlook, elev. 3890

373.8 Bull Creek Valley parking overlook, elev. 3483. S.

374.4 Tanbark Ridge Tunnel, 746 ft. long

375.3 Bull Gap, elev. 3107

375.7 N.C. 694 (Elk Mountain scenic road), right 8 mi. to Weaverville

376.7 Tanbark Ridge parking overlook, elev. 2782

377.4 Craven Gap, elev. 3132. N.C. 694 (Town Mountain Road) right 7 mi. to Asheville

382.6 U.S. 70, right 5 mi. to Oteen and Asheville; left 9 mi. to Black Mountain

383.5 Swannanoa River, elev. 2040

384.7 U.S. 74, right 5 mi. to Asheville; left 17 mi. to Bat Cave

386.9 Biltmore Estate reservoir

388.85 U.S. 25, right 5 mi. to Ashe-

Milepost

ville; left 16 mi. to Hendersonville

393.5 French Broad River, elev. 2000

393.6 N.C. 191 & 280, right 9 mi. to Asheville

393.8 French Broad parking overlook, elev. 2100. S.

395.1 Glenn Gap, elev. 2495

396.4 Walnut Cove parking overlook, elev. 2915

396.8 Reynolds Gap, elev. 2865

397.1 Grassy Knob Tunnel, 600 ft. long

397.3 Sleepy Gap parking overlook, elev. 3920

398.3 Chestnut Grove parking overlook, elev. 3035. E.

399.3 Pine Mountain Tunnel, 1320 ft. long

399.7 Bad Fork Valley parking overlook, elev. 3350

400.3 Bent Creek Gap, elev. 3270. U.S.F.S. road (gated)

400.9 Ferrin Knob Tunnel No. 1, Trace Ridge, 360 ft. long

401.1 Wash Creek Valley parking overlook

401.3 Ferrin Knob Tunnel No. 2, 310 ft. long

401.5 Ferrin Knob Tunnel No. 3, 230 ft. long

401.7 Beaver Dam Gap parking overlook, elev. 3570

402.6 Stony Bald parking overlook, elev. 3750

403.0 Young Pisgah Ridge Tunnel, 400 ft. long

403.6 Big Ridge parking overlook, elev. 3815

403.9 Fort Mountain Tunnel, 350 ft. long

404.2 Standhill Mountain parking overlook, elev. 3975

404.5 Mills Valley parking overlook, elev. 4085

Milepost

405.5 Elk Pasture Gap (formerly Cutthroat Gap), elev. 4235

406.9 Little Pisgah Tunnel, 500 ft. long

407.4 Buck Springs Tunnel, 380 ft. long

407.6 Mount Pisgah parking area

407.7 Buck Springs Gap parking overlook, elev. 4980

407.8 Mount Pisgah picnic area, 50 sites

408.4 Flat Laurel Gap, elev. 4925

408.6 Mount Pisgah Inn, 29 units, restaurant, service station

408.8 Mount Pisgah campground, 73 tent sites, 75 trailer sites

409.3 Tunnel Top parking overlook, elev. 4925

409.6 Frying Pan Gap, elev. 4931

410.1 Frying Pan Tunnel, 275 ft. long

410.3 The Pink Beds parking overlook, elev. 4825

411.0 Rich Mountain parking overlook, elev. 4710

411.85 Cold Mountain parking overlook, elev. 4542

411.9 U.S. 276, right 22 mi. to Waynesville; left 17 mi. to Brevard

412.2 Wagon Road Gap parking overlook, elev. 4550

412.5 Pigeon Gap, elev. 4520

413.2 Pounding Mill parking overlook, elev. 4700

414.2 Bennett Gap, elev. 4402

414.9 Bennett Cove, elev. 4525

415.6 Tunnel Gap, elev. 4325

415.7 Cherry Cove parking overlook, elev. 4330. E.

416.3 Log Hollow parking overlook, elev. 4445

416.8 Bridges Camp Gap, elev. 4450

Milepost

417.05 *Looking Glass Rock* parking overlook, elev. 4493. S.

417.8 Seniard Gap, elev. 4775

417.9 Yellowstone Falls

418.3 East Fork parking overlook, elev. 4955

418.8 Graveyard Fields parking overlook, elev. 5115. S.

419.4 John Rock parking overlook, elev. 5330

420.2 Balsam Spring Gap, elev. 5550. U.S.F.S. road (gated) right

421.1 Old Silver Mine

421.7 Andromeda parking overlook

422.1 Devils Courthouse Tunnel, 650 ft. long

422.4 *Devils Courthouse* parking overlook, elev. 5462. Trail. S.

422.8 Mount Hardy parking overlook, elev. 5415

423.2 Beech Gap, elev. 5340. Right 23 mi. to Waynesville; left 17 mi. to Rosman

423.5 Courthouse Valley parking overlook, elev. 5362

423.7 Tanassee Bald

424.0 Herrin Knob parking widening, elev. 5510

424.2 Black Mountain Gap, elev. 5490

424.4 Herrin Knob parking widening, elev. 5510

424.8 Wolf Mountain parking overlook, elev. 5500

425.3 Wolf Bald

425.4 Rough Butt Bald parking overlook, elev. 5300

425.5 Buckeye Gap, elev. 5377

426.5 Haywood Gap

427.1 *Rough Butt Bald*

Milepost

427.6 Bear Pen Gap parking area, elev. 5560

427.8 Spot Gap parking overlook, elev. 5610

428.0 Caney Fork parking overlook, elev. 5650

428.3 Little Bear Pen Gap, elev. 5600

428.5 Beartrap Gap parking overlook, elev. 5580. E.

429.1 Reinhart Gap, elev. 5455

430.0 Reinhart Knob

430.4 Beartrail Ridge parking area, elev. 5865

430.7 Cowee Mountain parking overlook, elev. 5960

431.0 Haywood-Jackson parking overlook, elev. 6020. Self-guiding trail

431.4 Richland Balsam parking overlook, highest point on Parkway, elev. 6050

432.7 Lone Bald parking overlook, elev. 5635. Enter Waynesville watershed

433.0 Lone Bald

433.3 Locust Gap parking overlook, elev. 5580

433.4 Locust Gap, elev. 5575

434.2 Old Bald

434.8 Racking Horse Gap, elev. 5400

435.3 Doubletop Mountain parking overlook, elev. 5365

435.7 Licklog Gap parking overlook, elev. 5135

436.7 Deep Gap, elev. 5260

438.8 Brassy Ridge Mine parking overlook, elev. 5250

439.0 Steestachee Bald parking overlook, elev. 4780

439.1 Cove Ridge

439.2 Leave Waynesville watershed

439.4 Cove Field Ridge parking overlook, elev. 4620

Milepost

439.7   Pinnacle Ridge Tunnel, 750 ft. long
440.1   Saunook parking overlook, elev. 4375
440.9   Waynesville parking overlook, elev. 4110
441.4   Standing Rock parking overlook, elev. 3915
441.9   Rabb Knob parking overlook, elev. 3725. S.
442.2   Balsam Gap parking overlook, elev. 3630
443.1   Balsam Gap, elev. 3370. U.S. 19A & 23, right 8 mi. to Waynesville; left 12 mi. to Sylva
444.6   The Orchards parking overlook, elev. 3810
445.2   Jones Knob parking overlook, elev. 4000
446.0   Woodfin Valley parking overlook, elev. 4325
446.7   Woodfin Cascades parking overlook, elev. 4535
448.1   Wesner Bald parking overlook, elev. 4912
448.5   Scott Creek parking overlook, elev. 5050
449.0   Fork Ridge parking overlook, elev. 5280
450.0   Yellow Face parking overlook, elev. 5610
451.2   Waterrock Knob parking overlook, elev. 5718. E.
452.1   Cranberry Ridge parking overlook, elev. 5475
452.3   Wollyback parking overlook, elev. 5420
453.4   Hornbuckle Valley parking overlook, elev. 5105
454.4   Thunderstruck Ridge parking overlook, elev. 4780
455.1   Soco Gap parking overlook, elev. 4570
455.4   Overlook
455.7   Soco Gap, elev. 4340. U.S.

Milepost

        19, right 8 mi. to Dellwood; left 12 mi. to Cherokee
456.2   Jonathan Creek parking overlook, elev. 4460
457.6   Docks Gap, elev. 4930
457.8   Plott Balsam overlook, elev. 5020. S.
457.9   Indian Road; no access
458.2   Wolf Laurel Gap, elev. 5100. S.
458.8   Lickstone Ridge Tunnel, 402 ft. long
458.9   Lickstone parking overlook, elev. 5150
459.3   Bunches Bald Tunnel, 268 ft. long
459.5   Bunches Bald parking overlook, elev. 4925. S.
459.7   Bunches Gap, elev. 4850
460.8   Jenkins Ridge parking overlook, elev. 4445
461.2   Big Witch Tunnel, 348 ft. long
461.6   Big Witch Gap, elev. 4160. Bunches Creek Road to right, Indian Road (Wrights Creek) left
461.9   Big Witch parking overlook, elev. 4150. E.
462.35 Barnett fire tower road
463.9   Thomas Divide parking overlook, elev. 3735
465.6   Rattlesnake Mountain No. 4 Tunnel, 410 ft. long
466.25 Sherill Cove No. 6 Tunnel, 572 ft. long
466.7   Sherill Cove parking overlook, elev. 2970
467.4   Ballhoot Scar parking overlook, elev. 2550
467.9   Raven Fork parking overlook, elev. 2400
468.4   Oconaluftee parking overlook, elev. 2200
469.1   End of Blue Ridge Park-

way. U.S. 441, right 29 mi.
to Gatlinburg, Tenn.; left
2 mi. to Cherokee, N.C.

HEINTOOGA SPUR

0.0   Begin at Mile 458.2, Blue
        Ridge   Parkway,   Wolf
        Laurel Gap, elev. 5110
0.1   Indian service road
0.5   Plott Ridge
0.9   Mollie Gap, elev. 5352. In-
        dian Road (left) to Soco
        Bald
1.3   Mile High parking over-
        look, elev. 5250. S.
1.4   Maggie Valley parking
        overlook, elev. 5220
2.3   Lake Junaluska parking
        overlook, elev. 4905

3.3   Horsetrough Ridge park-
        ing widening
3.4   Horsetrough Ridge park-
        ing widening
3.6   Black Camp Gap parking
        area
3.65   Boundary, Great Smoky
        Mountains National Park
3.9   Parking overlook
6.2   Parking overlook
8.4   Balsam Mountain camp-
        ground, elev. 5340. 47 sites,
        campfire circle
8.9   Heintooga Ridge picnic
        area, 37 sites
9.0   Parking area; end of paved
        road. Fire road (one-way
        traffic in summer) con-
        tinues to Round Bottom,
        Great Smoky Mountains
        National Park

Bibliography

PRIMARY SOURCES

Public Documents and Reports

Congressional Record. Vols. LXIX, LXXI, LXXX, LXXXI, LXXXVI.

Glenn, Leonidas Chalmer. *Denudation and Erosion in the Southern Appalachian Region.* U. S. Geological Survey Professional Paper No. 72. Washington, D. C.: Government Printing Office 1911.

House of Representatives, Committee on the Public Lands. *Hearings on House Resolution 6668, A Bill to Grant the State of North Carolina a Right of Way for the Blue Ridge Parkway across the Cherokee Indian Reservation in North Carolina,* 76th Cong., 1st Sess., 1939.

Keith, Arthur. *Nantahala Folio.* U. S. Geological Survey Report No. 143, 1907.

Loomis, C. P., and L. S. Dodson. *Standards of Living in Four Southern Appalachian Mountain Counties.* U. S. Department of Agriculture Social Research Report No. X. Washington, D. C.: U. S. Department of Agriculture, 1938.

North Carolina. *Public Laws and Resolutions,* 1935–36.

Pratt, Joseph Hyde. *Highway Work in North Carolina: Containing a Statistical Report of the Road Work during 1911.* North Carolina Geological and Economic Survey Economic Paper No. 27. Raleigh, N. C.: E. M. Uzzell and Co., 1912.

————. *Proceedings of the Annual Convention of the North Carolina Good Roads Association.* North Carolina Geological and Economic Survey Economic Paper No. 30. Raleigh, N. C.: Edwards & Broughton Printing Co., 1912.

Rose, Albert C. "Historic American Highways," *Annual Report of the Board of Regents, Smithsonian Institution, for the Year 1939.* Washington, D. C.: Government Printing Office, 1940.

Senate. *Message from the President of the United States Transmitting a Report of the Secretary of Agriculture in Relation to the Forests, Rivers, and Mountains of the Southern Appalachian Region.* Senate Document No. 84, 57th Cong., 1st Sess., 1902.

Taylor, Carl C., *et al. Disadvantaged Classes in American Agriculture.*

U. S. Department of Agriculture Social Research Report No. VIII. Washington, D. C.: U. S. Department of Agriculture, 1938.

U. S. Department of Agriculture. *Climate and Man. 1941 Yearbook of Agriculture.*

_____. *Economic and Social Problems and Conditions of the Southern Appalachians.* U. S. Department of Agriculture Miscellaneous Publication No. 205. Washington, D. C.: U. S. Department of Agriculture, 1935.

U. S. Federal Land Committee. "Public Works and Rural Land Use," *Report of the Land Committee to the National Resources Planning Board.* Washington, D. C.: Government Printing Office, 1942.

U. S. Federal Land Planning Committee. "Maladjustments in Land Use in the United States," *Supplementary Report of the Land Planning Committee to the National Resources Board,* Pt. VI. Washington, D. C.: Government Printing Office, 1935.

U. S. National Resources Board. *Report on National Planning and Public Works in Relation to Natural Resources Including Land Use and Water Resources with Findings and Recommendations.* Washington, D. C.: Government Printing Office, 1934.

U. S. *Statutes at Large.* Vols. XLVIII, XLIX, LIV.

Virginia. *Acts of the General Assembly,* 1933, 1936.

Unpublished Material and Interviews

Abbuehl, Edward H. "History of the Blue Ridge Parkway." Paper read before Blue Ridge Parkway Rangers' Conference, Roanoke, Va., February 8, 1948. Manuscript in the files of Superintendent, Blue Ridge Parkway, Roanoke, Va.

Abbuehl, Edward H., Parkway supervisory landscape architect. Personal interview, July 16, 1962, Roanoke, Va.

Batten, Earl W., Parkway engineer. Personal interview, September 3, 1963, Roanoke, Va.

Blue Ridge Parkway. Historical Files, Office of Superintendent, Roanoke, Va.

Blythe, Jarrett, chief, Eastern Band of Cherokee Indians. Personal interview, May 19, 1962, Cherokee, N. C.

Byrd, Harry F., United States senator. Personal interview, June 3, 1962, Waynesboro, Va.

Cherokee Indian Agency. Historical Files, Office of Superintendent, Cherokee, N. C.

Demaray, A. E. "Federal Parkways." Paper read before Council Meeting of the American Planning and Civic Association, January 24, 1936. Manuscript in National Archives, National Park Service, Record Group 79, Washington, D. C.

Doughton, Robert L. Private Correspondence. University of North Carolina, Chapel Hill.

Gibbs, J. Gordon, North Carolina Parkway claims adjustor. Personal interview, July 5, 1963, Raleigh, N. C.

Mathis, William, retired Parkway construction superintendent. Personal interview, September 3, 1963, Waynesboro, Va.

North Carolina. Governors' Correspondence. State Archives, Raleigh.

——. State Highway and Public Works Commission Correspondence. Commission's files, Raleigh.

——. State Park Commission Correspondence. Commission's files, Waynesville.

——. State Park Commission Minutes of Meetings. Commission's files, Waynesville.

Straus, Theodore E., former Public Works Administration official. Personal interview, July 30, 1962, Baltimore, Md.

Straus, Theodore E. Private correspondence files. Baltimore, Md.

U. S. Department of the Interior. "Brief of Hearings Relative to Parkway Routing," September 24, 1934. Manuscript in National Archives, Department of the Interior, Record Group 48, Washington, D. C.

U. S. Federal Emergency Administration of Public Works. Stenographic Report of Hearings Relative to Parkway Routing, September 24, 1934. Manuscript in National Archives, National Park Service, Record Group 79, Washington, D. C.

U. S. National Park Service. Correspondence. National Archives, Record Group 48, Record Group 79, Washington, D. C.

U. S. Special Board for Public Works. Minutes of Meetings, 1933, in National Archives, National Park Service, Record Group 48, Washington, D. C.

Virginia. Governors' Correspondence. Virginia State Library, Richmond.

——. State Highway Department Correspondence. Department's files, Richmond.

——. State Highway Department Minutes of Meetings. Department's files, Richmond.

———. State Highway Department, "Right of Way, Extension Skyline Drive," July 2, 1934. Department's files, Richmond.
Weede, Fred L. "Battle for the Blue Ridge Parkway." Manuscript in Park Library, Asheville, N. C., 1957.
Weems, Sam P., Parkway superintendent. Personal interview, September 5, 1963, Roanoke, Va.

Newspapers

Asheville *Citizen*, 1933–63.
Blue Ridge Parkway News, 1935–37.
Greeneville (Tenn.) *Sun*, 1933–34.
Johnson City *Chronicle*, 1933–35.
Johnson City *Press*, 1934.
Kingsport *Times*, 1933–34.
Knoxville *Journal*, 1933–34.
Knoxville *News-Sentinel*, 1933–34.
Mount Airy *News*, 1933–34.
The Nation (New York), 1934.
New York *Times*, 1939–40.
Richmond *Times Dispatch*, 1933–36.
Roanoke *Times*, 1933–51.
Roanoke *World News*, 1933–61.
Washington *Post*, 1933–34.
Waynesboro *News-Virginian*, 1933–62.

SECONDARY SOURCES

Books

Abernethy, Thomas Perkins. *Three Virginia Frontiers*. Baton Rouge: Louisiana State University Press, 1940.
Allen, Martha N. *Asheville and the Land of the Sky*. Charlotte, N. C.: Heritage House, 1960.
Alvord, Clarence Walworth and Lee Bidgood. *The First Explorations of the Trans-Allegheny Region by the Virginians, 1650–1674*. Cleveland: The Arthur H. Clark Co., 1912.
Arthur, John Preston. *Western North Carolina: A History from 1730 to 1913*. Raleigh, N. C.: Edwards & Broughton Printing Co., 1914.
Billington, Ray Allen. *Westward Expansion: A History of the American Frontier*. 2nd ed. rev.; New York: The Macmillan Co., 1960.

Binkley, Wilfred E. *American Political Parties: Their Natural History.* New York: Alfred A. Knopf, 1943.

Boyd, William K. (ed.). *William Byrd's Histories of the Dividing Line Betwixt Virginia and North Carolina.* Raleigh, N. C.: The North Carolina Historical Commission, 1929.

Brigham, Albert Perry. *Geographic Influences in American History.* New York: Ginn and Co., 1903.

Campbell, Carlos C. *Birth of a National Park in the Great Smoky Mountains.* Knoxville: The University of Tennessee Press, 1960.

Campbell, John C. *The Southern Highlander and His Homeland.* New York: Russell Sage Foundation, 1921.

Caruso, John Anthony. *The Appalachian Frontier: America's First Surge Westward.* Indianapolis: The Bobbs-Merrill Co., 1959.

Clark, Thomas D. *Frontier America: The Story of Westward Movement.* New York: Charles Scribner's Sons, 1959.

Cumming, William P. *The Southeast in Early Maps.* Chapel Hill: University of North Carolina Press, 1962.

Dodson, Leonidas. *Alexander Spotswood, Governor of Colonial Virginia, 1710–1722.* Philadelphia: University of Pennsylvania Press, 1932.

Duerr, William A. *The Economic Problems of Forestry in the Appalachian Region.* Harvard Economic Studies, Vol. LXXXIV. Cambridge, Mass.: Harvard University Press, 1949.

Fearnow, Theodore C. and I. T. Quinn. "Action on the Blue Ridge," *Trees, 1949 Yearbook of Agriculture.* Washington, D. C.: Government Printing Office, 1949.

Fenneman, Nevin M. *Physiography of Eastern United States.* New York: McGraw Hill, Inc., 1938.

Fries, Adelaide L. (ed.). *Records of the Moravians in North Carolina.* 9 vols. Raleigh, N. C.: Edwards & Broughton Printing Co., 1922.

Hatcher, J. Wesley. "Appalachian America," in W. T. Couch, ed., *Culture in the South.* Chapel Hill: University of North Carolina Press, 1934.

Ickes, Harold L. *The Secret Diary of Harold L. Ickes.* 3 vols. New York: Simon & Schuster, 1954.

Kephart, Horace. *Our Southern Highlanders: A Narrative of Adventure in the Southern Appalachians and a Study of Life among the Mountaineers.* New York: The Macmillan Co., 1929.

King, Edward. *The Southern States of North America: A Record of*

163

Journeys in Louisiana, Texas, the Indian Territory, Missouri, Arkansas, Mississippi, Alabama, Georgia, Florida, South Carolina, North Carolina, Kentucky, Tennessee, Virginia, West Virginia. London: Blackie and Son, 1875.

Lefler, Hugh Talmage, and Albert Ray Newsome. *North Carolina: The History of a Southern State.* Chapel Hill: University of North Carolina Press, 1934; rev. ed, 1963.

Lord, William G. *The Blue Ridge Parkway Guide.* Asheville, N. C.: The Stephens Press, 1962.

Morison, Samuel Eliot, and Henry Steele Commager. *The Growth of the American Republic.* 2 vols. 4th ed. rev.; New York: Oxford University Press, 1950.

Peattie, Roderick (ed.). *The Great Smokies and the Blue Ridge: The Story of the Southern Appalachians.* New York: The Vanguard Press, 1943.

Robinson, Blackwell P. (ed.). *The North Carolina Guide.* Chapel Hill: University of North Carolina Press, 1955.

Roosevelt, Theodore. *The Winning of the West.* 4 vols. New York: G. P. Putnam's Sons, 1900.

Semple, Ellen Churchill. *American History and Its Geographic Conditions.* New York: Houghton Mifflin Co., 1933.

Toynbee, Arnold J. *A Study of History.* D. C. Somervell's abridgement of Vols. I–VI. New York: Oxford University Press, 1947.

Vance, Rupert B. *Human Geography of the South: A Study in Regional Resources and Human Adequacy.* Chapel Hill: University of North Carolina Press, 1932.

Waynick, Capus. *North Carolina Roads and Their Builders.* Raleigh, N. C.: Superior Stone Co., 1952.

White, C. Langdon, and Edwin J. Foscue. *Regional Geography of Anglo-America.* 2nd ed. rev.; Englewood Cliffs, N. J.: Prentice-Hall, Inc., 1954.

Periodicals

Abbuehl, Edward H. "A Road Built for Pleasure," *Landscape Architecture,* LI (July, 1961), 233–35.

Avery, Myron H., and Kenneth S. Boardman (eds.). "Arnold Guyot's Notes on the Geography of the Mountain Districts of Western North Carolina," *North Carolina Historical Review,* XV (July, 1938), 251–318.

Dillman, Grover C. "Roadbuilding as an Agency of Employment during the Depression," *American City*, XLVII (December, 1932), 75–76.

Editorial. *Nature Magazine*, XXV (March, 1935), 101.

Hickerson, Thomas F. "The Crest of the Blue Ridge Highway," *Journal of the Elisha Mitchell Scientific Society*, XXVIII (December, 1911), 160–68.

Ickes, Harold L. "The National Domain and the New Deal," *Saturday Evening Post*, CCVI (December 23, 1933), 10–11.

Ross, Edward A. "Pocketed Americans," *New Republic*, XXXVII (January 9, 1924), 170–72, 224–26.

White, William A. "Blue Ridge Front-A Fault Scarp," *Bulletin of the Geological Society of America*, LXI (December, 1950), 1309–46.

Index

Abbott, Stanley W., 59, 108
Adney Gap, 65, 146
Afton Overlook, 143
Air Bellows Gap, 68, 149
Alder Gap, 150
Alexander, Hugh, 21
Alligator Back, 150
Altapass, N.C., 12
Anderson, J. A., 36–38
Appalachian Highway Company, 13
Appalachian Park-to-Park-Highway, 62–63
Appalachian Trail Club, 108
Apple Orchard Mountain, 145
Apple Orchard Overlook, 152
Arnold Valley, 145
Ashe County, N.C., 12, 115
Asheville, N.C., 6, 12, 18, 29, 36, 47, 48, 54, 57, 61, 68, 71–74, 77–79, 87–89, 153–54
Austin, William M., 108
Avery County, N.C., 52
Azrael, Louis, 30

Bachman, Nathan L., 61, 81
Back Creek, 146
Bad Fork Valley, 154
Bailey, Josiah W., 18, 36, 61, 70, 79, 82
Bald Mountain, 143
Ballhoot Scar, 156
Balsam Gap, 153, 156
Balsam Spring Gap, 155
Bamboo, 151
Basin Cove, 150
Beacon Heights, 151
Bear Den, 152
Bear Pen Gap, 155
Beartrail Ridge, 155

Beartrap Gap, 155
Bearwallow Gap, 145, 152
Beaver Dam Gap, 154
Bedford, Va., 47, 146
Beech Gap, 155
Bee Tree Gap, 153
Belcher Curve, 147
Bell Spring House, 137, 147
Bennett Cove, 154
Bennett Gap, 154
Bent Creek Gap, 154
Big Laurel Gap, 153
Big Pine Bear Stand, 153
Big Ridge, 154
Big Witch Gap, 107, 134, 156
Biltmore Estate, 153
Black Camp Gap, 157
Black Horse Gap, 146
Black Mountain, N.C., 84
Black Mountain Gap, 153, 155
Black Mountains, the, 152
Black Rock Hill, 145
Blair, Clyde M., 100
Bland County, Va., 61
Blowing Rock, N.C., 12, 18, 61, 64, 68, 70, 83–84, 87
Blue Ridge Baptist Church, 150
Blue Ridge Church, 149
Bluemont Presbyterian Church, 148
Bluff Mountain, 144
Bluffs, the, 5, 119
Bluffs View, 150
Blythe, Jarrett, 93, 100
Bobblets Gap, 145
Boone, N.C., 12, 18, 151
Boone, Daniel, 4, 10, 140
Boston Knob, 134, 144
Boston Post Road, 9
Botetort County, Va., 61

Brassy Ridge Mine, 155
Brevard, N.C., 12
Bridges Camp Gap, 154
Brinegar, Caroline, 116
Brinegar Cabin, 138–39, 142, 149
Bristol, Va., 75, 85
Browning, R. Getty, 61, 67, 73, 79, 93, 100
Browns Creek, 144
Buchanan, Va., 145
Buck Creek Gap, 61, 152
Buckeye Gap, 155
Buck Mountain, 146
Buck Springs Gap, 154
Buffalo Mountain, 147
Bull Creek Valley, 134, 153
Bull Gap, 153
Bullhead Gap, 149, 153
Bull Run Knob, 146
Bully Creek, 149
Bulwinkle, A. L., 61, 69
Bunches Gap, 157
Burch, T. G., 61
Burlew, E. K., 44, 122
Byrd, Harry Flood, 23–29, 31, 33–42, 54, 70, 86, 108, 127
Byrd, William, 4
Byrnes, James F., 84

Cahas Knob, 147
Calloway Gap, 150
Cammerer, Arno B., 39–40, 48, 59, 65, 70–71
Camp Creek, 152
Campgrounds, 141
Caney Fork, 155
Carroll County, Va., 45, 61, 104
Carroll Gap, 151
Carson, William E., 41
Carvers Gap, 64
Cascades Trail, 138, 150
Caudill Cabin, 138
Chapman, David C., 15, 65, 74, 91
Cherokee, N.C., 39, 68, 93
Cherokee Indian Agency, 95, 99–100, 120

Cherokee Indians, Eastern Band of, 3, 93–100
Cherry Cove, 154
Cherry Hill, 150
Cherry Log Ridge, 153
Chestnut Creek, 149
Chestnut Grove, 154
Chestoa View, 152
Chimney Rock Mountain, 143
Civilian Conservation Corps, 22, 24, 55, 120
Clarkes Gap, 144
Clark, G. D., 59
Clark Mountain, 144
Clarkson, Francis O., 37
Coiner's Deadnin', 134
Cold Mountain, 154
Cold Spring Mountain, 68, 70
Collett, John, 9
Colonial National Parkway, 19
Concessioner Services, 141–42
Cone, Moses H., 135
Cone Memorial Park, 132, 135, 151
Cool Spring Baptist Church, 130, 138, 150
Cotton Tree Gap, 153
Courthouse Valley, 155
Cove Field Ridge, 155
Cove Ridge, 155
Cowee Mountain, 155
Coxey, Jacob S., 53
Crabtree Creek, 119
Crabtree Meadows recreation area, 132, 141, 152
Craftsman's Trail, 134
Craggy Dome, 153
Craggy Gardens, 5, 119, 133, 137, 153
Craig County, Va., 57, 61
Cranberry Ridge, 156
Craven Gap, 153
Crest of the Blue Ridge Highway, 11–13, 22
Crockett, David, 3
Cumberland Knob recreation area, 119, 132, 141, 149

Curry Gap, 146
Curtis Valley, 153

Dancing Creek, 144
Daniel Gap, 150
Daniels, Josephus, 66–67, 69, 72,
    77, 78
Deep Gap, 61, 64, 150–51, 153, 155
Deer Lick Gap, 152
Delta Theta Chi Sorority, 58
Demaray, A. E., 30, 110, 127, 128
Devil's Backbone, 147
Devil's Courthouse, 131, 155
Devil's Garden, 149
Dividing Springs, 146
Dock's Gap, 156
Doubletop Mountain, 155
Doughton, Robert L., 18, 31, 36, 47,
    54, 61, 69, 79, 96, 123–25
Doughton Park recreation area,
    132, 141, 149
Dripping Rocks, 143

Eastern National Park-to-Park
    Highway, 16–18, 22, 41
East Fork, 155
Ehringhaus, J. C. B., 36, 38, 57, 61,
    72, 78–79, 85, 114
Elk Mountain, 150, 153
Elk Pasture Gap, 154
Elk Run Trail, 134, 138, 145
Erwin, Tenn., 85

Falling Rock Creek, 144
Fancy Gap, 61, 69, 148
Federal Land Planning Committee,
    11, 57
Fishers Peak, 68, 119, 132
Flannagan, John W., 61, 76
Flat Laurel Gap, 154
Flat Rock, 152
Flat Top Mountain Trail, 145
Floyd, Va., 46
Floyd County, Va., 11, 46, 61, 104
Fork Mountain, 143
Fork Ridge, 156

George Washington Memorial
    Parkway, 19
Grandfather Mountain, 7, 68, 116,
    121, 137, 152
Grandmother Mountain Gap, 151
Grandview, 151
Grassy Gap, 150
Graveyard Fields, 140, 155
Grayson County, Va., 46, 61
Great Road, the, 9
Great Smoky Mountains
    Conservation Association, 65
Great Smoky Mountains National
    Park, 15, 20, 23, 25, 28, 30, 33,
    35, 39–40, 44–45, 59, 70–71, 84,
    89, 92–93, 126–27, 129, 140, 157
Greeneville, Tenn., 85, 91
Green Knob, 153
Greenstone Trail, 134, 138, 143
Greenwood, Arthur H., 125
Greybeard Mountain, 153
Groundhog Mountain, 148
Guyot, Arnold, 5
Gwyn, R. L., 36

Hancock, Franklin W., Jr., 61
Hanks Branch, 149
Hare Mill Pond, 149
Harvey's Knob, 145
Haywood Gap, 155
Headforemost parking widening,
    145
Hearkening Hill, 145
Heffner Gap, 152
Heintooga Ridge picnic area, 157
Hendersonville, N.C., 12, 84
Herrin Knob, 155
Hickory Spring, 143
Highlands, N.C., 12
High Piney Spur, 149
Hillsville, Va., 46
Holloway Mountain, 151
Hornbuckle Valley, 156
Horse Gap, 64, 150
Horsetrough Ridge, 157

House Mountain, 144
House Resolution 6668, p. 98
House Resolution 12455, pp. 123,
    125
Howardsville Turnpike, 10
Hubbard's Mill, 147
Humpback Gap, 134, 143
Humpback Rocks, 7, 118
Humpback Rocks recreation area,
    119, 132, 143
Humpback Rocks visitor center,
    133, 137, 143
Humphrey's Gap, 144
Hutchins, Charles, 37

Ickes, Harold L., 23–24, 35, 40, 42–
    43, 49, 54, 55, 59, 64, 66, 69–70,
    72–76, 78–80, 82–92, 96, 109–110,
    114, 122, 127, 128
Ickes, Mrs. Harold L., 72
Indian Gap, 144
Irish Creek Valley, 144
Irish Gap, 144
Iron Mine Hollow, 145
Iron Mountain, 68

Jackson, Andrew, 3, 81
James River visitor center, 133,
    137, 144
Jarman's Gap, 105, 108
Jefferson, N.C., 18
Jefferson, Thomas, 3
Jeffress, E. B., 38
Jeffress Park, 132, 150
Jenkins, Thomas A., 125
Jenkins Ridge, 156
John Rock, 155
Johnson, Andrew, 81
Johnson City, Tenn., 76, 91
Jonathan Creek, 156
Jones Knob, 156
Jumpin' Off Rocks, 150

Kanawha Canal, 10, 145
Kelly Spring House, 138, 147

Kennerly, W. T., 80
King's Mountain Men, 135
Knoxville, Tenn., 15, 64–65, 74–
    76, 80, 83, 86, 92

Lake Junaluska, 69, 157
Lancaster Gap, 146
Lancaster Turnpike, 9
Lane's Pinnacle, 153
Latham, Robert, 79, 80, 88
Laurel Creek, 147
Laurel Springs, N.C., 37
Laurel Springs Gap, 143
Lee, W. I., 108
Lenoir, N.C., 37
Lewis Fork, 150
Licklog Gap, 155
Licklog Ridge, 153
Lick Log Spring, 119
Lick Log Springs Gap, 144
Linville, N.C., 12, 18, 70, 87
Linville Falls recreation area, 132,
    152
Linville Gorge, 61, 119
Linville River, 152
Little Bear Pen Gap, 155
Little Glade Mill Pond, 149
Little Grandfather Mountain, 64
Little Stony picnic area, 145
Little Switzerland, 12, 63, 84
Locust Gap, 155
Log Hollow, 154
Lone Bald, 155
Looking Glass Rock, 7, 140, 155
Lost Cove Cliffs, 152
Lost Mountain, 146
Love, Va., 118
Love Gap, 143
Low Gap, 64, 113
Low Notch, 149
Lynn Gap, 152

Mabry Gap, 148
Mabry Mill, 130, 133, 137, 142, 148
McAlister, Hill, 36, 76, 80, 82, 91
McCall Gap, 152

MacDonald, Thomas H., 23, 26–28, 34, 38, 40, 59, 70
McKellar, Kenneth D., 63–66, 73, 77, 80, 82–83, 86, 90
McKinney Gap, 152
McNeil, Marshall, 92
Maggie Valley, 157
Mahogany Rock, 149
Maloney, Frank, 62–64, 70, 74, 82
Marble Spring Lean-to, 145
Marion, N.C., 18, 36
Marshall, Robert, 48, 76
Mason's Knob, 146
Massie's Mill, 143
Matthews Cabin, 130, 138, 148
Max Patch Mountain, 68
Maybery Presbyterian Church, 148
Meadows of Dan, 148
Metz Run, 146
Michener, Earl C., 125
Miller, Hunter, 24
Mill Mountain, 146
Mills Gap, 145
Mills Valley, 154
Mollie Gap, 157
Moravians, 3, 9
Morganton, N.C., 9
Moseley, Edward, 9
Mount Airy, N.C., 46
Mount Carroll Methodist Church, 149
Mount Hardy, 155
Mount Jefferson, 150
Mount Mitchell, 68, 84, 87, 119, 153
Mount Pisgah Inn, 154
Mount Pisgah recreation area, 132, 154
Mount Vernon Memorial Highway, 19
Mountain Farm Trail, 138
Museum of North Carolina Minerals, 133, 137, 152

National Industrial Recovery Act, 20

Natural Bridge, 15, 108
North Cove, 152
North Toe Valley, 152
Northwest Trading Post, 142, 150
Norwall Flats recreational area, 119

Oconaluftee River, 137
O'Connor, John J., 125
Old Bald, 155
Onion Mountain, 145
Orchard Gap, 148
Ordinary, Polly Woods', 130, 137, 145
Osborne, Ozzie, 23
Osborne Mountain, 151
Otter Creek recreational area, 132, 141, 144
Otter Lake, 144

Page, Frank, 79, 80
Parker, Haywood, 37
Parkway, defined, 107
Parkway Craft Center, 135, 142
Patrick County, Va., 46, 61, 104
Peaks of Otter recreation area, 119, 132–33, 141, 145
Peaks of Otter visitor center, 133, 137, 145
Petites Gap, 145
Phillips Gap, 150
Picnic Areas, 141
Pigeon Gap, 154
Pigeon River Falls, 119
Pilot Mountain, 148
Pineola, N.C., 15
Pine Spur recreational area, 119, 132, 147
Pine Spur Gap, 112, 147
Pink Beds, the, 154
Pinnacles of Dan, 45, 148
Pioneer Industry Trail, 138
Piper Gap, 107, 148
Plott Balsams, the, 156
Plott Ridge, 157
Poages Mill, 146
Poe, Edgar Allan, 50
Pole Spring House, 138

Polk, James K., 81
Pollard, John G., 23, 27–30, 33, 37, 42, 43
Porters Mountain, 145
Potato Field Gap, 153
Pounding Mill, 154
Powell's Gap, 108, 145
Pratt, Joseph Hyde, 12–13
Preacher Brown Cabin, 138
Price, Julian, 135
Price Memorial Park, 132, 135, 141
Priest, the, 143
Public Law No. 848, pp. 126, 128
Puckett, Orlena, 130
Puckett Cabin, 130, 138, 148
Pulaski County, Va., 61
Purgatory Mountain, 131, 145

Rabb Knob, 156
Rabun Gap, 12
Racking Horse Gap, 155
Radcliffe, George L., 23, 26, 28, 30, 33, 39–41, 43, 59, 64, 66, 70, 75, 82–83, 127
Rake's Mill Pond, 147
Randolph, John P., 37
Rattlesnake Mountain, 150
Raven Fork, 156
Ravensford, 107
Ravens Rock, 151
Ravens Roost, 131, 143
Reeds Gap, 143
Reinhart Gap, 155
Reinhart Knob, 155
Reynolds, Robert R., 30, 36, 39, 40, 61, 74, 76, 80, 90–91
Reynolds Gap, 154
Rice Mountain, 144
Rich, Robert F., 123
Rich Mountain, 154
Richland Balsams, 119, 155
Riffles, the, 144
Right-of-way, defined, 102
Roan Mountain, 64, 68, 70
Roanoke Mountain recreation area, 132, 146

Roanoke Valley, 139, 146
Roanoke, Va., 7, 112
Roaring Gap, N.C., 64
Robertson, James, 10
Robertson, Reuben B., 37
Robertson, Willis, 33, 124
Robinson Gap, 144
Rock Castle Gorge, 147
Rockefeller, John D., Jr., 135
Rockfish Gap, 107, 137
Rockpoint, 143
Rocky Knob Cabins, 141, 147
Rocky Knob recreational area, 119, 132, 147
Rocky Knob Trail, 138
Roosevelt, Franklin D., 19, 23–24, 42, 48, 53, 66–67, 72, 78, 85, 90, 126–27
Roughbutt Bald, 131, 155
Round Meadow, 148
Rutherford Expedition, 135

Saddle Mountain Church, 149
Saddle Parking Overlook, 147
Sandy Flat Gap, 151
Scenic easement, defined, 102
Scott Creek, 156
Seniard Gap, 155
Sevier, John, 81
Sharp Top Mountain, 145
Sheets Cabin, 138
Sheets Gap, 150
Shenandoah National Park, 15, 20, 22, 24, 25, 28, 30–31, 33, 35, 37, 39–40, 42, 44–45, 54, 61, 70, 87, 93, 127–28, 130
Shirley, Henry G., 27, 37, 41, 86, 108
Short's Knob, 147
Shull's Mill, 151
Silver Mine, old, 155
Singecat Ridge, 153
Skyline Drive, 22, 25–26, 28, 31, 37, 41, 47, 58, 108, 126, 130
Slacks, the, 143
Sleepy Gap, 154

Sling's Gap, 146
Smart View recreational area, 119,
    132, 141, 147
Smyth County, Va., 61
Snell, Bertrand H., 125
Soco Gap, 61, 84, 93, 156
Southern Highland Handicraft
    Guild, 135
Sparta, N.C., 18
Spelman, H. J., 108
Spot Gap, 155
Spy Run Gap, 143
Standhill Mountain, 154
Standing Rock, 156
Steele's Tavern, 143
Steestachee Bald, 155
Steppe's Gap, 12
Stewart's Knob, 146
Still House Hollow, 144
Stone Mountain, 139, 149
Stoney Fork Valley, 151
Stony Bald, 154
Straus, Theodore E., 23, 26, 28,
    29–31, 37, 40, 59, 66
Sunset Field, 145
Surry County, N.C., 105
Swafford Gap, 152
Swannanoa River, 153
Sweet Annie Hollow, 131, 147

Table Rock, 140, 152
Tanasee Bald, 118, 155
Tanbark Ridge, 153
Taylor, J. Will, 74, 81, 92, 123
Taylor Mountain, 146
Teer, Nello, 113
Terrapin Hill, 144
Terrapin Mountain, 131, 145
Thatcher, Maurice H., 15, 18–19,
    40
Thomas Divide, 156
Thomas Grove Baptist Church, 147
Thompkins Knob, 119, 150
Three Ridges, 143
Three Knobs, 152
Thunder Hill, 151

Thunder Ridge, 131, 145
Thunderstruck Ridge, 156
Toe River Gap, 153
Tolson, Hillory A., 21
Toxaway, N.C., 12
Toynbee, Arnold J., 50
Trails, 134, 138
Trail's Cabin, 138–39, 147
Trees, Trail of, 134, 138
Tsali, 99
Tuggle Gap, 147
Tunnel Gap, 154
Twenty Minute Cliff, 131, 139, 143
Tye River Gap, 108, 143

Umstead, William B., 61

Vint, Thomas C., 59
Volunteer Gap, 148

Wagon Road Gap, 154
Waite, Henry M., 44
Walker's Mountain, 68
Walnut Cove, 154
Ward's Gap, 148
Wash Creek Valley, 154
Washington, George, 3
Waterrock Knob, 156
Watson's Dome, 150
Waynesboro, Va., 6
Waynesville, N.C., 15, 68, 87, 96
Weaver, Zebulon, 61, 69, 98
Webb, Charles A., 71
Webster, Frank W., 75
Weede, Fred L., 29, 48, 61, 73,
    77, 90
Wesner Bald, 156
Westchester County Parkway, 19
Wheeler-Howard Act, 95
Whetstone Ridge recreational
    area, 132, 141, 143
White Oak Flats, 144
White Rock Gap, 143
Whites Gap, 144
White Top Mountain, 12, 68

Wilderness Road, 135, 151
Wilkinson Gap, 145
Willis Gap, 148
Wirth, Conrad L., 24
Wolcott, Jesse P., 123, 125
Wolf Bald, 155
Wolf Laurel Gap, 156
Wolf Mountain, 155
Wolman, Abel, 59
Woodfin Cascades, 156
Wythe County, Va., 61

Wytheville, Va., 15, 18

Yadkin Valley, 151
Yankee Fence, 144
Yankee Horse Logging Exhibit,
   135, 144
Yankee Horse Ridge, 144
Yellow Mountain, 146
Yellow Mountain Road, 9
Yellowstone Falls, 155